in the spring, to see whether they migrate north with their wild companions or return to Guisachan to nest with us. Yesterday a skein of whooper swans passed over the house, twenty birds in wide vee formation, and bugling loudly as they went. I saw our wigeon fidgeting and they whistled loudly in response. Perhaps tomorrow they will be gone when I go out to feed them in the half-light of morning.

We have had no snow yet, although it is nearly the end of November, and there are still some amber leaves left on the birches and geans which have added themselves to the planned silviculture of the Tweedmouth parkland. Soon the hills above Affric will turn white and the deer will come down to the woods for shelter, and we shall find their slot-marks around the house where they have passed through the fields in the long night. I must remember to try to photograph some for a slide lecture Peter has started on the year of the red deer. The winter is good for such things because there is time and we can recharge our energies and plan for the move and the coming year.

Whooper swan

Lorna Haines.
Inverness, November, 1982.

By the same author

The White Island
Seal Cull

The Seeing Eye

Notes of a Highland Naturalist

John Lister-Kaye

Illustrated by Sarah Norton

One August day on the Isle of Skye we came across two old men sitting in the purple heather enjoying the sun. Removing his pipe, one asked me what we were doing.

'We run field-study courses,' I said. 'We are looking at the birds and the flowers and the mountains.'

'Och yes,' he said, 'I see.' And turning to his friend beside him he said, 'It is the seeing eye they have.'

Allen Lane

Allen Lane
Penguin Books Ltd
536 King's Road
London SW10 0UH

First published 1980

ISBN 0 7139 1306 1

Set in Monotype Bembo
Reproduced from copy supplied
printed and bound in Great Britain
by Billing and Sons Limited
Guildford, London, Oxford, Worcester

The author and publishers are grateful to Faber & Faber
for permission to publish the poem by Edwin Muir

For Sorrel

Yes, yours, my love, is the right human face.
I in my mind had waited for this long,
Seeing the false and searching for the true,
Then found you as a traveller finds a place
Of welcome suddenly amid the wrong
Valleys and rocks and twisting roads. But you,
What shall I call you? A fountain in a waste,
A well of water in a country dry,
Or anything that's honest and good, an eye
That makes the whole world bright. Your open heart,
Simple with giving, gives the primal deed,
The first good world, the blossom, the blowing seed,
The hearth, the steadfast land, the wandering sea,
Not beautiful, or rare in every part,
But like yourself, as they were meant to be.

Edwin Muir

Acknowledgements

The writing down of these events has been a lonely job and I have only Sorrel to thank for being here and propping me up. But the years themselves could not have shaped our lives the way they have without the help of many people. In particular I want to thank James and Pamela Fraser, Richard and Joan Frere, Elizabeth Taylor and Lilian and Lovell Foot for their part; and Lord Burton, the late Captain Matheson, John Grigg and The Forestry Commission for permission to walk over their land when we first started. Peter Wortham, Roddy Miller, Simon Fraser, Roy Dennis, Julian Clough, Janis Burlton, Martha Crewe, Tina Pocock, Charlie Barrington, Finlay MacRae, Ian Smith and Don Cameron have all helped in their various professional ways to keep us going, or in line, or moving forwards; and, at the very end, Wendy Sedgwick who typed the manuscript, Kathy Fraser and Paul Johnson who criticized it, and Eleo Gordon and John Guest who did the rest. I am more than grateful to Sarah Norton for the illustrations throughout the text.

List of Illustrations

The author wishes to thank the following photographers for kind permission to use their work: Peter Wortham for nos. 3, 6, 11, 12, 13, 14, 15, 16, 22, 23; Sorrel Lister-Kaye for nos 21, 24; Julian Clough for no. 9; Roderick Miller for no. 17 and *The Berkhamsted Gazette* for no. 5. All other photographs were taken by the author.

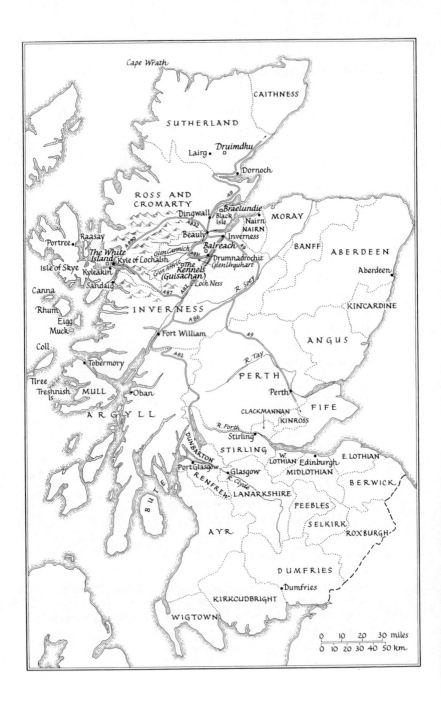

Foreword

This book is about the Highlands of Scotland as I have seen this huge upland area from when I first came to live here in 1969, through a handful of years of change, and on into an uncertain future. It is uncertain because, just as there have been past eras of grandeur and poverty, of injustice and bloodshed, this is an era of development and a great opening up of Highland wilderness to the world at large.

Every ònce in a while, through our work, I have been able to look back and catch a glimpse of what it must have been like to live here when life was a simpler day to day matter of birth and death; when man was shaped by his environment, by the forest and the hill and the animals which lived out their days beside him under the tumbling wind and the sky.

Aigas 1979   JOHN LISTER-KAYE

Book One

Chapter One

After Gavin Maxwell's unexpected death in September 1969 I had remained on Kyleakin Island until the end of the year, winding up the wildlife sanctuary we had been creating there and sorting out the thousand odd difficulties which arose from those tragic circumstances. The island was finally sold and I was homeless. In a year my world had turned itself head-over-heels, and I viewed the future with some concern and trepidation.

Early in 1969 I had abandoned my career in steel and gambled with the vagaries of natural history and writing. Gavin had helped me enormously and given me a very good insight into the problems of being so highly dependent upon one's own resources, but the months I had spent on the island had killed any desire I might once have harboured for the rewards of commerce, and the thought of returning to an industrial area like South Wales was now quite repugnant. Donald Mitchell, who had been the last of the Maxwell otter keepers and with whom I had shared the last months on the island, had gone to a job in the Nature Conservancy. A little while later he wrote to say that he was rowing round Loch Leven in a glass-bottomed boat looking for the bottom. Whether he ever found it I never heard, for shortly afterwards he wrote that he had been transferred to a laboratory where he cared for large numbers of rats and mice. This struck me as being vastly less interesting.

I was pleased that Donald should have found an involvement so quickly, but I held little chance for myself. For Christmas I went to Skye, to the house of some friends who had generously offered me a haven in which to lick my wounds and sort out whether to turn back or go on. Skye and the other Hebridean Isles have become a drug over the few short years that I have known them. I have never known another place where it is possible to lose oneself in the timelessness of the present. There is a quality of separateness from the rest of the world which exists in the Western Isles which writers have been struggling to define for centuries. I believe it defies definition and exists only in experience. Although how long Skye in particular can maintain its mysterious separateness in the face of the growing tourist flood which invades its ferries every year, is no longer a rhetorical question.

I stayed on Skye until mid-January. When I left, the Cuillin hills were heavy in snow and the tinkling, crystal burns of summer which had lately crashed and thundered down the hills in long lines of white spume were now, for a while, silent in frost. Ice waterfalls hung from ice-crusted rock lips, and great bulbous blue-green stalactites showed where the last flow had died.

I had decided to write *The White Island* and I was travelling to the Central Highlands to a cottage I had been offered for the rest of the winter. An eyrie would be a better description for Balreach. It was perched high on a rock ledge overlooking Loch Ness and the Monadliath hills. I could not have wished for a better place in which to struggle with a first book. Ostensibly the cottage was in a village, but the track from the main road led up so steeply, twisting and turning through six hundred feet of hair-pin after hair-pin bends, that the view from the cottage was like a cliff-top view in that one did not know what went on at its foot.

Balreach, too, was gripped in snow and frost. I dug my way into the front door the day I arrived, and had to climb out of a window to dig my way out of the cottage the following morning. But the snow, if not the frost, was ephemeral. On the track it became trodden and grey, and the small white lawn in front of the building was so pitted with rabbit tracks and criss-crossed with my labrador Max's ever hopeful forays that it too became unsightly. Soon, however, it froze into ice. For many successive nights, ten and even twenty, degrees of frost froze everything so hard that to fall in the snow was sharp and painful, like falling among rocks. Yet while the nights were severely cold, and the temperature remained often below freezing during the day, the clear skies and thin air allowed the sun to shine piercingly. On those bright days I could often see twenty or thirty miles from my cottage window; and from upstairs, where the extra height took me above the surrounding birch trees, the view spread out across eighty miles of Monadliath mountain and high moor to the Cairngorms beyond. With field glasses I could easily discern the famous Cairgorm peaks, Cairngorm itself, at just over four thousand feet, and Ben Macdhui, its snows blue with distance, at four thousand three hundred.

At the point opposite my window Loch Ness was over two miles wide, and of its 22-mile length I could see five or six miles. As well as the many small craft which were kept along its shores and in the bay below, there were regular fleets of east coast fishing boats which passed through the Caledonian canal to fish in Hebridean waters and the Atlantic.

It was several weeks before I could pass that upstairs window without pausing, often too long, to gaze out over the scenery; mesmerized by the shifting cloud shadows spreading and folding across the surface of Loch Ness, or captivated by a car, a tiny insect creeping along the loch-shore road; or a boat, rowing boat or fishing smack, noiselessly inching across the window pane, white wrinkles peeling back from its bows and its wake running in long lines to the land.

To have left Skye and the island was no escape from the sound of water. Even in hard frost the Balreach burn rushed and tumbled past the cottage, hidden and protected by its deep gorge which dropped sheer from behind the building down through forty feet of wet walls to its own dark world of ferns and mosses and occasional birches and alders which swerved madly skywards from cracks and fissures in the rock walls. When I arrived the sound was a gentle murmur, the endless movement of underground water unaffected by frost, a natural drainage which produced the sweetest and softest drinking water I have ever tasted. But later on, when the spring thaw started and the snow receded on the high hills, the sound grew daily, reaching a pitch and intensity which made one glad that it was contained within its forty-foot walls. At its peak, for a few days one lived in a weird world deafened to all other sounds. A constant crashing roar surrounded and engulfed the cottage, and one moved about as if in a film without its soundtrack, steps with no thud of footfall, sticks breaking and the axe falling on wood without the ring and clatter one expects.

Behind the cottage the ground rose steeply from the far side of the gorge through natural birchwoods up to a sharp tree-line at a thousand feet. Above the trees a bare rock boss capped the hill a hundred feet higher up. To cross the burn one had to follow the gorge up past the cottage for a quarter of a mile where the stream was at ground level, a gentle babbling burn with no suggestion of its anger below. Here a sheet of corrugated iron had been wired to three stout birch poles and laid across stones to form a makeshift bridge. Its crude efficiency reflected much of the Highland temperament seen more commonly in gates and fences – but it was a bridge, and, if one crossed quickly, it was possible to remain dry-shod.

The land immediately around the cottage was rough, and varied between birch scrub, long impenetrable banks of gorse and broom, and rough, unkempt pasture. There were occasional sheep, but the land was really dominated by rabbits which cropped the grass and kept the brambles at bay, and which, until Max arrived, lived in comparative peace within the maze of tunnels the gorse provided.

My early days at Balreach were unproductive. They were a holiday during which I rose late to potter happily about, cutting wood for the stove and brewing indelicate stews from the rabbits I shot behind the byre, and turnips filched from a field nearby. I was happy not to approach the village any closer than this larceny required and I retired early to my fireside, feet up on the stove rail, and lost in the small selection of literature I had with me and in plans for my book.

Max was one year old a few weeks after I moved to live at Balreach. It had been an exciting first year. He had come from a select home in Wales from where he was to have gone to the grandest of Scottish labrador kennels. But those plans had been upset and he had come to me instead. He was named after Gavin Maxwell and it was to Gavin that he also owed the idyllic freedom of his puppyhood. The island was a perfect place to rear a puppy, traffic-free and with every variety of scent and animal smell a dog could dream of. I had gun-trained him on the island, and at Balreach we worked the gorse and broom thickets together to shoot rabbits for the pot.

One afternoon I was standing on top of the bank below the house waiting for Max to reappear from the dense bushes in front of me. We were working our regular routine. The disturbed rabbits regularly fled uphill to the top of the bank and down the other side. By standing on top I had a chance to shoot as they ran up towards me and again as they disappeared over the other side. Max had gone in with his usual jubilant enthusiasm, tail gyrating wildly and with squeals of excitement and impatience when I had made him wait until I was in position.

I could hear his tail thrashing about in the thickest part of the bank, and I knew from the intensity of the sound he was hard on the tail of a rabbit. Suddenly it appeared running, not uphill as usual, but down the bank and toward the open hill. I watched it go without attempting to shoot; it was already too far. Then Max saw it too and gave chase. At the bottom of the bank was a tight wire fence, six taut wires with a barbed wire along the top. The rabbit slipped between the bottom wires and sped out into the field. Max charged down the bank and, seeing the fence ahead, took off while still above the fence, stretching out to leap it in one bound. There had been no fences like this on the island and he was still inexperienced with barbed wire. With his legs stretched out in front and behind, the skin of his tummy in mid-leap must have been as tight as a drum. An inch would have cleared him; but he had misjudged it, and, as the speed of his leap swept him across the wire, a single razor-edged barb slit him open from sternum to pelvis.

He landed on the snow on the other side of the fence on all four feet, and struck out in pursuit of the rabbit. Even from where I was standing I could see the blood trail in the snow getting thicker and thicker. After five or six bounds the seriousness of the situation must have hit him. He faltered, turned and screamed like a fallen child. Dropping my gun I ran down the bank and cleared the fence without noticing it. There seemed to be blood everywhere, and still the heart-rending cries as he writhed in the snow. The cut was far worse than I had imagined it could be, and his intestines were spewing out in long bloody coils. I turned him upside down and pushed them back inside the abdomen wall. There seemed to be little else I could do straight away, so I picked him up, cradled him upside down in my arms and walked and half-ran back to the cottage

Thankfully it was not very far and I was indoors within a few minutes. I laid him on the old settee beside the stove and propped him up, still in the same position, with cushions. He was still bleeding profusely, but at least he was quiet and seemed to accept my help without question. I rushed about collecting sterilized lint and bandages, and putting the kettle on to boil. Then I started to examine the damage.

Miraculously the barb had penetrated no deeper than through the abdomen wall. None of the intestines seemed to be damaged at all. I returned them carefully to their place and swabbed most of the blood from around them with lint and cotton-wool. But the barb had ripped through his genitals, causing erectile tissue to be badly torn. This was where the excessive bleeding came from. I bound him up as best I could and then set about stitching. I stitched the cut from his chest down to his navel without trouble; the flesh met tidily and formed a neat line. Max didn't seem to mind too much. But I was not happy about lower down. I would have to go for a vet.

Leaving Max lying quietly on his side I ran to the nearest house and asked to use their phone. They seemed surprised to open the door to a man out of breath and liberally smeared with blood, but they accepted my story and let me in. The nearest vet was, inevitably, out on a farm round and was unlikely to be home before eight or nine that night. I explained the situation to the vet's wife and returned quickly to Balreach to wait. All the bandages and cushions were covered in blood when I returned and I again bound Max in an effort to stop the bleeding. It was just getting dark at about five o'clock.

At midnight I heard a Land Rover grinding up the track. I had changed the bandages so often during the evening that I had run out and had had to tear up a sheet instead. For an hour and a half the vet snipped and stitched and swabbed away the blood. Finally it was done. He gave Max an anti-biotic injection and a sedative and we sat back to see if the flow of blood had been stopped. I poured two liberal whiskies and we waited. At two-thirty the vet changed the dressings again and decided that things were beginning to improve. There still seemed to me to be too much blood, but I thanked him as the Land Rover lights jogged and jerked away down the track. It was three o'clock in the morning. He had started work the previous day at 7.30 in the morning, driving eighty miles to inject a herd at 10 a.m. He had finally got home again at half-past ten in the evening, received my message and come out again straight away, driving another thirty miles to attend to Max. It would be after four before he was home again. That, I thought, was real dedication to one's work.

When I returned to the cottage Max lifted his head to greet me, and his tail fluttered feebly. A little while later we were both asleep, I in the armchair drawn up to the fire, and Max on his side on the settee where he had now been for twelve hours.

The bleeding did not finally stop for another three days. The cut healed unbelievably quickly, and the stitches were out in little more than a week, but he continued to pass blood sporadically and there were anxious moments when I feared more permanent injury.

During Max's convalescence I had to make sure that he didn't stretch his wound, so any exercise he took had to be very gentle. Because the cottage was surrounded by rabbits I had to go out first thing in the morning leaving Max indoors, and beat about in the bushes to scare any there might be away from the building. I knew the temptation of a chase would be too much if one got up from under his nose. Once the ground was clear I allowed him out for a few minutes. At first it was a very painful stiff-legged affair, but within a day or two he was trotting about quite comfortably.

My book was progressing well during this period and since I had little inclination to walk the hills alone I worked long hours at my desk. When after a week or two Max was quite healed I let him run alone again, often spending an hour of more outside while I worked. He developed the habit or returning to the cottage at regular intervals of about half an hour, and I would have to get up from my desk to let him in. But really all he wanted was to check that I was still there and had not gone off anywhere exciting without him. No sooner had I sat down to work than he would whine to be let out again. This happened so often I decided to teach him to let himself in and out.

By hanging a shot rabbit on the back of a half-open door and encouraging him to jump up at it with the words 'close the door', he soon caught on to the idea of pushing the door shut. The front door had a press-down handle on both sides, and by attaching a tassel to the end of each handle and encouraging Max to pull it with his teeth, he soon learned to let himself in too. This done, it remained only to practise it to perfection. So every morning we had opening and closing door sessions for half an hour. Within a week he had perfected the trick and I was troubled no more.

By the middle of March the snow had thawed at Balreach. It remained only on the high hills, pink and purple in the sun, and the burn was loud with melt-water cascading down from the mountains as clear and as fresh as the first snow-drops on its banks. Yet it was by no means the end of winter. There would be more snow and more ice before spring; but the thaw, short though it was, gave an inkling of what was to come.

Balreach Burn

The snow-drops had appeared overnight. They were there, pushing up through the ground during all the frost and cold, waiting for the first release, the first slackening of the frost-grip.

Suddenly the roof-eaves were dripping and the ground was covered with tiny thrusting spears. Thousands of green needles in patches so thick that one could not put a finger between them, bursting out through the melting snow-crust in every direction. In twelve hours they were in bloom and the ground was white again. All along the burnside and under the birches up and down the track they stood, bell-mouthed and whiter than the trampled snow, vivid green against the uniform rust of last year's leaves.

Only now that the snow had gone was I able to see Balreach in its true colours. Balriadach, as the old Gaelic spelling was, means 'settlement of the grey stones'. And it was the grey stones which struck me first. The hill behind the cottage was dotted with large bare patches of rock where the soil had been eroded by wind and water. Whether the Highlander who first chose to build on that site, and who gathered the grey stones from the hillside and placed them carefully one on another, binding them with lime and water as he did so, was as moved by their beauty as I was, or not, is unknown, but he was right to choose them for a name. He might have chosen the view, or the gorge down which he must have climbed daily to draw his water, or any of a dozen outstanding features of that place, but it was the grey stones he liked and it is the grey stones by which it is known to this day, although sadly the meaning is lost to a native population impoverished through the decay of its language.

From a distance the Balreach rocks gave depth and interest to the hill. They were a subtle grey which varied with the light on them. Sometimes when they caught the sun they gleamed white like water, and in shadow they were dark and menacing, reflecting in their hard edges the struggle for exist-ence in a windswept land. But under close inspection the stones were a dozen different colours. The bare faces were covered in lichens, not ordinary fence-post lichens of dusty green, but mountain lichens in rings and patches bigger than the spread of my hand. Circles of bright ochreous yellow with brown pin-point heads dotted around their periphery.

Growths of deep wine-red and terracotta with convoluted surfaces clinging to the contours of the rock like miniature sponges; and orange suns as bright as a garden marigold with inner whorls of yellow and brown and red. Others stood out from the rock in tiny leafy fingers, pale green like willow leaves, and cigar-brown lobes which rustled and tore like brown paper when touched. And then there were round patches, almost white, so that I thought at first they were bird droppings and ignored them. But a closer look showed that they were made up of tiny individual heads so that the whole was like a colony, crowded together for protection. I was so impressed by the colours that I tried to prize the lichens from the stones to take them home to keep. After long, painstaking care, I managed to collect a few of orange and red and arranged them in a haphazard pattern on the mantle-shelf over the stove. But, like the seaweeds I had tried to collect on Skye, they dried in the artificial climate of the room and became curled and brown so that, conscious of their great age, I wished I had left them alone.

At the end of March I had to leave the cottage. The owner had made arrangements to stay there for Easter, and after that it would be in use sporadically throughout the summer. Yet with my eviction came another generous offer. The same friend had a second cottage in a still wilder and more remote area and he offered me that instead. I accepted wholeheartedly and, packing my few books and possessions, I slung my rucksack on my back, closed the door and whistled for Max to follow. As when I had arrived, it was snowing when we left, and as we walked off down the track the snow filled in our footprints behind us.

Chapter Two

My new cottage was a complete contrast. Instead of the square symmetry of Balreach with its painted stonework and neatly tiled roof, Druimdhu was delightfully primitive. It was probably far older, too. It was a typical Highland hut of a type and style which probably existed from the time when the Gaels first started placing one stone on top of another until English building techniques filtered north with occupation. Originally it had had a turf roof, but at some point between the wars the turfs had been replaced by corrugated iron. There had been no question of nailing the corrugated sheets smoothly on to rafters in the normal way, because on Druimdhu there weren't any rafters. The roof timbers were birch poles haphazardly arranged from a central support running along the apex. The effect of laying corrugated iron on to a framework of this sort was quite bizarre, since in no two places were the rafter poles at the same level. The roof dipped and rose like a choppy sea and the apex was as uneven as an old cow's back. At the edges the iron sheets had been cut, trimmed and turned under as if by a conscientious tailor. Finally, to keep the whole in place, large stone weights were suspended on either end of fencing wires which ran over the roof from front to back. At the lowest point the eaves started five feet from the ground and nowhere all round the building could a man stand beneath them. In exactly the same way the wall head varied from between four and five feet, the walls being three feet thick at the bottom and tapering inwards to two feet at the top. It was a masterpiece of improvisation and resourcefulness. In its disregard for any building principle it proved to be the strongest, cosiest and most durable building in the district.

The interior was as impromptu as the outside. There happened to be three windows in the front, but one felt that there might have been only one, or even none at all had the builder been in a different mood. They were small, uncompromising holes; mere apertures through which one could see a little of the world outside, but from which one shouldn't expect to get light. No man spent the day indoors when that house was built, and his wife sat to her chores in the doorway. Light at night was a luxury and anyway, if you had big windows you lost heat and the candles blew out.

There was one large room inside with an earth floor stamped hard by centuries of feet, and a rough wooden partition separating off a small area at one end; but that, I am sure, was not part of the original plan. Highland architects of that period and inclination had no use for bedrooms. A bracken bed on the floor and perhaps a curtain. The other end would almost certainly have housed a cow and two or three goats. Presumably, too, there had once been a hole in the turf roof to let the smoke out, but with the galvanized iron roofing had come an iron chimney pipe and a pot-bellied stove which sat rudely in the middle of the floor.

Had I moved into a modern cottage, or even a Victorian or earlier house like Balreach, and found no water and no electricity I think I would have been a little put out, disgruntled at having to fiddle with candles and paraffin and carry water in pails. But it would have been utterly presumptuous to have even thought of such services at Druimdhu. A spring bubbled out of the ground not twenty feet from the end of the building, and the smell of oil lamps was so much a part of the house that I looked forward to trimming the wicks and watching the glow spread in the glass and across the ceiling. Half-way through my stay at Druimdhu a friend remarked how inconvenient it must be to have no electric light. Caught for a moment unawares and unconscious of any inconvenience about the place, I blurted out that I had got it. Then I faltered and, feeling silly, had to say 'Oh no!' and 'How stupid of me!' while my friend adopted an expression which plainly suggested that the isolation was affecting me.

The cottage was adequately furnished and equipped: a table and two chairs, a bed behind the wooden partition and an old armchair before the stove. A small bottle-gas cooker and a selection of plates, mugs and cutlery saw to any other needs I had. It was ideal. I could not have devised a better setting to work in, and its isolation ensured the peace and quiet I wanted.

Yet the terms isolation and peace and quiet referred only to humans. There were, in fact, many distractions and almost constant sound; nor was I alone. Actually the place was rather crowded at times as I quickly found out. On my first evening I set about cutting some firewood and lighting the stove. I worked busily outside for some minutes and, bringing the cut kindling into the cottage, I opened the iron door on the stove. To my surprise I found that the last inhabitant had kindly relaid the fire with leaves and wood-shavings and sticks before leaving. I was on the point of striking a match when I noticed that there was movement inside the bundle of wood-shavings. They parted and a whiskered nose and two shining black eyes impaled me. It was, appropriately, a wood-mouse and it faced me with a dilemma. The wood-shavings had been gratefully accepted for a nest and the mice were clearly happy with the arrangement. But I was not happy without a fire and someone was going to have to give way. Of all the British mice I have always most liked the wood-mouse. It is the live-liest and the gayest, with large round eyes and big ears like cartoon mice. It has lovely markings too, pure white breast and belly and a golden hamster-brown above. Most striking, though, is its superbly long tail, often longer than the whole of the rest of the body, tapering to a delicate needle point. It is flamboyant, that vertibral excess, a product of fashion rather than essential design, and it is carried as if it knows it, with a graceful upward curve, its length never touching the ground and the tip held in a permanent flourish. Wood-mice sparkle, it seems to me, all over. From enormous twinkling eyes, over a shining coat and down the length of its glossy tail. There was never really any question of evicting them completely, but I had to move them from the stove.

Once I was sure that the nest contained no young, I lifted it intact from among the kindling sticks and put it in a small cardboard box. I cut holes in either end and put the box on the floor against the wall. Then I had to wait half an hour for the two mice to vacate the bowels of the stove where they had hidden during this disturbance. They appeared cautiously at the entrance, paused to test the air for danger and then scuttled away along the wall. Exactly as I had hoped, one mouse ran towards the box. There was the dark inviting security of a hole, and in it went without a second's hesitation. Moments later it appeared at the other end. It popped out, ran round the side and in through the first hole again. There were scuttling sounds inside the box while it inspected the whole interior and then it was out again, away down the wall and under the door. I felt sure that something was wrong and was considering moving the box to a new site when back it came, nipping along with complete confidence, with its mate a few feet behind. They dived into the box where, for the next two hours, they busily set about remaking the nest to their precise requirements.

Meanwhile I lit the stove and bustled about unpacking my few possessions. Max was fascinated by the mice and I had to tell him firmly that they were not to be exploited either for sport or amusement. In a few days Bubble and Squeak – for those were exactly the noises they made – had become so used to Max that more than once they ran over him as he lay stretched out in front of the fire.

While there were mice in the hearth, there were not, happily, jackdaws in the chimney. They were under the roof. The corrugated iron had buckled in one particularly uneven place half-way down the roof, and the buckle provided an opening. Jackdaws are insatiable explorers of holes and the Druimdhu roof had been explored before I arrived. It was lined on the inside with sheets of hardboard so that there was a warm and dry cavity between the two. When I first heard the scuttlings from the roof I thought there were rats which, I confess, worried me. Wood-mice are one thing, but rats, however clean and countrified they may be, do have some disturbing habits and I was not anxious to share my home with them. But the unmistakable 'Jack' of one bird sitting outside on the roof put my mind at ease. When I moved in, the jackdaws were beginning to build a nest inside the roof and during my first two weeks I often saw them carrying twigs to and fro, sometimes dropping them from flight on to the roof so that they landed with a clatter and startled me at my work.

My move had taken me eighty miles from Loch Ness. Druimdhu was in Sutherland and the scenery was quite different. Instead of the birchwoods and the scattered remnants of the Scots pine forests of Inverness-shire, the Sutherland hills were bare and austere. And unlike Balreach, my new cottage was on the glen floor with the hill rising sharply behind so that my view was restricted to the width of the glen, a few fields and a river, before the hills rose again on the other side. But its striking feature was the daffodils. I had been sad at leaving the bulbs that were sprouting at Balreach, but those at Druimdhu amply made up for my loss. There was half an acre of rough pasture in front of the cottage which, a few days after my arrival, was yellow with springing daffodils. I had seen their greenery when I arrived and noted with pleasure that the clumps were thick and abundant, but I had been so tied up with settling into the house that I had paid them no further attention. Suddenly, on about the fourth morning of my tenancy I could scarcely believe my eyes. The ground was a carpet of colour, not just in clumps as I had expected, but covered, to the right and left, within the confines of the old stone wall, with thousands and thousands of nodding yellow blooms.

They were the greatest distraction that could have been devised. It was impossible to sit inside and work with the knowledge of that wealth of colour outside, so I took to working in the porch; but the effect was mesmeric and I found myself staring blankly at the flowers for minutes at a time with my pen held limply in my hand. I think their scent had something to do with it. When the sun shone and the flowers opened fully the air was heady with their smell, like walking into a big flower shop in London, that earthy, green smell which is as distinct and evocative as violin music.

To try to work outside with the daffodils so thick about me was bad enough, but as soon as I had torn my attention from them a breeze would spring up and scatter my papers or I would watch a jackdaw struggling with a twig larger than it could manage. It was while I was busy doing no work on my doorstep one morning that I noticed a pied wagtail alight two or three times in quick succession on the path leading up to where I was sitting. On each occasion it flew up under the eaves so that I knew it must be building a nest there. The wagtails, the jackdaws and Bubble and Squeak all produced young at about the same time so that there was a constant clamour of activity in and around the cottage. They numbered five, four and five respectively, a total of twenty-one tenants under the same roof and not a penny of rent paid between us. I remained the only celibate in the centre of a dynamic ring of fecundity and procreation, but I enjoyed vicariously the family security it created.

I made no attempt to tame any of my cohabitants. To have done so would have been in a sense a betrayal of the wildness of the place, but I did put out finely grated cheese for the wagtails, which they came regularly to take. When the young were fledged they sat in a row along the top of the wall opposite my front door and cheeped incessantly. The parents hawked up and down the length of the building and down the road behind, collecting large beak-fuls of insects to cram into the cavernous mouths of their brood. They were like dragonflies, the adult birds, flitting across my vision times without number to alight on the wall, tails flicking, heads held high and faces almost hidden behind the indelicate bundle of writing wings and legs captive in their beaks. I have never stopped marvelling at the dexterity of this feat. In some bundles there must have been a dozen or more winged insects, all caught flying. How the bird secures each successive capture without losing it when it snaps at the next victim remains a complete mystery to me. Perhaps the spiky little tongue that wagtails have is used to this effect. If so, and if the same usage is extended to other bird families, Æsop's fable of the Fox and the Crow with the cheese sadly fails in ornithological observation.

I saw much less of the jackdaw family – the upstairs tenants – as they were separated from me by the ceiling, though they made up for this in other ways. From the day when the first egg hatched there was the constant threat of uproar in the cottage relieved only at night when they slept restlessly. Young jackdaws don't cheep endearingly like young birds are supposed to; rather, they whine and wheeze as if each one is being slowly strangled by its own personal boa constrictor – a disturbing sound at its lowest ebb, but one which rises to a crescendo of frenetic hysteria at the sound of the return of a parent bird. Happily there were quite long periods when the adults were away searching for food; but unhappily, for as long as the four rowdy youngsters remained in their nest they were quite incapable of telling the difference between the sound of their returning parents and that of their downstairs neighbour. I had only to get up to stoke the fire, or even shift noisily in my chair to set them off. At first I tried thumping on the ceiling with the broom handle, but this merely provoked a louder and longer outburst. Then I tried making predatory noises like owl-hoots and fox-barks, but although these attempts were greeted by an inquisitive silence to begin with, they were quickly followed by riotous mockery from above.

As the young birds grew, so did their volume and I found myself actively suffering because of them. I would sit working at the table for an hour or two and would begin to long for a cup of tea. Attempts to creep across to the cooker had always failed and so I would sit there hour after hour dying for a drink, or to go and relieve myself, sometimes in an acutely uncomfortable position, while I waited for the adult birds to return. When at last they did I would leap to my feet, dash madly round the cottage boiling kettles and refuelling the stove while the ghastly hubbub went on up above, and be back in my place at the table by the time they had settled into silence again so that I could make the most of the peace and quiet.

At one point they made so much noise so regularly that I was strongly tempted to evict them by force; but that would have meant taking the roof apart or burning the cottage down, and my anger never reached quite that pitch. When they ultimately flew from the nest and perched insecurely about the place in trees and on the roof making altogether much more jackdaw-like noises I became rather fond of them; but there is one crime, far worse than any disturbance, of which I shall never be sure of their innocence.

I had been working outside on one particularly fine day and, for once, had made some progress. Several hours had slipped past and Max had grown bored with such prolonged inactivity. He trotted off through the daffodils, but was soon back, clearly asking for a game. I gave in and left my work to throw his rabbit dummy for him. We played vigorously for some minutes in a small clearing among the flowers, and in the course of pushing Max away from me my gold signet ring flew off my finger and fell into the long grass. I ran straight to the spot and searched anxiously. The grass was thick and rough and I thought that I would stand a better chance if I cut it down with scissors. I marked the spot and went into the house to get some. It took me several minutes to find a pair and I then returned to the spot. I searched all afternoon. I cut the grass down to its roots all round the place where the ring fell. I raked up the stems and searched through them blade by blade. There was no trace of the ring. The jackdaws sat around and squawked aggravatingly from the trees and roof.

In the late afternoon I drove down to the nearest village and went to see a water diviner whom I had heard could dowse for anything. She was a voluminous lady of great character and she kindly agreed to come straight away and help me search for the ring. Among her many distinctions this lady told me that she had, for many years, lived beside Loch Ness and had come to know the monsters intimately – for she assured me that there were several – and could predict their appearance accurately. For her family and friends she had done this successfully many times, but she chose to remain anonymous because publicity in the past had become a nuisance to her.

The good lady worked diligently in the Druimdhu garden for over two hours, straining over her whalebone switch and frequently 'getting a line' on gold. She clutched another ring in her left hand and walked about the patch with her eyes tight closed and muttering to herself in a way for which she would certainly have been burned at the stake in the Middle Ages. After a while she opened her eyes and came towards me. She was very red in the face and I noticed that she was perspiring heavily. A few years before, I had known a man in Northumberland who could dowse for deer in the forests and he had had to restrict his activities because it endangered his health. He became very hot and his blood pressure rose alarmingly. This lady looked to me to be in the same condition so I was relieved when she admitted defeat and said that, while she had received strong vibrations several times she had been unable to tie them down and pin-point the exact spot where the ring lay – but, she added encouragingly, she was sure it was there somewhere!

I took the lady home and when I returned the jackdaws were still sitting around looking innocent. I searched for a week and found nothing. Finally I abandoned the ring as lost. I have never been able to explain its disappearance for certain but I do think that when I went indoors to get the scissors one of the jackdaws might have swooped down and picked it out of the grass. All the crow family are attracted to shiny objects and, being a bright sunny day, the ring would have shone like gold at its best. If this is what happened, then the ring, finely engraved with a heraldic device and the valued possession of many generations of my family, lies in some sordid twiggy hole or chimney with fragments of silver cigarette paper and other rubbish. At the end of the day the Cardinal Lord Archbishop of Rheims was a very much happier man than I.

In the evenings when the jackdaws were at last quiet, I put my feet up on the pot-bellied stove and read. If I stoked the stove high with oak logs and birch, by the end of the evening its belly was glowing red hot and the heat was so great that Max would retreat to a cold corner. When it rained the stove spat and spluttered because the chimney pipe was straight and the rain drops fell direct into the fire. But even those evenings were not free from distraction. Bubble and Squeak only really became active after dark and I would be vaguely conscious through my reading that there were small creatures at work around about me. In the early days at Druimdhu I took care to clean up after meals, leaving no crumbs or dirty dishes about the table, but as time went by I became increasingly lazy about housework and often left plates unwashed for two or three days. It was this free food supply which encouraged Bubble and Squeak to explore the table. They were remarkable acrobats and could climb almost anything. They had a variety of routes which led to the table, including one up the rough cast wall, but they preferred an upholstered chair because it gave a better grip to their tiny claws, and so I always left the chair touching the table edge for easy access. Storing crumbs in their cheek pouches they would glean whatever was available, toast, biscuits, bacon rinds, cheese, butter, and apple. I enjoyed watching them climb and I would leave a crust of bread perched on top of a pile of books or in a shopping basket so that they had to scale the obstacle first. Quite accidentally I discovered their delights and preferences. After eating prunes one day I was astonished to see them carrying off the stones, one by one, down into their box where I later heard their sharp inscisors grating through the nut to the kernel inside. Cherry stones, too, they loved and in the space of twenty minutes they collected, hauled and hoarded in their box the stones of a large tin of cherries, perhaps forty or fifty stones in all.

I think most bizarre was their addiction to kipper remains. On more than one occasion I caught them dragging off the entire skeleton of a kipper from my plate. But I had to intervene in the interest of hygiene because hoards of kipper bones would attract vermin of every kind to the cottage as well as produce a fulsome smell. Nor was I anxious that they should pay so much attention to my salt-cellar, a low open bowl in which I regularly found signs of their interest. One day I discovered the remains of a cattle salt-lick in a field nearby and I brought a piece home for the mice. I left it on the floor in one corner and it was an immediate success. I often heard them gnawing at it and they left my table salt alone from then on.

It is interesting to note that, given the chance, wood-mice will be truly omnivorous. Bubble and Squeak would industriously remove any meat left on a chop bone, and the raw egg I cracked into a saucer and left out for an experiment was completely eaten in less than forty-eight hours. Raw cabbage and turnip peelings they loved and almost any fruit was tried, even lemon peel. Nuts were great favourites, a small uneven hole being gnawed in one end until the kernel could be removed. Olive stones and pickled onions, shrimps, haddock and plaice, liver pâté and black pudding, ham and pasta – the list is endless – of foods tried and mostly enjoyed by those delightful scavengers. In the end they came to ignore me almost entirely, no longer waiting for me to leave the table after meals, but joining me at my board and stealing what they could. They were never tame, and I never handled them at all, but they were quite unafraid of my presence and my movement. If they became too bold and attacked food I did not want them to I had only to rap the table with a fork and say 'Shoo!' for them to dart away down the chair and into the dark security of their box; but it usually only took them a few minutes to recover their boldness and be back on the table top again.

When Squeak was heavy in milk it was possible to distinguish between the two of them, but until then they had appeared to be identical. Only when her nipples became visible and when she sat up on the table on her haunches to hold food in her fore-paws – used exactly like human hands – did I notice that she had a yellow star in the centre of her chest. Wood-mouse fur is often very golden-yellow around the throat and flanks, just where it changes to the pure shining white which extends right along the mouse's underside from chin to tail; but Squeak's chest-star was bright yellow. Bubble, smart though he was, had no chest markings at all. Rather sadly I think Squeak's beautiful yellow star must have been controlled by a recessive gene because not one of her five offspring inherited it unless perhaps it developed with adult pelage after I had gone.

The young mice were tiny when they first emerged from the box. They can have been no more than a fortnight old and they were perfect in every way; little mouse-people straight from Beatrix Potter. Unlike most young things they seemed to be complete adults in miniature; practised and co-ordinated in movement and reaction to a degree which seemed too good for their two weeks' life. Max and I watched them for hours during their first days while they were still exploring the interior of the cottage. Their box was always the ultimate security and, if their nerve failed when they experienced something for the first time – a stick that moved unexpectedly in the wood stack or a crackle from the stove – they darted back to the box like arrows. They were often in trouble and more than once I had to come to their rescue. I fished the same mouse out of Max's drinking bowl twice within an hour and another spent a cold and frustrating night in the bottom of a polythene bucket he had accidentally fallen into. I examined the outside minutely and found inscisor marks in several places which told me that Squeak had located her missing child and tried to free it, but it had probably moved about so much inside the bucket that she had never seemed near enough to it to persevere with her gnawing at any one place.

Mouse mortality rate is naturally high and I knew that their numbers would be reduced sooner or later. Sure enough, as soon as they started to leave the safety of the cottage and forage outside casualties occurred. There were always tawny-owls about the place at night – I heard them often and saw them regularly – and I expect they were responsible for the two losses to Bubble and Squeak's family that happened within the first few days of their exploration outside.

By no means all the Druimdhu animal life was restricted to the area of the cottage. The hill behind, for instance, like many remote mountainous districts of the Highlands, had its herd of wild goats. Although there were indigenous goats in the Highlands at one time, this herd was almost certainly a product of domestic stock either released or escaped to their natural habitat among the rocky slopes and screes of the high hills.

The Druimdhu goats were a big herd, thirty or forty strong, and very wild. The road which ran past the cottage wound along the glen floor roughly following the contours of the river plain. In places it came close to the foot of the hill on the north side, which rose steeply, sometimes sheer, for three or four hundred feet before the gradient slackened and the rounded mountain swept back to a distant horizon. The effect of driving along the road was that of moving through a one-sided gorge, and it was on that stretch that one could sometimes see the goats. They lived on precipitous ledges, their shaggy black, chocolate and cream marked coats standing out against the uniform grey of the rock behind. They were very picturesque, but they knew all too well the dangers of a car stopping on the road below. They had obviously been shot at not infrequently because they moved off sharply whenever a vehicle did stop. I think that goat-sniping was one particularly pointless and obnoxious pastime of some local youths – at which I caught one once – for several of the herd limped, or dangled broken limbs, and the fox-scattered remains of carcases were not an uncommon find.

My efforts to observe them closely had, for this reason, to be conducted from above rather than below. When I first saw them I was in the cottage at work. I heard the rattle of falling stones from the rock face behind, and, wondering what had caused it I went out to look. An old billy stood only a few yards away from me. He looked plainly shocked. He had

magnificently curved horns sweeping back from his shaggy, bearded face, and wore an expression which made me laugh aloud. A billy such as this is a very proud animal; having passed through the undignified years of being a minion in the herd he had, at last, gained superiority and, with sexual achievement, had grown the biggest and finest horns. With his horns came dignity and the responsibilities of a patriarchy. To turn tail and flee from adversity at such close quarters could not be entertained. It must be done with courage and dignity.

The old goat looked at me as if to say: 'Oh dear! If I had known that cottage was occupied I would not have come so close.' But this first regret quickly changed to arrogance. It was a bluff, and had I been a local youth with a ·22, it would have failed. He stamped his feet, tossed his head and coughed; a sharp petulant cough which seemed to spit contempt. He advanced in short, menacing rushes, a few feet at a time, halting and stamping again and lowering and tossing his enormous horns. Then the show was over. Satisfied that his honour was unblemished he turned slowly and, with his tail standing foolishly erect, walked stiffly away up the slope. The rest of the herd watched in awe from a hundred feet higher up. As soon as they saw him turn away they too turned and disappeared quickly from view. The old billy kept up the stiff-legged dignity bid for another fifteen or twenty yards and then with a flick of his heels he was away, running as fast as his hooves would carry him until he was over the top and out of danger. I chuckled to myself all day – a fact which, had he known, would have hurt the old goat almost as much as the ·22.

The next day I set out before dawn to try to photograph the whole herd. I climbed the hill in half-light and sat to watch the day begin from a thousand-foot pinnacle overlooking much of the top of the gorge. I remember that the dawn was reflected in the river long before there was any light on the surrounding fields. It was like a broad silver ribbon winding along the glen floor.

I located the goats easily. They had been down almost to the river-fields during the night and were slowly browsing their way back to the safety of the rocks. I was far above them and, guessing their route upwards, I positioned myself at the top of their path and sat back to wait. I had a powerful telescope with me and I watched them pick and choose their food with great delicacy of touch if not of taste. The gorse was in bloom; whole banks of yellow as vivid as daffodils, each waxen flower loud with colour, were dotted about among the rocks. The goats picked the flowers nimbly, chewing each one three times before nipping off the next one with a neat sideways twist of the head.

They were eating brambles and nettles, too, and when I

examined them later they had taken only the top, the upper-most succulent growing point or newly unfurled leaf. Whole beds of young stinging nettles were tidily clipped just where they were beginning to sprout above the tangle of last year's dry and brittle stems.

It took them twenty minutes to move up to me, walking two or three steps between mouthfuls. The breeze was in my favour and they came on quite oblivious of my presence. They were mainly nannies, with short compact horns and swinging teats. The young males were quite without the presence of the old billy I had met first, mere adolescents as yet unaware of their masculine potential. Besides these juniors there were three 'master' billies, all of much the same size and with long curved horns, but they showed distinct deference to the old master himself. He came up the slope last of all, and, as he passed, I could have touched the tip of his right horn. He was, at that range, quite the most pungent animal I have ever smelt. After keeping ferrets and mice as a boy I thought I knew all about animal smells, and those goats we had kept on Kyleakin Island had warned me of what the breed could be like, but this old roué walked off with the grand champion-ship. I had great difficulty in not giving myself away when the cloud of rank air hit me full in the face. Mercifully he walked on past and I did not have to hold my breath too long, for to have taken a lungful of that would have brought on immediate asphyxia. It was almost as if he had planned to repay me for the ignominy I had caused him the previous day.

On the day I heard the crack of rifle shots as I sat working at the table indoors, I went to investigate out of curiosity rather than from any preconceived wish to interfere. The gorse bushes were full of rabbits at which I had shot myself, and I assumed straight away that this was the reason for the shoot-ing. I approached quietly along the rabbit-cropped turf on the roadside and saw the figure of a youth standing at the foot of the rock wall, examining something at this feet. As I neared I realized that it was a goat he was standing over. Suddenly he heard me and spun round with a look of surprise and guilt.

He was holding a light repeating rifle in his hand. The goat, a nanny, was not quite dead and it gasped and heaved and kicked its legs. The youth, who must have been sixteen or seventeen, looked uncomfortable and made as if to shoot the dying animal again, but my presence prevented him.

'Aren't you going to kill it?' I asked, coldly.

'Aye,' he mumbled and turned to despatch the beast with a bullet in the head. It kicked violently and died.

'What are you going to do with it?' I asked, probably looking more disgusted than I had intended.

'N-nothing,' stammered the boy, now looking acutely worried. He was a tall languid youth with a maze of blonde hair. I noticed that he was wearing odd shoes. I had once shot a tawny-owl roosting in a tree out of sheer devilment when I was about this boy's age, and I remember how small I felt later. The fact that I had witnessed the deed would give him conscience enough I thought, and so I tried a different tack: 'I'm living in the Druimdhu croft and I came here to photograph the goats and make a short study of them . . .' The apology that interrupted me was painfully profuse. 'There aren't many places in Scotland where there are herds of wild goats,' I continued, 'they're rather special you know.'

He soundly assured me that he would never shoot a goat again and that he would pass the word round the village that the Druimdhu goats were 'special'. He pedalled away on his bicycle as if I had threatened to shoot him. I hope the old billy survived a year or two longer.

But the Druimdhu hill was famous, rather more than for its goats, for its colony of breeding fulmar petrels. The fulmar is a strictly coastal bird which has such well adapted wings for long periods of flight at sea that, like other sea-birds such as the gannet and the albatross, its legs are small and underdeveloped and its wings so long that the bird has great difficulty in rising into the air from a flat surface. For this reason these birds breed almost exclusively on cliff ledges so that they can just push off into mid-air. Since there was a shortage of suitable cliffs on the east coast of Sutherland these fulmars had come a few miles inland to breed on the Druimdhu cliff. It was, in fact, the furthest inland breeding site of fulmars in the British Isles. Again, the only way that I could really watch them was from above, and I spent long hours peering down from the cliff top at the nesting ledges thirty or forty feet below.

The fulmar is a curious bird in other ways too. It has a defence mechanism nearly as revolting as and not unlike that of the skunk. As one approaches the bird, either on its nest or, as I did, on the ground, unable to get off into flight, it opens its bill wide and flicks its head forward with a sharp hiss which culminates in an ejaculation of evil-smelling oily fluid. The fulmar can spit this fluid accurately a distance of five or six feet.

The bird that I found was sitting in the middle of a flat water-meadow beside the river about a mile from the nesting colony. There was no explanation for its presence there, so I must assume that it landed there out of choice. It was the first time I had seen a fulmar really close to and so I approached with interest. They are very like sea-gulls, big white birds but with nostril-like protuberances on the top of their bills. On the ground they look silly because they appear to have no legs. It was only as I came near that I realized how helpless the bird was on a flat field. It pushed itself along the ground with its inadequate legs, spreading and flapping its long, sabre-like wings. I very quickly caught it up and, knowing its unsavoury habits, I thought I would not go too close. But I underestimated the range of its spit. It rounded on me and I had to jump back to avoid a salvo of oil. I could smell the foul fishy stench of the fluid as it passed my face a few inches away.

Keeping well out of range I encouraged the bird to spit at me for some minutes in the hope that it would run out of ammunition and I would be able to get near enough to give it a lift off into the air. To my surprise the supply did not seem to diminish. I realized that, as one can go on producing saliva, but in a more efficient way, this bird was producing oil. Finally in desperation I took off my coat and held it out in front of me. I lunged at the bird and managed to swamp it with the coat. There was a brief struggle of hands and wings and I had it pinioned so that it couldn't peck or spit at me. As I got to my feet I flung the bird high into the air over my head. In seconds it was soaring away out of sight, a white speck finally invisible against white cloud.

A few days later I was fortunate in being invited to lunch by the Countess of Sutherland, a lady who had a few years previously turned her family home, Dunrobin Castle, which stands on the east coast of Sutherland with a magnificent view looking out across the mouth of Dornoch Firth to Tarbert Ness, into a boys' public school. We talked for some minutes before lunch about the school and the problems inherent in being situated so far north. She then asked me about my interests.

'I am very keen on all natural history, but particularly on birds,' I answered hoping that she wasn't a famous bird writer I had never heard of.

'Oh dear!' she said honestly, 'I'm afraid I don't know very much about ornithology. What birds in particular are you watching in Sutherland?'

I thought for a moment, not wishing to drown the conversation by mentioning some rare species she might never have heard of. Then I remembered the fulmars.

'One most interesting bird I've been watching a lot lately is the fulmar petrel,' I said confidently, knowing that I could talk about them in some detail. 'I wonder if you know it?' The Countess winced visibly at this question and replied with obvious displeasure: 'The fulmar petrel is the one bird with whose habits I am unhappily, and intimately acquainted. It has persistently and messily nested on the bedroom window-sills at Dunrobin and has spat evil-smelling ink at me every time I opened a window for the last thirty years. Yes, I do know the fulmar petrel!'

As the spring broke out around me life in and around Druimdhu burgeoned. The green leaf comes late to the North and it was mid-May before the birches had a full canopy. At about the same time a family of kestrels came to the hill behind the cottage. They must have nested on the rock face of the gorge a little way from the cottage, but when the young were fledged they chose a line of electricity poles crossing the hill to a farm on the other side of the valley as perches on which to sit the young while the parent birds hovered and hunted over the surrounding moor. There were three young birds and they habitually perched on three consecutive poles, one behind the other, thereby maintaining a strict order of feeding. As each bird was fed by the parent bringing in a morsel of prey the other two on the other two poles became so excited that they frequently lost their balance and flapped wildly to remain perched. More than once I saw them fall as if they had forgotten they could fly and pick up on uncertain and clumsy wings half-way to the ground. Like the jackdaws they shrieked vociferously, a harsh repetitive cry which was both angry and demanding. So consistent were they in the poles they used that I was able to fix my field glasses on a tripod, permanently locked in one position on my desk so that as soon as I heard their cries I could put my eyes to the glasses and watch them feed at close range. Kestrels commonly eat a lot of insects, but I saw few taken to this brood. There was a glut in that locality of short-tailed voles and the birds preyed upon them ceaselessly and monotonously until I finally lost count. At that early stage in their predatory career I had to leave the young kestrels and the other inhabitants of Druimdhu and drive south to England for the brief interlude of a family wedding. When I returned a fortnight later the kestrels had gone.

Whilst in England I took the tatty sheets of my first manuscript to a publisher. The response was promising. It seemed possible that it might be acceptable when it was complete. I drove back to Druimdhu from London without stopping. After sleep and food I set about my work with renewed vigour. By the end of July it was done; parcelled and posted to the great city. I had done little but eat, sleep and write for eight weeks. I needed a break and a change of scenery so I packed up my few belongings and vacated the tiny cottage, leaving it to Bubble and Squeak and their family. Like me, the other seasonal occupants had moved on.

Chickweed wintergreen

Chapter Three

After the long months of inland isolation, I yearned for the sea again. From Druimdhu I had travelled as far north as the mainland would allow, to Cape Wrath where the North Atlantic rollers broke in slow thunder over the oldest cliffs and rocks in the world. Sutherland is very humbling country. Its ageless scenery of bare windswept moors and hills is careless of life and the individual. It is remorseless and inclement and utterly predictable. I was reassured by its solidity and massiveness and was happy, for a brief while, to be dominated and stand in awe of it.

It was there, among the puffins and razorbills of those Archaean cliffs that I determined to find a foothold near the sea. It was a hot September day and Max and I were drowsy, having walked many miles across the heather, and, at the land's edge, we sat down to study from above the rocks and ledges ringed in surf and spume below us. We had not expected to see geese. I was fascinated by the puffins, and Max, having chased innumerable rabbits, was exhausted, flat out on his side in the heather, tongue lolling, chest heaving and eyes tight shut. When he raised his head and stopped panting for a moment I knew he had heard something. He sat up sharply and puckered his brow, ears up, staring fixedly out to sea.

'What is it?' I asked, and he whined uneasily, drinking in the wind through searching nostrils. I had lived with Max too long to scorn his perception. While I pride myself in possessing sharp eyes and ears I have been out-sensed by him too often to ignore so positive a reaction. I thought perhaps he had seen a boat or heard the far-carrying pop-pop-pop of a ring-netter's engine. I turned my glasses on to the horizon and scanned the haze not knowing whether it was sea or sky. But for a few scattered groups of gulls, cormorants and guillemots the sea was empty. I could hear only the intermittent screaming of the birds below us, and the wind and sea fused in a harmony of inseparable sound. I turned my attention back to the puffins.

Fully five minutes later I heard the first fragment of music. Max was glaring intently into the sky, ears right forward in his most attentive pose. I closed my eyes and strained to filter the sounds into identity. It was maddening. It was like a smell one suddenly meets in a strange place that spins one dizzily back to childhood and for a few poignant moments saps every sense, every attention, in a desperate search for identity of time and place.

More fragments of sound floated in, rudely broken by wheeling, screaming gulls and the buffeting wind. I was bursting with anticipation, biting my lip with frustration. Then I knew. Recognition broke with a rush. It was wild geese.

I knew it would be some time before we saw them. Wild goose voices carry far on the wind. They are among the most stirring sounds nature has produced, more so than the sea in a shell pressed to a child's ear; more evocative than the bubbling curlew. We sat staring at the sky for several minutes before we saw them, a long straggling arrowhead of greylags high out over the sea, mere specks against the blue above. Lying on my back I watched them pass, probably at three or four thousand feet, their formation shifting and changing and their strident voices haggling incessantly.

These would have been among the first Icelandic greylags migrating south for the winter. For while it was still high summer in Sutherland, in more northerly latitudes the season had begun to wane.

The thought of the autumn worried me. It was nine months since I had left Kyleakin Island, and although I had completed the initial draft of my manuscript I had earned no money at all during that time. I needed to find a base for the winter so that I could work as a free-lance journalist to earn my keep. I returned to Inverness, the Highland capital, where I had a number of old friends, and I began to inquire about a winter cottage.

It would have been a strange coincidence indeed if the greylag geese I had seen high above Cape Wrath that September day had been heading for the Black Isle and the Moray Firth, the wintering ground of a large number of greylags, for it was there that I found my winter home. An old friend who possessed an untenanted and lonely farmhouse on the Black Isle coast offered me the house for the winter and a modest wage in return for my services as gamekeeper on a small sporting estate. It was an ideal situation and I accepted the job without hesitation.

The house was gaunt and grey and large for my bachelor needs. It stood overlooking a small tidal bay which opened into the Moray Firth, grey water stretching east as far as the eye could see. But the geese, if they had settled there, had done so only briefly. When Max and I moved into Braelundie there was only the shrill piping of oystercatchers to be heard.

The house was completely bare inside. Even the light fittings had been removed by the previous tenant who, I was given to understand, had left the locality hurriedly and on the brink of ruin. Only the range in the kitchen and the sink remained inviolate, taps and odd lengths of copper pipe having fallen early prey to some predatory plumbing instinct. This last degradation was as random as it was perverse and caused me far more trouble than if the entire plumbing system had been removed. In fact, towards the end of the re-instalment operation I had begun to suspect a motive more subtle than purely the value of the copper pipe and fittings. Replacement of the taps was easy and, seeing three obvious gaps in the pipe-work running along the kitchen ceiling, I cut and fitted new lengths without too much trouble. I gave the rest of the house a cursory inspection and was satisfied that the system was intact. I went outside and turned the water on. Nothing happened. I waited, tapped pipes, peered into the roof-tank from the top of the precarious ladder and turned the stop-cock off and on once again. Still nothing happened.

The water source was a spring on the hill fifty feet or so up behind the house. Convinced that this must have dried up or be blocked, I set off up the hill with Max to examine it. We found it without difficulty. The spring bubbled heartily into a sunken bath, overflowed and bubbled away down the hill. The primitive filtration system on the end of the house supply pipe was a ball of wire netting. I removed it from the water and examined it. It was clean and unblocked. There seemed to be no possible obstruction there. Puzzled we returned to the house. I mounted the ladder once more and found the tank as dry and dusty as before. Max, however, was more successful. Loud and excited barking from downstairs led me to the larder. A strong flow of water was, and had been for half an hour, pouring out under the door, across the concrete floor of the back hall and, fortunately, out under the back door. Not unnaturally I opened the larder door. A powerful jet of water struck me, as if by design, in the groin. I slammed the door shut and swore volubly. The front of my trousers was drenched.

When I had turned the water off and changed my trousers I returned to the larder. At ground level, in a far corner of the small rectangular room, a single right-angle joint had been removed from the pipe. The open end of the inlet pipe seemed to me to have been bent out of line to aim directly at the door. The character of my unknown predecessor was beginning to take shape. Suspicious now of the whole system I examined it carefully from inlet to the tank in the roof. There had been no further interference. I drove to Inverness to purchase the joint I needed.

My second attempt to turn the water on was, despite my precautions, no more successful. This time the water hammered and coughed its way up through the house and finally spilt into the dusty tank with pleasing force and flow. I climbed down the ladder and turned on the cold tap in the bathroom. Instead of emerging predictably and satisfactorily from the tap and flowing into the bath, the water appeared in rivulets and drips on the ceiling and flowed down the walls. I rushed out to halt the supply once again. Examination showed that again a single connection had been removed, this time from immediately underneath the roof-tank, so that the water now poured out all over the attic. The task of moving into Braelundie had long since lost its novelty and my humour was degenerating fast. I was not going to be had again and so I undertook an inch by inch scrutiny of the whole waterworks. The third perversity I was able to detect and repress: the back-boiler in the range had been similarly disconnected, and its reconnection gave me further and more specific insight into the shape of the enemy. He was a small man. By my calculations he was three feet high, with a minute head, and tiny hands of inhuman strength. I knew this because to undo the water-pipe going into the back-boiler it was necessary to crawl into the bottom of the airing-cupboard, flat on one's face, and reach in behind the range with one hand in order to manipulate a large brass nut where there was no possible room for the spanner to make the joint watertight. Only after a dozen or more cripplingly claustrophobic attempts was I able to get it done successfully. But the final and most perplexing subtlety of this man's tortured wit remained a complete enigma to me throughout my occupation of the house.

It was on my third evening in Braelundie that I chose to have a bath. It was appropriate in that I had just finished sweeping a chimney and I was well covered in soot. The range in the kitchen burned beautifully and the hot-water tank in the cupboard beside it creaked and groaned as the water approached boiling point. The pipe joints had given no further trouble and water, hot and cold, flowed freely from the kitchen taps. I went upstairs to run the bath. The hot tap coughed promisingly and a spider was rudely and abruptly evicted. I put the plug in and went through to my bedroom to undress. When I returned, clad only in a towel, there was no water in the bath. I checked the cold tap which was running perfectly, and went downstairs to find out what was wrong. The tank was too hot to touch and the tap over the sink was working perfectly. I felt the pipes up through the airing-cupboard and they were hot right up to the ceiling. Upstairs again the pipe was hot where it came through the floor right up to within a foot of the tap on the bath.

An hour later, having dismantled the tap and its pipe and found them both clear, I still had no water in the bath. In fact seven months later when I left the house for good there was still no water in the bath. I never succeeded in extracting one drop of hot water from the Braelundie bath tap. The plumber who came in the lee of my failure and exasperation explained to me that the existing system could never work. There was an insufficient head of water to push the hot water back up to the bathroom and the only solution was to raise the level in the roof. Without cutting a large hole in the ceiling there was no possibility of getting a larger tank into the roof, so I abandoned it; deserted the bathroom and scoured the Inverness sale rooms until I found a tin hip-bath. By extending the sink taps with two lengths of hose I was able to bath in front of the kitchen fire; actually a greater luxury than any bathroom, although the marks of years of use on the upstairs bath in that house never ceased to puzzle and irritate me.

I furnished the three rooms I chose to occupy for ten pounds from a local sale. A week later I bought for a pound the entire contents of the kitchens of a large and remote shooting lodge. I must have been the only bachelor in Scotland with seven egg whisks and four mincing machines. I also had the remains of a dinner service for thirty-six and a fish kettle which, had I not already bought one, might have served equally well as a hip-bath.

My job was very much more exacting and time consuming than I had imagined. I had spent some time with gamekeepers as a boy and I knew the round of their duties quite well. But I quickly found that the occasional boyhood foray with a keeper to destroy a fox in its earth or to control grey squirrels and rabbits was quite different from being fully and solely responsible for three thousand acres. There were no grey squirrels at Braelundie, but there were hordes of hooded crows, the least attractive of the crow family, and my devious and strategic attempts to trap and shoot them were constantly outwitted. In the few months I was employed to destroy them I killed only a few, but it was certainly not for want of time and effort. Not long after I had moved on from there, the experience I had gained from the Braelundie hoodies led me to devise the most effective and foolproof means of catching birds that I have ever seen; and I live in fear of my discovery. Applicable to almost any species it could be devastating; a means of total annihilation, and the realization of its horrific potential in the wrong hands causes me to guard my secret carefully.

In addition to vermin control I had a variety of other duties, by far the most difficult of which was to ward off poachers. The estate was a peninsula with sea around much of its perimeter, a fact which should have eased the problem. Instead, it made it worse. The obvious trick of finding and immobilizing the poacher's means of escape, usually a car or a bicycle, was quite inappropriate since the hardy breed of marauder who preyed on the Braelundie pheasants came and went on foot, never arriving or departing by the same route. They had another advantage over me in that as a newcomer to the area it took me a long time to familiarize myself with the ground. They ran rings around me on more than one occasion.

And yet I had two triumphs. The first was a youth whom I saw from a distance stalking through some undergrowth not far from the shore. Anticipating his route of escape I did my best to cut him off. When he saw me rapidly approaching he turned and fled towards the shore. There was a large area of marsh between him and the beach, which I knew to be very boggy. In his panic he attempted to cut straight across the middle of it, and to my absolute delight his pace began to slow with the wetness of the ground. I stopped and watched.

Within five yards he was up to his knees in evil-smelling mud and seconds later he was completely bogged from the waist down. I stayed only long enough to take a good look at his face and to make sure he couldn't sink any deeper. Half an hour later I saw a very bedraggled figure creep away along the bay. I never saw him again.

Waders in mud flats

My other success was, to me, even more satisfying. Down on the marshes below the house was a small reedy pond where teal, the smallest and one of the most attractive British ducks, regularly flighted in to feed at dusk, and could often be seen there during the day. I had heard shooting at this pond on two or three nights in one week, but on each occasion when I had run down to intercept the culprit he or they had heard me coming and vanished into the darkness. On the two nights that I chose to sit and wait for them, of course they didn't come.

Early one morning, however, just after dawn I was idly scanning the shoreline through my field glasses when I noticed a figure creeping up through the reeds towards the teal pond. I could see one or two ducks swimming about on the pond and it was clearly these the figure was after. Unfortunately there was no cover between the house and the bay and it was extremely difficult to approach without being seen. But there was a small ditch which ran part of the way down to the pond and I thought that by creeping down this I could probably get to within fifty or sixty yards of the man.

I ran down the field keeping behind gorse and broom bushes as best I could until I reached the ditch. It was very muddy and difficult to move quickly along, but I found I could manage quite well. At the end of the ditch I peered up over the bank. The man was now only about seventy yards from me and was so intent upon his stalk that he had not been aware of my approach. But the ducks were more alert than he, for they suddenly saw me as I climbed out over the bank, and they rose from the pond in a flurry of wings and water. I stood up and began walking briskly towards the man. I saw him hurriedly push his gun in among the reeds, and then, pretending to have just re-tied his bootlace, he rose and sauntered idly towards me, whistling as he did so – a sign of certain guilt.

As we neared he hailed me. 'Good day,' he started cheerfully. 'A grand day to be out.'

'What are you doing here?' I demanded, ignoring his genial manner.

'Och, I'm just out for a walk Mon, it's a grand day for a walk.'

'Just walking are you?' I asked brusquely.

'Aye, just stretching ma legs in the early morning. I always take a . . .'

'Was it you shooting here the other night?' I asked, fixing him with a cold gaze.

'Me? Shooting?' he repeated incredulously. 'I'm not a shooting man,' he added indignantly.

'Oh, I'm sorry,' I lied, 'I thought it was you I had seen here with a gun in the past few days.'

'Och, no! You've not seen me here with a gun. I haven't even got a gun. It's the walking I enjoy, not shooting.'

'Oh, you haven't got a gun?' I corrected myself. 'I'm so sorry, I thought that perhaps this was your gun,' and I strode forward and snatched his gun from among the reeds. 'But obviously I have made a mistake, I'm so sorry. This must be a poacher's gun left here by mistake.' The man looked ill and eyed the gun in despair. He opened his mouth to say something but I cut him short. 'There's only one thing to do with a poacher's gun, isn't there?' I broke the gun across my knee with a sharp crack. The fore-end sprang off into the reeds and I was left with the barrels and the stock in either hand. Then I lobbed them out into the middle of the pond, one after the other, where they splashed and disappeared leaving only a spreading ring and a line of bubbles breaking on the surface.

This was too much for the wretched man. He turned and fled, leaping from reed clump to reed clump, across the tidal ditches and away over the mud flats running for all he was worth as if I had threatened to throw him into the pond with his gun. I stood and watched him out of sight, a little black figure hurrying away into the distance. When, two days later, I answered the door to three policemen I thought that the man had, in some remarkable way, sought to take action against me. But I was wrong, as, indeed, were the policemen; although their story was no less remarkable.

Shortly after leaving Kyleakin Island a year before, I had wished to return to the island to collect something I had forgotten. The island boats had been sold by then, so I went to my friend Colin Mackenzie on Skye and borrowed his boat to make the short crossing from Skye to the island and back again. Afterwards I returned the boat to the boathouse on Skye, thanked my friend, and departed to Balreach. At some unknown point after I had left Skye Colin Mackenzie's boat was stolen from the boathouse. The theft was reported to the Skye police and I was named as the last person known to have used the boat. The wheels of the Highland police system were set in motion. But each time the police found out where I was living I had moved on, Inverness-shire, Ross-shire, Sutherland, and, finally to Braelundie on the Black Isle.

Unfortunately, during the search through several counties to catch up with me, my involvement in the crime had been alarmingly exaggerated from that of last user of the boat to most likely culprit. It was with some alarm and surprise, then, that I found myself confronted by a sergeant and two constables at five o'clock on a winter's afternoon, all three apparently requiring to search my person for a rowing boat belonging to a close friend.

I tried to explain that there must have been a misunderstanding between the various parties involved, but they would have none of it. They were out to find the boat and find the boat they would if it took them all night. It very nearly did. Eventually I abandoned my argument and flung the doors wide. A cursory inspection of the inside of the house was followed by a thorough examination of all the buildings and outhouses. They then returned to my door.

'Does this path lead down to the bay?' the sergeant asked, pointing to a track which led away across the fields.

'Er-yes,' I replied, adding 'eventually' as an afterthought.

'Do you keep a boat on the bay?' he inquired again.

'No, I don't. But one or two other people do, I think. You're not thinking of going down there tonight are you?' I asked. 'It's getting dark already and it's a good walk to the bay.'

'Never mind that,' came the curt reply. This sergeant was obviously not easily deterred. The two constables looked gloomily at the path and the distant bay.

'Would you like a torch?' I ventured, knowing that they would need one. The sergeant wavered for a moment and then, as if there were some rule against accepting help from suspects, 'No, no, there's no need for that, we have our own in the car.'

Their car was back on the county road half a mile above the farm.

'Right-ho,' I said resignedly, 'but I wouldn't advise you to go down there tonight.' By now the sergeant, I'm sure, was convinced of my guilt and of the location of the stolen boat. They disappeared into the twilight heading back towards their car.

Half an hour later I saw torches flicker across the yard and glanced at my watch. It was just after six o'clock, and very dark outside. I drew up my chair and put my feet up on the stove in the kitchen. The wind howled menacingly in the chimney and the first fat drops of rain struck the window pane. I shuddered at the thought of the policemen out on the marsh, and poked at the fire until it flared up and glowed so hot that I had to shield my face.

The track down to the bay wound through a mile of scrub and rough ground to the edge of the marshes where it petered out. From there on, the last three hundred yards to the tideline was across waterlogged salt marsh which altered and shifted with the season's tides. There was no certain path through it; some parts were dangerously boggy, and others so muddy that one regularly sank in up to one's calves, and even to knee depth. I hoped the policemen had changed into wellington boots.

At half-past nine there was a gale blowing outside and rain was drumming hard against the window. The three had now had ample time to reach the shore, examine any small boats which might have been there, and return. I peered out in the hope of seeing a distant flickering torch. But the night was endlessly black. At ten o'clock I had begun to worry for their safety. Unwillingly I climbed into oilskins and started to walk up the track to see if their car was still there. In the shelter of the trees the going was easier and I climbed the hill quickly to the county road. There was their car, sleek and glinting in the nearest gateway. I set off back down the track with a quickened pace. Facing into the wind now, I was soon chilled and wet. The rain was stinging my face.

When I arrived back at the house I went in to fetch a walking-stick, a valuable aid on the marshes, and was just emerging once again when I saw the first flicker of a torch. It was a long way off, and far removed from the path. I went back into the house, put all the upstairs lights on so that they would have a beacon to home in on, and sat down to wait.

At eleven-fifteen they finally reached the house. As policemen, they were quite unrecognizable. They were completely wet, with the blue dye from their caps staining their faces. The rest of their uniforms were no longer blue, but the indeterminate colour of mud. The sergeant, it seemed, had ventured on to the tidal mud, not realizing that the tide was out and that the beach-line, where any boats would be kept, was at that moment some two hundred yards from the water's edge. He had crossed the beach without knowing it and, set upon inspecting the water's edge, had marched out on to the mud flats.

It was a miracle that they had returned at all. The mud flats in that bay are as treacherous as quicksands and far more unpredictable. One footfall can be on a solid crust, and the next collapse into thin semi-liquid ooze many feet deep. It was into one such sea-drain that the sergeant had stepped, luckily not a deep one, and the two constables, happily close by, had been in time to pull him back on to firmer mud. But that had been only the beginning of their troubles. Although they sensibly chose to turn back at that point, their footprints had filled with water and were no longer visible in the dark. The short journey back to the beach had been a horrific succession of slipping, sinking and floundering in mud and ooze. And when they found the shore they had lost the path and had been forced to cut back through acres of evil-smelling marsh and bog in the general direction of the house.

There was no use in my attempting to warm or dry their bedraggled clothes. It would have taken the rest of the night and in any case I had nothing suitable in which to reclothe them. It seemed better that they should return to their base as quickly as possible. They stopped only long enough to drink a bowl of hot soup, and to warm their hands by the fire. I never saw them again, although the diligence and thoroughness of the investigation system has to be applauded. Several months later, after the boat had changed hands several times, it was traced to the London district of Paddington. The culprit was named, the case finally heard on Skye and the boat returned to its owner.

Chapter Four

I remember that dawn particularly because of the shooting down on the bay. I had rushed down, still half asleep, to intercept the wildfowlers and ask them to go away. Not that that was the only time. I had done it so often that it was becoming routine. The leap out of bed at the first shot; pulling on cold clothes over my pyjamas; thrusting my bare feet – no time for socks – into damp wellingtons and bursting out into the knife-edge chill of those winter mornings.

I had worn a path through the field like the cattle, and the fence sagged where I crossed. Down across the marsh there was a track too, a thin line winding between the frozen reed clumps and brown mud patches where I had leapt the cuts and puddles in the saltings. By now I knew where I could tread with safety and I crossed the burn at the only firm mud on that side.

Once on the bay it was never hard to find them. They knew where the geese would fly as well as I did and they were always there, crouched like soldiers in the ditches and creeks at the tide's edge. On the first morning I had stopped at the burnside, momentarily lacking conviction. I had felt the intruder, the stranger, and, uncertain of such precipitate emotion, I had approached warily, expecting scorn and abuse, and had consequently worded my appeal cautiously and politely. It had worked, too. They had nodded dumbly and gone home, shuffling silently away in their waterproof leggings until they thought I was out of ear-shot. Then I could hear them. Voices rising and falling in the mist, voices of indignation and rough with dissent.

It was naive of me to have imagined it would stop there. My

euphoria was short lived indeed when I found myself face to face with the same six men at the same place exactly twenty-four hours later. Still they didn't argue; again they sloped off muttering and kicking at the reed clumps as they went. That time I knew it was going to be a long battle, for this was not poaching. Wildfowling on the foreshore in season is quite legal and I had no lever other than reason to use against them.

Greylags

I had moved to Braelundie before the shooting season got under way, so I was unaware of the onslaught which was to follow. The first geese had arrived in late September. I had heard them long before I saw them. The old familiar honking, like baying hounds at a distance, gradually rising in intensity until I saw them, a thin waving line like bees high above the hills, forming, breaking and re-forming in vee formation. That first skein of greylags had circled once over the bay and then passed on, further south to some previous winter's feeding grounds. But it was the start. From then on I heard them every day, and often as I lay awake at night. Many more passed overhead than landed on the bay; but slowly, over a period of days, a gradual build up took place. From a small party of eight to begin with until there were always several hundred out on the mud flats.

At their peak there were few short of two thousand greylags on the bay. They roosted far out on the tide's edge by night and flighted in to the stubble and potato fields at dawn. Their constant haggling cries were as much a part of the day as sunrise and sunset, and when they circled low over the house to pitch in the adjacent field I would stop what I was doing to watch them plane in on vibrant pinions. For a few blissful weeks the geese at Braelundie were the centre of my attention, and the odd shot from down on the marshes or away on the other side of the estuary was of no consequence to me. Caught unaware one day by a friend who dropped in for a night, I took my gun and my dog and stood in the dusk at the head of the bay. Choosing the two leading birds from a flight which passed low overhead on their way back to the mud to roost, I fired twice. We dined on goose the following night and laughed as we did so. A week later I ate the second bird alone. But by then the taste had soured.

To begin with the men came in twos and threes, dressed like marines in khaki and green with balaclavas and strangely camouflaged hats. They stole out across the mud in the dark and crouched in the hollows to await the dawn. I would listen with interest from my bed, knowing the thrill of the sound of the first geese moving restlessly out on the water before flighting inland to feed. Then I would count the shots; sharp jabs of sound in the cold air, and the sudden tumult of a thousand goose voices as they clamoured away circling wildly in broken skeins.

Later in the day I would take Max, and walk down to the shore to examine the signs: the scattered cartridge cases and the footprints; the stain of goose-blood on the mud and the trail of feathers. Sometimes there would be a wounded bird flapping out at the water's edge and I would send Max to fetch it, a type of hyena scavenging I resented most of all.

It was on the ninth consecutive day of dawn and dusk shooting that I finally decided to interfere. I leapt angrily from my bed pulling on inadequate clothes for the bitter cold of that December morning. By the time I had crossed the burn the first grey light was spreading across the open water ahead, and the headland was silhouetted sharply against the east. I felt foolish and suddenly very cold. The sky was loud with geese, and the spasmodic bursts of flame from guns spread out all along the bay pin-pointed their exact positions. I walked towards the nearest crouched figure. 'Ahoy there!' I shouted, and a face turned towards me with a look of surprise. 'Nine mornings in a row,' I heard myself saying. 'Too much shooting . . . geese won't stand it . . . driven away from the area . . . spoil the shooting for everyone.'

The man kept looking away at a greylag thrashing about on the mud. Two other men came up. I repeated myself. One of them muttered something about plenty of geese; the other shuffled off to collect the wounded bird. Soon they went away, carrying nine birds between the six of them. Nine geese and two or three wigeon, and nearly thirty empty cartridge cases littered across the mud. From that day on it was a daily and often a twice-daily occurrence. I saw new faces sometimes and tried to moderate my words. All too often it was the same men and they avoided me, snatching up what birds they had and moving off as I arrived, gesticulating rudely as they went. On Saturday mornings I learnt to expect a party of ten or twelve. They came forty miles in a minibus and sometimes they were there in the evening too.

By the New Year the geese had changed their habits completely. They no longer circled over the house by day but sat sullenly out on the mud occasionally rising in small groups to wheel round the bay and pitch again far out from the shore. They fed almost exclusively at night now, and I heard them coming into the fields long after dark and returning to the sanctuary of the tidal ooze before dawn. The wildfowlers changed their timetable too. They came on bright moonlit nights and fired their guns haphazardly into the night sky, and the wounded geese Max and I collected by day grew steadily in number. Nor was I the only scavenger. Often I saw fox footprints, and sometimes I found the remains of a carcase and the evidence of a brief struggle written plainly in the mud.

That little bay was overshot, plundered would be a better word, for eleven consecutive weeks that winter. Not an uncommon situation for well known wildfowling spots, but

I remember that particular February dawn for the incongruous sight of a man struggling to carry away seven geese. Greylags are big, heavy birds, and seven was as many as he could manage. He had passed me standing by the burn and smiled weakly.

'Have you got enough?' I said, but he missed the scorn in my voice and laughed.

'We got fifteen last week.' But his laugh died as he saw I didn't share the joke. Then I think he recognized me as the madman who ran about the marshes at dawn shouting and waving his arms in the air. Later that day I found four geese thrown into a ditch near the road. Hidden booty, I thought, to be collected later. But three weeks later the crow-picked and vermin-scattered remains of all four geese were still lying in the ditch.

I walked back to the house regretting my interference. The situation seemed worse for having stood in the middle of it. I was standing by the stove soberly stirring porridge and still trying to get some warmth back into my limbs when there was a loud knock at the door. The middle-aged American lady who stood at my remote cottage door that morning was a complete stranger. It seems possible that if Nancy Redmayne had not had the diligence to seek me out in my hideaway, the years and activities which have followed might have been very differently shaped. My kitchen was squalid and I was unshaven and strangely dressed. I did not want to admit a total stranger at that hour and I must have sounded gruff and unwelcoming. I am now grateful that she persevered. 'I've come a long way to find you,' she appealed, and I gave in. As we sat drinking coffee she told her story. It was one I had heard before and was to hear often again, but for some reason I liked this lady and wanted to help her.

Several years before, she had read Gavin Maxwell's *Ring of Bright Water* and had fallen in love with the idyll. Quite suddenly her husband had died and she was at a loss. To get over her own tragedy she had decided to take a long holiday and the *Ring of Bright Water* story, with its own tinge of melancholy and tragedy, had directed her to the Highlands. She had visited Skye and learned for the first time of Gavin Maxwell's death a few months before. With self-admitted irresistible curiosity she had walked the winding path down to Sandaig and stood overlooking the site where Camusfèarna had stood and the rowan, laden with bitter red berries, still stands beside the Edal memorial. Back in her hotel she had been told that I was the last occupant of the island house and that I had moved to the east. With the help of the post office she had slowly traced me from cottage to cottage until, finally, after two weeks of driving round the Highlands she had arrived at my door.

She wanted a guide. She wanted to see for herself those places, animals and islands of which Gavin Maxwell had written so descriptively. She knew that there would be no tourist agency who could help her in this need and she had set out to find someone who would take her round the Highlands, who was a naturalist and who had a knowledge of the man and his books. I suppose it was understandable that some of my friends and neighbours from Kyleakin should have sent her in search of me. Few of the other Gavin Maxwell Enterprises employees would have had the time or the inclination to do it.

For my own part, Nancy Redmayne's request came at a moment of hiatus. I had finished my book, and, while I was happy in my cottage and with my gamekeeping existence, I was sickened by the goose slaughter at my door. Although I had not recognized it myself I needed a change and some company. Since Gavin's death I had been spinning in the wind. I knew I did not want to go back into industry and I wrote the book to gain time in which to think. I view it now very much as a product of that vacuum. For a year I had wandered from cottage to cottage enjoying the seasons with the keen eye of a naturalist, and, not surprisingly I now viewed the Highlands as a great upland wildlife paradise. Only from my little east coast farmhouse did I now begin to witness the first discordant elements. The slaughter of the geese rankled because it shattered the dream-image I had of the Highlands.

The problem itself was far from new; in fact, I was painfully familiar with the whole scene. The wildfowling grounds of South Wales are a legend. They have been overtaken by development and the huge numbers of people it brought. But the problem under my window was not one of pressure from development of population; it was one of greed and ease of access. A short walk, less than a mile from your car, and there appeared to be unlimited sport. Compared with some other famous wildfowling haunts it was child's play. But, in the curious way that an ill wind works, it had brought me to terms with the Highlands. I had, for the moment at least, stopped spinning, and the arrival of Nancy Redmayne at my door demanded a much more professional outlook. I agreed to be her guide for a few days to see how it went.

Red deer in the Highlands are easy to find and watch in winter because the snow and the shortage of grazing at high altitudes keeps them on much lower ground. Nancy and I spent four days watching deer that February. For our first expedition I had chosen an area near home where I knew it was easy to see deer at close quarters. Some days the animals were down beside the road, and on others one had to search a little first. I hoped for the latter. I did not want to make it all seem too simple.

We parked the Land Rover off the single-track road at the foot of a vast sloping moor sweeping upwards to a ridge of hills all well over three thousand feet high. We were approaching a corrie which I knew to be a likely place for deer to lie up in during the day. The ground we had crossed had been well covered with slot-marks and droppings only a few hours old, so they had certainly been there during the night.

We were walking across very open ground and the nature of the country was such that I knew the odds lay strongly in favour of the deer seeing us first and moving off over the brow of the hill and away down the other side. By sheer good luck a hind had grazed out of the bowl of the corrie and was standing on the lip at a point where she was silhouetted against the sky behind. I froze and put out my hand to halt Nancy. She stopped without a word and I dropped slowly on to one knee and on down until I was lying full-length in the heather, signalling her to copy me.

'See that beast on the skyline?' I asked.

'No, I hadn't, but I see it now.'

'Right, good. Now there are almost certainly a good many more hinds and perhaps a stag or two lying in that corrie, just out of our sight from here. I'm afraid we'll have to crawl if we're not going to be seen.'

We crept through the damp heather without speaking for about a hundred yards.

I turned to see how the lady was faring. She was right behind me and apparently quite at ease.

'Are we O.K. for wind?' she whispered.

'Yes, we're lucky. It's in our favour,' I replied. 'Only a few more yards now.'

Our crawl was worth all the mud and the wet. There were between thirty and forty hinds placidly grazing only a hundred and fifty yards ahead of us, and from the top of a small knoll we could see right down into the corrie. There, fast asleep, were three stags. One lovely beast with eleven points on wide, sweeping antlers, and two young 'knobbers' – last year's stag calves with poorly grown antlers which were little more than spikes. All three were lying down, and with our field glasses we could see that their eyes were tight shut. Many of the hinds were lying down too, in little sheltered hollows and contours of the hill, where they chewed the cud mechanically.

We watched them in silence for a long time; so long in fact that I was getting extremely cold.

'Would you like to see them move?' I whispered. Nancy nodded and I added 'Keep very still or else they'll spot us straight away.' Then I coughed loudly. Suddenly every head was turned in our direction, every ear erect, and the big stag and most of the hinds were on their feet in a flash. There was no chance of our scent moving in their direction, and so, search as they would with raised heads and visibly dilating nostrils, they could find no cause for the sound. One or two hinds began to move off towards the top of the hill, obviously ill at ease. I coughed again, louder. This time there was a much more active response. Those hinds already departing broke into a fast run and were quickly out of sight. One or two paused in full silhouette on the top of the hill, where the extra height they had gained enabled them to see us clearly. They snorted indignantly and were gone.

But those remaining below were still uncertain of the direction of the intrusion and they paced about pawing the ground and looking uncomfortable. I coughed a third time and to my delight one of the young knobbers started running towards us. We shrank lower into the heather and the beast came on at a fast trot. Unbelievably, a few hinds began to follow him reducing the ground between us to a mere forty or fifty yards. Suddenly the knobber stopped. He had at last caught our scent. He stood as rigid as a gravestone for a few seconds, his nostrils wide, staring straight at where we lay. Perhaps he could see us too, although we were well camouflaged. The hinds came up beside him, standing in a row, evenly spaced like victims before a firing squad. Then they turned and fled. Within half a minute there was not a beast in sight. They had passed over the skyline in a stream of heads and legs, fluid in continuous motion. Only a few stood, like the first ones, for a chilling moment on the top, the old stag among them. His antlers branched out against the sky in classical silhouette – then he, too, was gone.

We lay in silence for a moment before realizing that we were wet and cold.

We walked slowly on up to the crest of the hill, a long slow plod which seemed endless compared with the few seconds it had taken the deer. At the top we were almost in cloud and the heather had given way to a thin wind-cropped vegetation of lichen and moss with weathered rock faces and stones everywhere. The glen on the other side lay far below, the ground tumbling away from us in a vast sweep, almost sheer in places with long ski-runs of deer-grass and heather creating an effect of light and dark brown stripes. Beyond, lay more and more hills with peaks rising to over three and a half thousand feet, snow-capped and rugged like battlements.

The animals we had watched were a good two miles away now, just brown specks moving slowly across the wide expanse of moor below us. Their sudden flight had drawn other small parties of hinds to join them and with our field glasses we counted over ninety deer, mainly hinds, steadily grazing their way to a more remote and undisturbed area.

But the wind was cutting on the exposed heights and it was uncomfortable to linger. We returned to the Land Rover discussing the future of deer in an overcrowded world. The success of the morning had encouraged me, and as we ate our packed lunches in the vehicle I agreed to be Nancy's guide for the following week. I arranged to dine with her in her hotel that evening to make a plan for the rest of her stay.

As it turned out, I was to be granted a reprieve. When I met Nancy the following morning she was dressed for London and not for the hills. A relation in England had been taken ill and Nancy was rushing to help her. She thought it would be at least two weeks before she would be able to return. I was curiously disappointed although later it proved to have been a god-send. I drove the lady to her aeroplane and watched it sweep away into the dreich February sky. In the interesting way that one suddenly makes snap decisions I had made one, and I hurried away to put it into action.

Chapter Five

By the time Nancy contacted me again not two weeks but a month had elapsed. The Highlands was a different country. The winter had blown itself out in the remaining days of February and the first week of March, and the hills were now snow-covered where Nancy and I had walked together watching deer. Blizzard conditions had halted traffic in and out of Inverness and the first newborn lambs had to be rescued from drifts over their astonished little faces. Then, suddenly, the wind shifted from the east and a strong gale from the southwest, warm and wet, pushed the Siberian weather back where it came from. The Gulf Stream influence on the Highlands is remarkable when the wind is strong enough to drag it across the mountains in the west, and it strips the snow from the hills like peeling back a sheet from a naked body. The contours return in pure relief and the shape and texture of the rock and heather stand apart by the subtle play of light and shadow. Then came the sun; hot, steaming, tangible sunlight which made people smile and laugh and forget that a week before it had been mid-winter. The rivers and burns were gorged with melting snow and the sun danced on their white bubbling spume and sparkled in the eye of the spate-evicted dipper.

By the time Nancy's letter arrived much more than a shift in season had happened. I had shifted myself and my dog and my ten-pounds worth of chattels out of Braelundie farmhouse and into the welcome hospitality of Richard and Joan Frere of Drumbuie House at Drumnadrochit. *The White Island* was done and away to the publishers. The day Nancy departed I had driven west of Inverness to see my landlord and friend. I thanked him sincerely and wholeheartedly for the use of Braelundie and for the keepering job and told him that I would vacate the cottage by the end of the month. I drove on down Loch Ness-side to Drumnadrochit and a friendly white house on the hill above the Urquhart Bay where, the tourist jangle tells us, monsters frolic. For some reason, however, there were none that day.

Richard Frere had been managing director of Gavin Maxwell Enterprises Limited – the company which was born on the wave of a tax problem following the unhealthy success of *Ring of Bright Water*, and which existed to offset the costs of all Gavin Maxwell's polyglot activities, interests and employees. Richard's own account of his diverse dealings on his employer's behalf are ably set out in his book *Maxwell's Ghost*. It was only now, more than a year after the famous author's death that Richard was beginning to emerge from beneath the ruins of the tragic Maxwell empire. He, too, was out of a job.

I told Richard and Joan that I was hoping to be able to move out of Braelundie by the end of February and find a home more centrally situated than the east coast from which to run, for a trial period, a natural history guiding service for foreign visitors. With spontaneous generosity Joan offered me a room in Drumbuie House from which I could set my scheme moving and search for a permanent base on a more satisfactory time-scale. Richard, with a characteristic pessimism I have come to value over the years, said he thought it was a good idea but one which would undoubtedly perish, all the more certainly because he had been in at its conception.

Discarding his gloom I tried to involve him even further by bringing him into the plan as a partner. But this he declined saying that it was too soon after G.M.E. Ltd and anyway his only field of interest would be in hill-walking and mountaineering. I was keen to find the compromise combination which would involve his interest in my project. Richard is a skilled mountaineer of great experience and has a knowledge of the Highlands garnered over thirty-five years of active climbing – in his own words, 'man and boy'. It was vital that any guiding enterprise should be based upon this sort of extended knowledge, otherwise the thing would be shallow and unconvincing and would then be certain to fail. My own subject, the natural history of the Highlands, I felt confident I could cope with, but it was clearly going to take me a few years to build up even a fraction of Richard's knowledge of the ground.

We sat late into the evening on either side of the library fire at Drumbuie discussing the possibilities of such a venture. The whisky bottle grew empty and our ambitions grew wilder and less relevant as amusing anecdotes crept in to fill the many gaps in our plans. Coffee came and went and came again until there seemed to be no more to be said. When I got up to go we had reached an excellent compromise and one which pleased me greatly. Richard and I were to become partners in principle (if not in law) and our project – to be called, we had decided, Highland Wildlife Enterprises – was to embrace the whole spectrum of natural history from the climate and geology of the ground walked over, its plant and animal life, its social and human history, to its present-day use. Activities would cover every range of habitat from the mountain top to the estuary mud, and weekly residential courses would be at the same time educational, stimulating recreation, and beneficial to the environment through the process of inquiry and appreciation.

The last week before Nancy Redmayne's return was a whirlwind of application. I registered my enterprise, drafted out copy for a brochure and prospectus, invited a solicitor to research the legal implications, bought an embryo library of Highland books and maps, made a seasonal arrangement with a splendidly Highland lady who ran a superbly Highland guest-house on the village green in Drumnadrochit, and wrote a portfolio of advertisements. It was this last item which was to do more to determine the shape of the enterprise in the years to follow than all the others put together.

I chose to advertise in a large number of papers and magazines associated with outdoor activities, and spent two whole days on Richard's telephone placing mainly classified advertisements couched in what I thought was suitably attractive jargon. But the problems of this exercise were many and confused, and complicated by an inherent electronic flatulence on the Highland telephone. Time and time again the girl taking the advertisement was frustrated by the system, overcome by the spelling of 'capercaillie' or 'Drumnadrochit', vanquished by the ineptitude of the advertiser, or just cut off. By the afternoon of the second day I was beside myself with rage and ready to call the whole thing off, when I dialled the *Sunday Times*. The telephonist switched me straight through to the Classified Ads department and a confident voice took up the call.

'Can I help you?'

'I would like to place a classified advertisement in the Scottish holidays column please,' I said with no expression and very little interest.

'Certainly,' affirmed the calm voice. 'Please give me your name and telephone number in case we are cut off and then proceed with your advertisement.' I was impressed.

'John Lister-Kaye at Drumnadrochit 940. Two difficult names I'm afraid . . .'

'That's quite all right. I have a difficult name too so I know what it's like on the phone,' said the voice. 'Spell them to me to make sure.'

I obeyed.

'Thank you. And now your advertisement.'

I obeyed again, passing, to my amazement, over capercaillie and dotterel without a query. When I had finished she asked for the address to which to send the invoice, and that was that.

'Do you want me to go back over any of it?' I asked tentatively.

'No, thank you. I'll read it all back to you now and you can stop me if I've gone wrong.' She read it back, perfectly. And

I said so. She said 'Thank you', and was gone. I turned to Richard. 'That was astonishingly easy, especially after the hash some of the other buffoons made of our ads.'

'I hope you got her name,' said Richard, 'you'll need her again.'

'No, dash it, I didn't . . . Oh well, at least one advertisement has gone in correctly.' And there the matter might very easily have ended. There was no reason for Fate to extend it further, but within five minutes of my replacing the receiver the phone rang again. Richard answered it.

'It's the *Sunday Times* for you, John.' I took the receiver.

'Hullo?'

'Mr Lister-Kaye?'

'Yes.'

'This is the *Sunday Times* here again. I have gone through your advertisement carefully and I think I can improve on it quite a bit. Do you mind if I change it around, I think it'll sound much better? I'll read it to you.'

I listened reservedly. It was definitely better. It flowed, as it were.

'Don't you think that sounds more inviting?'

'Yes, yes I do,' I agreed hurriedly. 'Do you charge for this editing service?'

'Oh, no,' she said. 'It's slightly cheaper now because it's shorter.'

'I'm amazed.' And I was.

'Our job is to sell your product as well as our space, you know. Good-bye.'

'Hey! Hold on,' I expostulated. 'You can't go now. You've made my day. What's your name?'

'Sorrel Bentinck,' came the answer in its quiet voice.

'Sorrel Bentinck, eh?' I mused. 'I see what you mean about having a difficult name too. I'll do my best not to call you Carol Bendix or Sarah Bentine when I ring up again. Thank you very much for all your help.' She laughed, and then I added: 'Oh yes, and why did you decide to ring me back? You surely can't ring everybody back.'

'Oh! I don't know,' she said, 'I suppose I liked the sound of your voice.'

I collected Nancy Redmayne from her aeroplane in resonant sunshine. The sky was a vivid blue and the world smiled at a spring day. On the way to her hotel I told her all that had happened. She was keenly interested and pleased to be Highland Wildlife Enterprises' first customer. I told her too that I had worked hard for her and planned an itinerary, a copy of which I gave her. We would try, I assured her, to find almost all the animals and birds she wanted to see, but it would be largely up to luck whether the sight she got of them would be momentary and fleeting or a chance to observe them properly. But to see killer whales she would have to join the crew of an Icelandic trawler. She laughed. Some of the land mammals, too, were going to be hard to find. Pine-martens, otters and wildcats were only seen by locals on chance occasions and we could go to their habitat a hundred times without glimpsing a whisker, but we would try.

'Oh yes, I would like to try,' she said, and I knew from her tone that she would not be flying back to California without doing just that.

At 6.00 a.m. the following morning we were standing in a dark pinewood. Outside the wood it was dawn and there was a strident chorus from a surprisingly small number of birds. Coal-tits and great-tits were singing loudly in the crowns of the gnarled old pines around us and a pair of cresties, the tit which belongs exclusively to the Pine Forest, were trilling excitedly as they chased each other through the trees. As the light spread through the heavy canopy and found the pale greens and reds of sphagnum moss on the forest floor I touched Nancy's arm and pointed to a mound of caterpillar-like excrement on the ground near our feet. I glanced up, but the branch above was vacant.

'A capercaillie roost,' I whispered.

The minutes ticked by and the chorus of bird song was swelled by the addition of a robin and a blackbird. Quite suddenly, and without apparent reason, there was a swoosh of huge wings and a great black shape rocketed past swooping low across the small clearing in front of us and up into a pine twenty yards beyond. It landed out of sight and I restrained Nancy's instinctive urge to crane round to see it. Almost immediately a second black shape, the size of a turkey, swung in from behind us and landed on a fallen log not ten feet away. It was the closest I had ever been to a cock capercaillie and it was colossal. A fat red wattle arose from above its eye and its secateur bill looked only slightly less dangerous than that of a raven. In a second it had seen us, ejected another fat caterpillar of excrement into the moss and disappeared as quickly and silently as it had arrived. This sudden movement had caught the attention of the first bird and we were aware that it had moved a little closer. Quite suddenly it broke into, for want of a better word, song. A capercaillie cock has no musical expertise whatsoever. What's more, it knows it and makes no attempt at it. Instead, it settles for a tuneless and repetitive series of clicks and pops. They are sounds produced in the back of the throat and flicked out, it would appear, by the tongue. It is said that with a high degree of skill and even more luck it is possible to stalk right up to a caper cock when it is displaying on its lek in the early spring. In order to produce its doubtfully seductive call it throws back its head, closes its eyes and emits two muted pops during which process its eustachian tubes are closed off as are a human's while swallowing, and the bird is deaf to the world. As soon as the 'pops' have ended absolute silence must be kept through the 'clicks' until the bird comes round to 'pop' again.

Happily it was not necessary for us to play grandmother's footsteps with our caper. For in the next ten minutes five more of these huge, incongruous forest grouse flew into our little knot of pines. Some stayed and others moved on. Several took up a clicking and popping stance, and although much of what we saw was in silhouette the active presence of such dramatic and diabolical birds all round us brought every sound into sharp relief. Probably due to the nature of its size and colour, the capercaillie is a secretive bird appearing on its lek before dawn and leaving it shortly afterwards, behaviour which contrasts sharply with that of its close cousin the black-cock whose flamboyant behaviour on the lek makes watching a simple affair.

We left the wood as quietly as we had entered it, moving across the deep pile of heather and bilberry slowly and with difficulty. But time was not important – it was not yet 7.30 a.m. and we had made a good start.

From the dark tangle of the Caledonian Pine Forest we drove through shafts of sunlight impaling the Land Rover on long gilded lances. We paused in open country to watch a small party of red deer hinds cross the road in front of us, ford the burn at our side and climb the short hill in quick steps which surged them effortlessly upward.

Before long we came to a small loch by the roadside, an oval of sky lying like a puddle in a fold in the land. It was about half a mile long and nowhere wider than sixty yards. On the far side of this loch a long stretch of birchwood came down to the water's edge ending in a margin of gorse and broom and rough pasture. I stopped the vehicle and scoured the rough for roe deer. It was a perfect place and it was not long before I had picked out the white tail scut of a buck and his doe browsing among the birches. I edged the vehicle along the road until we were opposite them and stopped. 'Now, how about some coffee?' I said. Using the vehicle as a hide it was possible to move about quite freely and we drank coffee and talked for an hour while the two roe and a third, which was certainly the doe's fawn from the previous year, browsed and grazed along the loch-shore.

'Do you notice how diverse their diet is?' I said to Nancy. 'The buck is eating willow from that scrub and has worked his way right through the whole bush; the fawn and its mother are both eating grass now but were pulling at birch buds a little earlier and, while we have been sitting here, they've eaten broom shoots, browsed on that clump of dogwood, and pulled moss off that log. And all at a time of year when the grass is barely growing and there are no leaves on any of the trees.'

'No wonder they're so successful as a species,' replied Nancy.

I have visited that small loch and its birchwoods countless times since that first lucky introduction to it. It is a habitat in which the Highlands is particularly rich and which, until recent years, has remained inviolate throughout the turbulence of the Highlands' unsettled history. It is that ribbon of land which must exist in all scenery as deeply cut and eroded by rivers and glaciers as Scotland, deriving its character from its altitude and yet in itself so marginal as to be overlooked as a feature of scenic note. In mountainous country the eye is drawn irresistibly to the peaks, the high snow-plastered pinnacles and the great horizons of curving moorland. In balance the eye swings down to the pastoral valley floor, to a cloud-reflecting loch or a river with its polished rock and shingles, its rapids and pools. All too hurriedly the eye has flicked across the transition from valley to mountain. Somewhere in between, often on steep ground, the grasses and sedges of the valley floor give way to the heather and moss of the moorland above. Where the land has been methodically burnt and then grazed by deer and sheep the scrub will in all likelihood not exist; but in many glens this intermediate ribbon is rich in birch scrub often mixed with hazel, oak or pine. Where the climate is suitable the birches will have grown into fine healthy trees providing a band of mature woodland of enormous value to its wildlife.

The old Highland husbandry under the clan system valued woodland for timber and as shelter for beasts, and probably did comparatively little to remove the indigenous forests; but later, when the English invasion of the north brought unrest, much forest was burnt to smoke out rebels, more to smelt iron, and more still in the nineteenth century to provide grazing for sheep. Only the remnant and impoverished crofting system of the last hundred years has permitted the recolonization of birch on some rough ground. Sheep, sphagnum moss and a heavy over-population of deer during the

Victorian sporting era gave the native pine no chance at all to return. These marginal birchwoods, often thin and straggling, are all that is left for the deer from the open hills above, hard pressed by winter snows, to find shelter in; for so many of the birds to feed and nest in; and in which the woodland mammals, the roe deer, the hedgehog and the weasel, the wildcat and the field vole, can complete their daily round of feeding and predating. But much more important than these obvious inhabitants are the unseen millions of invertebrates which inhabit every acre of woodland. In the boggy soil, in the fallen and decaying wood and leaf mould, under the bark of trees and on the backs of leaves, lurking in every conceivable space, pocket and crevice, boring through wood alive and dead, laying eggs in fruits and forming fissures, and in the eggs of others, are the rank and file of woodland ecology: the viruses and bacteria supporting the living plants and destroying the dead, about which we know as much as Columbus knew of the Americas when he first set foot on their virgin shores; the nameless hordes of crawling and flying bugs from the electric-blue carapace of dung-beetles to the filigree beauty of such Highland butterflies as the Scotch Argus and the Pearl-bordered Fritillary. Without these, and the plants which house them, there would be no flash of the redstart's fiery tail on a bright May morning; no trill from the wren who can spill from that tiny throat more jubilant song than any nightingale; no drum, chip and cackle from the greater spotted woodpecker nor splash of autumn colour from seed-hunting flocks of goldfinches.

Only in the last fifty years, against the light of knowledge and pressing conservational interest, has this valuable habitat been felled and cleared in the name of commercial forestry. It has happened on a small scale on privately owned land, largely as a tax dodge – an incentive now as precipitately removed as it was conceived; and on an alarmingly large scale by the Forestry Commission. The threat imposed by the Commission does not lie solely in the clearing of good indigenous woodland, for as a poorer substitute a plantation of spruce or pine would in some measure make up for the loss; but it is greatly heightened by the addition of an ostensibly rabbit, sheep and deer-proof fence around the mono-culture. Mile after mile of these barriers, ringing entire glens at the top and the bottom of the planted zone, serve to cut off the red deer from their natural wintering grounds, interfere with the migration routes vital for the dispersal which prevents inbreeding of the wild herds, and force starving deer to damage seriously what small patches of natural woodland are left to them.

The mono-culture of conifers, being an unnatural pheno-menon, creates an unbalanced situation, and the dominance of one species has the effect of eliminating whole groups of insect and invertebrate life and promoting to explosion-proportions some others. Such an imbalance is continued up the ecological scale until certain birds are totally absent while others are found in profusion. It is simple to know precisely what enters and leaves a plantation by the examination of footprints and the holes made in the fences. Knowing that the animal has to use such holes it is then equally simple to trap it. While sterile is too strong a word for any plantation I know, the effect of mono-culture is certainly one of partial steriliza-tion.

Of course it is easy to build up charges against the forester, just as can be and is done against the farmer or the indus-trialist; the argument, to be valid at all, must be objective. The fences are not there for fun; they are there to protect the young trees from the undoubted despoliation that would take place if they were not protected from deer, sheep and cattle. Nor is the trapper employed to make money out of pelts. He is there to meet the immediate complaints of the farming community that would ensue if he were absent: that the forests are harbouring foxes and wildcats which eat sheep and lambs by night, and return to sleep in the forest by day.

Whatever the rights and wrongs of commercial forestry policy in Britain, the Forestry Commission must be applauded for its progress in altering the over-rigid aims of its initial

brief. Game and wildlife conservation are now synonymous
with the work of the Commission and it is working in close
co-operation with the Nature Conservancy Council on a
number of projects. It is softening its heart to the growing calls
for recreational facilities, and against the tightening tourniquet
of financial restriction it has produced parks and trails of a high
standard. The gratifying result has been that even an organization as large and amorphous as the Forestry Commission is
seen as not entirely without conscience.

That small loch and its hundred or so acres of birchwood
where we watched three roe deer and a few rabbits that bright
March morning is strangely symbolic of so much that is
Highland. With a few shaggy cattle standing knee-deep in
water and a misty peak in the distance it would fit the requirements of many a Victorian landscape painter. I have returned
there many times in every season over five years and it is as
fresh and invigorating as it always was. One January day I
crossed the loch on the ice after a week of severe frost and had
nearly reached the middle, where the water had frozen so

quickly that it was glass-clear to the stony bottom five feet below, when I saw a fox setting out to do the same thing as myself from the far shore. I stood quite still and the vixen trotted on towards me. She was so intent upon the ice, as I had been, that she looked no further than her nose. When she was ten feet from me she stopped sharply and looked up. I smiled at her and said, 'Morning Ma'am!' For a second she did nothing, staring in horror at the mistake she had made and then she spun round, dug her shiny black claws into the ice and sprinted away back across the loch – at least, that was what she wanted to do, but the polished ice was so hard that her claws skidded like hobnails on marble. With an ignominious belly-flop she did the splits. Now she was in a rage of panic and desperation, and her black pads tore at the ice to carry her away, but the harder she worked the worse her wheel spin became. She slipped and slithered about until finally she reached a part of the ice where the surface was rough and frosted. Then she was away, a streak of pulsating feet and flying tail. I laughed out loud and the sound chased her away up the frozen grass and into the woods beyond.

For the next week Nancy Redmayne and I moved through the awakening countryside like robbers treading in stealth through force of habit. We watched whooper swans planing in to land on the shining waters of remote lochans; their bewitching bugle music filling the air. We drove to the tree-less valleys of Sutherland and listened to the high excited chatter of a red-throated diver as it circled a huge open loch and to the anguished moans of its mate, a speck somewhere out in the shadowy evening water. We climbed high into Cairngorm to walk the long ridges between the world and its ceiling, and with a flurry of powdery snow croaking ptarmigan arose from our feet and spun away into space like white mountain doves. We sat in a hailstorm in a pinewood in Glenmoriston where I had been told a pine-marten came to explore the litter-bins at dusk; and on the following day we drove to the Nature Reserve at Beinn Eighe to see pine-martens in captivity so that Nancy should not be disappointed.

Later I grew crafty and learnt to thwart disappointment by introducing the bonus of a certain surprise. When we went to sit in the pre-dawn to wait for a wildcat I chose a place so polluted with roe deer slots that I knew we must see something. We spent an exhilarating morning with a pair of young roe, the buck in heavy velvet and his doe so glossy with fecundity that although she had some six weeks to go her condition was plain. In the way that some women glow in pregnancy this doe was certain to produce twins.

To finish Nancy off, so to speak, I chartered a motor launch from Kyle of Lochalsh and we sailed with the ebbing tide down the straits of Kyle Rhea and up into Loch Hourn. We passed close by Sandaig lighthouse and the islands of the Camusfeàrna idyll, and I pointed out to her the Cuillen peaks and the pyramid hulk of Ben Sgriol. She asked if we might go ashore at Sandaig so that I could tell her about the site of Gavin Maxwell's house, but I invented an excuse about the channel being unnavigable at low water and pressed on into Loch Hourn. Perhaps she sensed my feelings because she didn't mention it again although we passed close by it on the return journey. The truth was that I did not want to. I had not known Sandaig intimately as had Jimmy Watt and Richard Frere and the others; but even so, it was little more than eighteen months since Gavin Maxwell's ashes had been buried there under the great rock where the house once stood, and I felt very much the intruder. Only once, later on, was I tempted to take a group of enthusiastic readers of the otter trilogy to the place and I did so in mid-summer. It had already become a Mecca to the inquisitive tourist just as it was in the days after the publication of *Ring of Bright Water*, when Gavin still lived there. The path was worn bare by many feet and the rowan tree had been sadly torn about by idle youths. The beach was shabby with the litter people had left behind them and I wished I had not come.

Our day in the boat was a happy excursion, watching black guillemots and eiders far out on the oily swell, and busy with the task of identifying passing gulls and auks. We steamed home in the dusk with a sunset silhouetting the Cuillens in amber and gold, and pink mackerel feathering across the sky from north to south. Even as we approached Kyle of Lochalsh the glossy heads of grey seals rose beside us to bid my friend from Sacramento farewell.

Chapter Six

April came in, bringing the springing grass and the daffodils. These, my favourites among spring flowers, were becoming a recurrent theme in my existence. After the unexpected flood of colour that had greeted my arrival at Druimdhu it was a joy to watch their thrusting spears peel and spill in scented abundance around the house at Drumbuie. Early in the month I was given the name of a lady living nearby who had some empty cottages and, seeking a more permanent base of my own, I wrote to her asking if I might lease one from her.

I met Mrs Cox at her own large house in Glenurquhart and together we walked down the back drive to look at the cottage she had kindly offered me. Even before the building was in sight I was enchanted with the place. We were walking down an avenue of tall beeches and fine exotic conifers, and the grass on either side of the drive was thronged with the jostling heads of daffodils and narcissi. The cottage was a single-storey building with large French windows opening on to a verandah which overlooked a wide and beautiful loch. The far shore was half a mile away and the length of the loch ran out of vision on either side. The hill beyond was deep green with coniferous forestry, and from the verandah the grass sloped gently to the water's edge a hundred yards away. It could not have been a more suitable home and I snatched at the generous rent-free offer Mrs Cox made. In return I undertook to cut firewood for her in my spare time, and assist her with a much larger project she was embarking upon.

I moved into my new cottage straight away and had a telephone installed so that I could begin to run Highland

Wildlife Enterprises from home. Inquiries were beginning to come in from my advertisements, and I began the daily chore of sending out brochures. It was exciting receiving those first inquiries; answering each with a personal letter written in whatever tone I felt most likely to produce a booking. The paperwork lent an air of finality to the project – a novelty which soon wore off; and yet I still enjoy seeing the mail come in addressed to the enterprise even after five years. Among the letters in that first week was a card confirming that my advertisement had gone into the *Sunday Times* due out that week-end. I imagined it had been sent off by the helpful girl on the telephone, but it was a printed card simply thanking me for my ad and giving the particulars of the department it had come from. A telephone extension number had been filled in by hand, but apart from that there was no clue to the identity of the sender. I think I was a little disappointed and I tossed the card into the waste-paper basket. But postcards are difficult to throw straight and it went wildly astray, landing face down on the carpet. I walked over to try again and found myself staring at the hand-written address. It looked oddly unfamiliar but I dropped it in the bin all the same. Then, as I turned back to my desk, I stopped in a theatrical double-take. 'What did that say?' I asked out loud and bent down to re-examine the address. I could scarcely believe my eyes. It was addressed to me, absolutely correctly, all spelling perfect, but the rest, in place of Highland Wildlife Enterprises, Drumnadrochit, Inverness-shire, although written quickly in an easy longhand, unmistakably read:

Wild Highlife Enterprises,
Run and drop it,
In-his-vest-sir.
Scotland.

Round one to the girl with the calm voice, I thought.

Even at this advanced stage, with inquiries coming in with every delivery of mail, I was not at all sure in my own mind how this thing I had created was going to work. The copy in the brochure listed many delights to be seen in Highland

Wildlife Enterprises' care, but, with no practical experience other than the few days spent with Nancy Redmayne, I had carefully avoided saying precisely how it would be done. For his part, Richard was quite clear. He felt that with absolute safety he could handle a group of up to ten hill-walkers provided they were properly equipped. Since in his hands it was to be huge open scenery the party would be enjoying, it would not matter too much if they became a little spread out, or if a particularly energetic individual wished to push ahead to some pre-determined point. We were both sure that after a few days out the problems of handling these mountain groups would be eliminated very quickly.

My responsibilities, however, had many more unknown factors. I knew very well that to attempt to see some of the things I had achieved with Nancy with a group of ten would be disastrous both for the party and for the animal or bird concerned. If any degree of silence, camouflage or stealth were to be maintained the parties would have to be much smaller. I guessed that five or six would be the maximum, and sometimes they would have to be operated in twos or threes. It was clear, too, that good discipline would be needed if the exercise was not to be damaging. It would be pointless from every angle if groups were returned to the same locations week after week only to find that suddenly the subject had had enough and had moved away. Breeding birds were clearly a responsibility, and good conduct in the field would be vital.

Working out these details of operation with Richard in front of the library fire at Drumbuie brought into question the whole motivation behind the scheme. Again Richard was decisive. He loved mountains and mountaineering and was never happier than when he was in the hills. To be paid to extend one's own pleasure to others was an excellent motivation. My own reasons were more complex: under-riding considerations were that I wanted to live and work in the Highlands and I wanted to work for myself. Subjugation in industry had given me that craving more earnestly than any other. I did not want to return to my profession nor to slip back into the entrenchments of commerce, even on my own terms. And I had no illusions about making money beyond an honest living. H.W.E. was not made of that stuff.

I did want to contribute to a general conservation issue, and I still believe it to be our most important function. I remember arguing this theme with David Chaffe at the conception of the Westbury-upon-Trym Wildlife Park with which I had been involved in 1964, and again with Gavin Maxwell shortly before his death when we were laying plans for the Reserve that was to have been on Kyleakin Island. That there was a worldwide conservation crisis no one denied. Wild land and animals were disappearing as fast as roads and concrete developments were taking their place, and money and support were urgently needed to combat these trends and establish reserves. Many organizations were constituted to meet these ends and they continue to do vital work. But as well as this direct approach to the problem there is the harder and more long-term necessity of persuading people that these places and animals are worth saving and that mankind can benefit from them. There are far fewer organizations dedicated to this task and it was this particular field of action, albeit on a humble and almost individual level, to which I wanted to contribute. I thumbed through a thousand portentous quotations from Darwin to Schweitzer and could find nothing which crystallized this ideal better or more appropriately than a snippet from the preface to *Ring of Bright Water*:

I am convinced that man has suffered in his separation from the soil and from the other living creatures of the world; the evolution of his intellect has outrun his needs as an animal, and as yet he must still, for security, look long at some portion of the earth as it was before he tampered with it.

By using this as the text for our enterprise, we linked ourselves to Gavin's message, using it as a means by which people might be better able to identify themselves with their environment. I do not think Gavin would have been displeased.

Towards the end of April I took delivery from a garage in

Inverness of a large and gleaming 12-seater minibus. Richard stood out against this purchase from the beginning, believing that the enterprise must prove itself before the expenditure of any capital whatsoever. With no bookings in my diary, he regarded it as blatant gambling and would have no part in it. As it turned out, he was right; the purchase of that new minibus was a serious error, but happily not for the reasons he feared.

I was anxious that at the end of a long and possibly disappointing day, particularly in bad weather, my groups should at least be able to travel home in some degree of comfort. My various old cars and a Land Rover I possessed, almost transparent with holes, were insulting almost to the point of injury and had to be abandoned.

The van, as it became known, was a product of the then British Motor Company and had been researched, I thought, thoroughly. Suitable vehicles in the right price range were few and were thinned even further by the service facilities available. On the promise of faultless service and the highest recommendations from the trade, I committed myself. Nothing ever went right for that poor, insubstantial, bedevilled carriage. On the day of delivery, in defiance of my instructions, Highland Wildlife Enterprises had been written in exaggerated lettering down each shining flank. Only the colour was right. Small Roman capitals had been interpreted to mean large jovial letters of so unclassical a nature as to suggest an air of carnival fairground gaiety; and the silhouette motif of an eagle on the rear door had been copied from my free-hand drawing. The result was a curiously corrupt, pseudo-heraldic pigeon which could have no more soared into the air than a kiwi. Altogether my classical image had perished, unlike Rome, before it even started. I had these caricatures instantly removed, whereupon the sign-writer took umbrage and faithful, no doubt, to his artistic temperament, refused to do anything further. The second attempt achieved by a youth working as a grease-monkey on a nearby construction site was much more acceptable.

Common to all minibuses used for hire and reward, ours was of P.S.V. specification. But the ministry concerned require both the vehicle and its drivers to be rigorously tested for public vehicle service. Richard and I arrived, long-faced, at the Inverness testing depot. One at a time we drove off round the joyless back streets of the Highland capital. The examination was part practical and part oral and the examiner, predictably uniformed in grey mackintosh and with sinister clipboard, sat tight-lipped in the passenger seat.

Richard passed without incident and I took my place beside the executioner. As I moved off I was just in time to see a leer spread across Richard's face as he roared away in his big green Mercedes.

For half an hour we reversed into cul-de-sacs, encircled roundabouts, traversed junctions and, to the disbelief of goggle-eyed pedestrians, effected three emergency stops in one street, none of which related to any incident visible to the world at large. A little later we came to a steep and apparently straight-forward hill. As we neared the top the examiner emitted another terse direction, 'Turn second right at the top of this hill.' As yet the choice of anywhere to turn was concealed by a tarmac horizon towards which I sped in ignorance. Quite suddenly there were five roads fanning out in front of me, all heading sharply downhill. It was a road-test examiner's dream and an examinee's nightmare. There was no warning, no time, no space for manoeuvre. I chose the second opening on the right and dived into it with flourish and abandon. It did seem somewhat narrow but otherwise quite normal. A sign flashed past on the wall at my right hand and a cold, distant voice said 'Please stop.' I did so. 'Would you care to observe that sign you have just passed?' the examiner said, staring glassily ahead. I craned my neck out of the window and read: 'Salutation Pavement – Cycling Strictly Prohibited.' The voice came again. 'This is a pedestrian right-of-way only. I am surprised that you could not observe that from the extreme narrowness of the entrance. Please reverse out.' As I did so I had a wry suspicion that I was being failed for reversing on to a major road. I was right. As I accepted the pink dismissal slip back at the depot I muttered: 'Not again, my friend, not twice will this bird be so easily snared.' I went straight to the reception office and booked myself in for a second test the following afternoon. I had hoped for the same man, a dozen times if need be, but it was a nice friendly man the next day who inquired about the enterprise and wished us luck. I passed without any trouble.

In the post a few days later we both received our Public Service Vehicle licences and, to our amusement, circular numbered button-hole badges such as bus-drivers wear on their lapels. When, a week or two later, an official came out from Inverness to inspect the vehicle for road-fitness, Richard, wearing what he traditionally wore for the job, a polo-neck sweater and climbing breeches and stockings, was displaying his bus-driver's badge from a fly-button hole. It was, he explained with a well-known bleak expression, the only possible solution.

We were now equipped to transport our customers from the guest-house on the green in Drumnadrochit to the particular destination for the day. Very often this was to be no distance, perhaps a mile or two, or even a few hundred yards, to the walking point we were to start from. It was essentially a pedestrian exercise. We published our schedules and distributed copies to the local tourist office and information centre. We did not have to wait long for a response; but it was very different from the one we either wanted or expected.

I received a summons to appear before the Traffic Commissioners Court in Inverness in a month's time. I had never heard of a Traffic Commissioner nor, for that matter, of his court. The summons revealed that I was, apparently, setting up a public transport service in competition with the authorized bus company. This was a twist of bureaucratic ingenuity beyond my most absurd dreams. It was a total misapprehension, a fantasy. We giggled limply as we went through our advertisements, our literature and our publicity. There was nothing anywhere spoken or in print which could conceivably be misconstrued in such a blatantly idiotic fashion. I could not take it seriously.

When on the appointed day, Richard and I sat before the court – a bench of six or more spectacularly uninterested pensioners – and listened to a thin whine of a man who was the prosecuting lawyer (whom Richard aptly named Mac-Ferret) demand that the court remove our licence on the grounds that we were competing with the authorized service, the whole scene took on the quality of a burlesque. Finally I was asked to speak in my own defence. I rose to my feet and was suddenly aware of a gallery around the court-room and a row of moon faces staring at me from above. 'I simply don't know what all this is about,' I said slowly, trying to address the bench as one. 'I am sure I am wasting a great deal of your valuable time.' There was a murmur and a rustle from the gallery.

'Would you mind explaining to the court what you mean by that remark?' asked the central figure.

'I mean, Sir, quite simply that I am not a tour operator, not in competition with anyone and have no wish to run a bus service to anywhere.'

'But you have a public service vehicle?'

'I have a minibus,' I said.

'Then would you explain to the court what you intend to do with your minibus.'

'To move my own customers whom I attracted to the Highlands by my own endeavour at my own cost from their accommodation to the place of interest for the day.'

'This clearly constitutes a bus service,' whined MacFerret. The central figure ignored him.

'And where is this place of interest, Mr Lister-Kaye?'

'It could be anywhere,' I answered, 'any stretch of river or loch, any moorland, forest or mountain. Anywhere, in fact, where birds fly and flowers grow.'

'I see,' grunted the central figure. 'Does this mean you will be operating to no set time-table?'

'Birds and animals do not use time-tables.'

'Er – quite,' nodded God in the middle. And then to MacFerret he continued, 'There does seem to be less of a conflict here than you have suggested, Mr MacFerret. We must discuss this in private. The court is suspended for fifteen minutes.' We all stood up as they filed solemnly out.

Richard and I could find little to say in the interval which went on for much more than fifteen minutes. If decorum would have allowed it I think we would have shouted obscenities or pulled faces. The whole thing, in fact, seemed like an episode of humourless satire. Even while God and his stooges were debating our fate in private MacFerret was fidgeting furiously, dipping into reams of paper and consulting furtively with his client. Periodically he would lapse into sullen scrutiny of our faces as if by the very keenness of his gaze he could extract from us some subtle tit-bit of evidence which would floor us for good. Perhaps he really did believe that we had designed the whole conundrum to compete for his client's fourpenny bus-fares.

When they came back we were overcome by the sanity of the anti-climax. For poor MacFerret it must have been a major nail in his professional coffin. It was to me that God addressed his judgment.

'You must understand that we cannot grant an open licence to an operator such as yourself for that would lay us open to misuse in every direction. On the other hand it is clear from what we have heard that you do not intend to compete with the bus service. This court finds that we cannot therefore pass a judgment on this case and I grant you a temporary licence of thirty days during which you must attempt to document your itineraries so that we can grant you a licence specifically for them.'

In the event that did not prove so very hard to do.

Now we had a licence, a vehicle, a guest-house and, slowly, one by one, from the great world outside we began to get bookings. They came nonchalantly, quite casually dropping in with a few cheques or inquiries. 'Manna in sheep's clothing' was the delightfully mixed metaphor someone used when I described the maddening way in which one never knew from the outside of the envelope what gratification or disillusion the postman had brought. I wonder how many of those early subscribers guessed what excitement they gave; what hopes eternal sprung from their chance embrace.

Yet there was one aspect of our operation I had not fully covered; and that was access. It is a very common misconception that the vast areas of Highland mountain and moorland are common ground, unowned and unused. A sort of wilderness there for the picking. The camper, caravanner and pick-nicker is persistently surprised to discover that he is in the middle of someone's field when no fence exists. The hill-walker in summer is indignant when he marches into an angry grouse-shooting party or deer-stalker. Every square inch is, of course, owned and to some extent used. Land usage must vary with the type and altitude of the ground and there are undoubtedly places where land is, from any com-mercial angle, useless, but it is a tiny fraction of the whole mass of Scottish upland.

The rights and wrongs of large land holdings have been a political issue for so long now that the arguments are well known, but the use of high land is still a sufficiently esoteric subject to be worthy of brief explanation.

There are principally four sources of income from mountain and moorland in the Highlands and I list them in order of importance in acreage. The greater part of hill land, particu-larly in the Western and Central Highlands where the hills rise to between two and four thousand feet, is broken up into sporting estates where, every year in the appropriate season, red deer are stalked – an important control process – grouse are shot, and salmon and trout in rivers and lochs are fished. The income from this ground comes in the form of sporting rents which can be substantial. In the glens between those hills, and on any available pasture on them, sheep-farming will be going on in its somewhat haphazard way and in many areas, cattle too. This may be done on a crofting basis or by the landowner whose tenant or agent may farm it for him.

Thirdly comes forestry which is rather more restricted to moorland up to about one and a half thousand feet and any poor quality low-lying pasture which may have become available for it. And lastly is the growing interest in income from tourism. This includes camping, chalets, caravanning, hill-walking, skiing, canoeing, pony trekking and wildlife study.

It is the provision of the last category, the tourist and recreational facilities, that will, in the long run, help to reconcile parties which are currently in conflict. Usually the farmer or sporting landlord does not mind a walker crossing his land, but in recent years, with the growth there has been in tourism in the Highlands, the incidence of tourist damage, largely through ignorance, has made farmers and estate owners concerned for the safety of their stock or game or the rights of their sporting tenants, and have shown the tourist to be unwelcome. At the sight of a car parked by a lonely roadside the farmer now worries for his sheep, the stalker about his deer, the forester about a fire.

One of the functions we wanted H.W.E. to fulfil from the outset was that of providing access for climbers and walkers besides those in our own care. By making ourselves known to the various farmers and landowners in our area we could help them by demanding a very high standard of conduct in the field from our own groups and making the hazards clear to those who used us as a clearing house. The concept was sound but in practice we quickly found that others viewed it with scepticism. Over the years, however, the nut has been slowly cracked and the problem has almost dissolved.

To begin with I selected a short list of known landowners around us and approached them personally with our ideas. Without exception they were enthusiastic and helpful and I remain grateful to them. Their example was to help us enormously later on. We drew up and published a country-code which was aimed to protect the interests of all parties, not least the countryside itself and the birds and mammals and flowers we sought out and enjoyed.

Chapter Seven

May broke with a spell of fine weather and activity. Green leaves burst from the long fingertips of birches in a pale haze. On every stone and fence-post was a chattering bird. The lapwings swooped and cried to their mates in the long dry grass, and every mirror of upland water flashed and shrieked with colonies of bickering gulls.

We started life with two small groups; the first week had four and the second five. They were good sturdy folk who had waited all year for a walking holiday and were anxious not just to walk but watch and understand as well. Richard and I alternated days. A day of instruction and observation with me peering into pools, sorting the abundance of nesting birds and examining a forest or wood or lonely river or moor. With Richard they strode purposefully into the mountains, up on to high ridges along the roof of the world to a summit in the eye of the wind. It is rare to cross high ground in the Highlands in spring without encountering some of its dramatic birds and animals. In the evenings I waited anxiously for their return to hear what excitements they had encountered. Here a plummeting falcon, or an eagle which swept past them on glider wings. Often they had seen huge herds of deer on the grass slopes below them or had surprised a young stag asleep in the heather and the warm sun. After supper the evenings became a time for discussion and debate; the assessment of days behind and the planning of those to come.

In our third week, from a stimulating group of five individuals we dropped to an unsatisfactory one. She was an unmarried school mistress in her mid-thirties from Manchester

'High above Loch Ness, an eyrie would be a better description for Balreach'

'Druimdhu was delightfully primitive'

'A constant backcloth of rugged upland wilderness'

Peter Wortham teaching map-reading among the high tops

'Sorrel Bentinck and I were married in June 1972'

'Drawing water from the Kennels burn in that long winter

5

7 and 8 Contact with the soil was essential for all our groups — fording the occasional stream or gathering reeds on the estuary

The high moors abound with curlews in spring

'Against a tuft of grass, not hidden, but just lying there, was the half moon shape of a newborn red deer calf'

◁ 11

12 ▷

▽ 13

Lennart Arvidsson, always with his spear ready to test the ice beneath us'

Sorrel – from the city to the arctic; a transhumance she took completely in her stride

The taiga. 'I cannot calculate how many miles of gently undulating forest lay below us. It is, of course, endless'

A Lapland scene identical to the forest around the Kennels

15 In Lapland we followed the reindeer which roamed the Highlands into historic times

16 The Lapland scenery was so similar, so stunningly Highland that we felt entirely at ease

and her name was Janet. Two weeks before she was due to come I telephoned her and told her that her week was unfortunately underbooked, and offered her the chance of changing to a more companionable week or cancelling altogether. But she was not deterred, saying that she was a solitary individual anyway and would not mind being alone. She added with some emphasis that she was a keen and practised hill-walker and wanted to cover a good many miles. I promised her that if we saw nothing alive at all we could still do that.

The lady arrived and was installed in the guest-house. Since the weather was fine and the week clearly unprofitable, Richard chose to do some repair work to the roof of Drumbuie House and I agreed to take care of Janet myself.

Our first day out was a great success. We walked to a high, lonely lochan and watched through our binoculars a pair of black-throated divers, perhaps the most strikingly beautiful of all our water birds, rolling and billing to each other as their weird echoing cries drifted across to us on the breeze. We returned in the afternoon by a circuitous route taking in a small hill and covering some six or seven miles. On the second day we walked all day, but slowly, through a remnant of pinewood where the trees of the old Caledonian Forest stood bowed and ancient, and crossbills snipped and cracked with their warped mandibles to extract the seed from the few remaining cones. We surprised a solitary black-cock sunning itself, and all day the silhouetted heads and ears of restive red-deer hinds high above us on the horizon watched with unease our faltering progress along the trees. We drove home in a gory sunset.

'What are we doing tomorrow?' Janet asked as I set her down at the guest-house.

'If the weather's still fine we would do well to climb a mountain,' I said.

'Oh good,' she answered quickly. 'How far will it be?'

'About twelve miles on foot and few miles in the van to

get there and back. It will be a good day,' I answered reassuringly. But her face clouded and she looked at the ground shiftily.

'When are we going for a proper walk?' came the unexpected reply.

'What do you mean, a proper walk?' I inquired a little taken aback.

'Well, in the Pennines and the Lake District we never do less than fifteen miles in a day and often over twenty.'

'Oh, I see. I'm sorry. I hadn't realized that distance was of such importance to you. Not many people walk that far, you know.'

'I did say to you on the telephone that I wanted to do some good walks, and as I'm on my own I imagined it would be easy for you to arrange.' The girl was clearly upset now and I hastened to put things right.

'I'm so sorry,' I said. 'Of course we'll do twenty miles a day for the rest of the week if you like.' I dreaded the thought, but we agreed to start at 8.00 the next morning.

May 1971 will be remembered in Britain for many years for its sudden and dramatic heat-wave. Since the British are only ever ready for rain it was not surprising that everyone ran out of sun-tan oil and got badly burnt. Dogs suffocated in parked cars, secretaries lay about naked on London roof-tops at lunch-time, and radio-broadcasters complained monotonously about being shut in windowless cells. At 8.00 that morning, in the proper way that heat-waves start, there was a thick mist. I collected Janet and drove cautiously through the thick wet atmosphere down a lonely single-track road which terminated at the foot of a mountain.

'It's going to be a super day once the mist clears,' I said as it swirled around us. 'I'm going to leave my anorak here; I think we ought to be as light as we can.'

Janet pulled hers firmly on and disappeared into the hood. She struggled into a large rucksack and wiping the fog from her spectacles said:

'Right then. I'm ready.'

'Are you sure you want to carry that frame?' I asked pointing to her load.

'I always climb with my rucksack, and anyway it has my lunch in it.' She was a determined soul and I didn't press the point. We set off uphill.

As we wound up the narrow sheep-path I explained that we were climbing to a height of about two and a half thousand feet to a wide plateau, taking in two summits at about three thousand feet and crossing to the other side of the plateau, a distance of about twenty-two miles, where Richard would be waiting for us in his car at 8.00 p.m. that night. We had eleven and a half hours in which to complete the crossing – ample time, requiring an average speed of under two miles an hour.

At about a thousand feet we broke out into radiant sunshine. Looking back across the valley it was as if we stood beside a huge lake gently steaming in the morning sun. The whole valley was mist-filled, stretching away to the east as far as the eye could see, a set specially contrived for Morte d'Arthur with Avalon's island-valley dimly visible on the other side. For all the gradient it had been chilly, this misty climb, and now we were out in the sun I was glad I had nothing to carry. I have never liked conventional walking equipment and will wear neither boots nor a back-pack. In a kilt and cotton shirt my stout shoes took me over moor and heather both quickly and comfortably.

After a little while, inevitably, Janet became too hot and we stopped while she removed her anorak and stowed it away in her pack. It was a little after nine and the sun was unusually strong. The sky had that languid look about its cloudlessness which accompanies really hot weather and I remember wishing I had brought a hat. We made good brisk progress for two hours, climbing to the first summit, a grey cairn of stones built, I suspected, by a shepherd or a stalker as a landmark rather than by intrepid walkers. The hill had little to commend it as a climb but as a viewpoint it was good, showing the almost flat table on which it stood pock-marked with tarns and lochans all gleaming in the shimmering heat. A raven drifted overhead and eyed us with an unpleasant vulturine look.

Janet was a silent girl and seldom replied to my comments on the mosses and sundews underfoot or the occasional wheatears which piped and chatted at us as we passed. By noon the sun was becoming uncomfortably hot and I began to hope for cloud.

None came.

At a quarter to one we began to climb towards the second small summit and as the gradient increased I noticed that Janet was flagging.

'Not far to the top of this one,' I said brightly, 'and we'll have lunch on the top.'

As we ate our sandwiches, mine revoltingly squashed from being jammed into a sporran, I erected a shade for Janet by building two small cairns and slinging her anorak between them. As I made it she confessed that she was not very comfortable. 'I'm not very good in the heat,' she said. There was a slight breeze on the top of that hill which made us feel a trifle better, but I knew that we were burning all the faster for it. My forearms were already sore. I tried to interest Janet in the small groups of red deer hinds I discovered dotted about across the great shadeless mosaic of heather and water in front of us, but she wouldn't leave the shade of her anorak to look. Once I saw her binoculars working up and down the horizon and I suspected she was looking for some sign of the end: a road or house or anything. I looked away so as not to embarrass her. We were not even half-way yet and the haze only permitted a visibility of five or six miles.

At two-thirty we struck out for the last long leg across the plateau. I had knotted my handkerchief and wore it for a hat, and by continually wetting it in tepid peat tarns I managed to effect a primitive cooling system. At three o'clock I was acutely uncomfortable myself and since we had come to a series of sizable lochans I said that I was going to cool off. I was sure that she would want to too. In a few seconds, for modesty's sake having moved a little way from her, I had stripped to my underpants and dived into that glorious pool. The deep dark water closed over my head and I let my dive take me to the black sticky bottom to enjoy the coldest water. It was at once stygian and lethean, black and narcotic as I rolled and looped in its magnificent glow. When I broke the surface I looked round but Janet was nowhere to be seen. I pulled myself out, infinitely refreshed, and redressed quickly. I expected to find her swimming in the neighbouring lochan and I approached cautiously.

To my surprise she was sitting in the heather with an expression of obvious sulk on her face.

'Aren't you going to have a swim?' I asked. 'It is really worth it you know.'

'I haven't brought my swimsuit,' she said. 'I would have loved to if only I had known.'

'Oh! Don't worry about that,' I tried to assure her. 'There are dozens of lochans to choose from. You can have one right over there.' I pointed to a seductively glistening pool about sixty yards away. 'And if you're concerned about wearing wet undies, forget it! They'll be dry within half an hour of walking again.' But it was no good. Nothing I could say would induce her to swim.

We set off again across the pitted moor and because I was fresh I strode ahead and had to keep stopping to let her catch up. For the first time I noticed how she was dragging her feet. 'Come on,' I said, 'let me take that back-pack.' She let me have it without demur. It was uncomfortable and it made my back run with sweat. I cursed the damned thing but said nothing aloud. Even without her load Janet fell further and further behind. Finally she sat down on a lump of sphagnum. I walked back to her.

'I must rest,' she said. 'It's so *hot*! What do you think the temperature is?'

'It must be in the nineties in the shade, so up here in full sun it must be well over a hundred, maybe even a hundred and twenty. Are you all right?'

'I think so,' she answered, 'but I do need a rest. How far have we to go?'

'Another five or six miles,' I lied. It was much nearer ten. As I spoke she unlaced her boots and removed her stockings. Her ankles were angrily swollen.

'You are suffering aren't you,' I said. 'Look, why don't you have a dip in that lochan over there? It'll do you the world of good.' She shook her head.

'No, it's all right. All I need is a few minutes' rest and I'll be fine. Don't you worry about me, my ankles often blow up on a long walk.' I had no way of knowing whether she was telling the truth. I had known hot days on the hill before, but never anything like this. The sun seemed hotter than ever and the whole world shrank beneath its wide glare. Max, who had wallowed in every stagnant peaty hollow along the way, now lacked the energy for even that cooling mire and lolled beside us heaving and panting. No bird flew and no deer moved on that sun-blasted upland. I suddenly thought that I must take the situation in hand for I was rapidly becoming afraid that the girl was not up to another ten miles.

'Janet, you've got to get into one of these lochans and cool off. This is no time for modesty. You're dehydrated and seriously over-heated and I can't have you collapsing on the way home.' She looked at me as if I had told her I was a rapist. 'Even if you paddle and swill your face and neck and arms,' I cried in desperation. Slowly she began to see that I was serious.

'I suppose you're right,' she muttered and, leaving her boots and socks, went off to investigate the lochan. I watched her drink some water and moisten her face and neck, but she would go no further.

We stumbled on in stony silence for a further three and a half hours until the sun had begun to sink and its potency was slightly diminished. I guessed that we had probably covered another six miles, and the approximate vicinity of our destination was in hazy sight. I had swum twice more, allowing her to rest at each loch, persuading her to drink and bathe her smarting skin. We moved off again, even more slowly now, my own knees giving noticeably at each step and my shoulders aching abominably. Then she was down. Within fifty yards of our last resting place Janet had collapsed. I ran back to her quickly and knelt beside her. She was quite unconscious, her face drained of blood and her heart thumping wildly. I ran back to the lochan for water, filling a polythene lunch bag and praying to myself that it was only a faint. When I got to her again she was, thankfully, coming to. I poured the water over her hair, down her neck and blouse and over her back. The last of it I gave to her to drink.

'I think I tripped.'

'No. You fainted from exhaustion and dehydration.'

'Oh,' she said. 'I suppose I must have done.'

'Are you hurt?' I asked.

'No, I don't think so. Let me get up and see.'

'You lie back and rest for a few minutes first.'

In our discussions Richard and I had covered, we thought, every possible risk and hazard which could conceivably confront our customers. From the third-party liabilities of fire and stock damage, through the whole field of accidents including avalanche, fall, exposure, exhaustion, snake-bite, allergic reaction to injurious insect-bite, to the extremes of misadventure such as being struck down by a stray bullet. We had taken all the obvious precautions and more, insurances, medical supplies, documentation of our expeditions and a sympathetic doctor who had agreed to ally himself to our undertakings. The one obscure possibility we had overlooked was heat-stroke. I had suffered it myself once, in a Mediterranean heat-wave when Italian youths delightedly fried eggs on car bonnets, but it had not occurred to us that it was relevant here. It was, under any circumstances, a stroke of ill-luck. Had it been more serious – had we been, I suspect, even a thousand feet nearer to that blinding sun when the luckless Janet fainted – the extra descent, always the most hazardous part of a climb, might have been too much and the outcome and the future of our enterprise very different.

As it was, we struggled wretchedly across the last four miles of sultry moor as the dipping sun leered from the horizon. Stopping every few yards for rest, I half carried, half dragged the exhausted girl to the lonely mountain road where a car awaited us. It was not Richard but another friend he had sent to collect us. We were nearly two hours late and both of us in a sorry state. Our proper walk was over. That night the radio announced a shade temperature of 94°F for northern Scotland, the hottest place in Europe that day.

The next morning I met the doctor emerging from our guest-house as I arrived. Janet was not well. She suffered a perpetual hammering headache and was running a slight temperature. She was also badly sunburnt. 'You were lucky, you know,' he said cocking his head on one side. 'It could have been very much worse. As it is she'll have to lie low for two or three days.'

Looking back over the span of years of our operation I still hold Janet's exposure as one of the most serious near-disasters we experienced; even though, in succeeding years, we have known sufficient incidents of small injury to compile a hand-book on first-aid in the field.

But it is the first experience of each type of crisis that one remembers and not necessarily the worst. Dealt with for the first time, the problem becomes a known factor. Without any implication of unfeelingness I now worry less about the hum-drum twisted ankle which might prevent a person from walking again for a week than about an undiagnosed physical symptom which appears and is gone again the following day. In these instances the unknown becomes the potential danger; the unfortunate with the twisted ankle, tucked away in a sunny corner with a book is, to the administrator, a problem solved. Only a month after the partially-cooked Janet had gone home a second incident occurred which was a lesson well learned and one which has helped me avoid many awkward situations since.

It was June and the weather had been continuously fine for several weeks but with few of the excesses of the previous month. The hills and moors were resonant with young breed-ing birds and the full canopy of summer lent the woods a depth and solidity, and an air of conspiracy as if the leaves were collaborating to hide some dark and personal secret. We had had a succession of excellent groups; enthusiasts with whom it had been possible to share and debate and from whom I had learned much. Both Richard and I were in the highest of spirits. Bookings were still coming in and the year had shaped well with a spread of activity sufficient to keep us busy all the time. After six days of such invigorating weather and scenery we looked upon our customers as friends rather than clients, and were regularly sad to see them go. Accordingly we viewed the arrival of each new group with a build up of expectation and enthusiasm. That Saturday was no exception, and Richard and I met them all in the evening at the guest-house. There were seven of them and we found them ideally suited to the week we had planned with the exception of one quiet girl in her early twenties, called Joy. Only much later in the week did I discover that the luckless Joy had recently suffered a broken engagement and had booked a week with us to provide a change of scene and interest. That it certainly did, but, for the first three days, she was a joy to no one. Partly through haste and partly through her somewhat individual motive for coming, Joy had arrived absurdly ill-equipped. Her shoes were flimsy plimsolls and her selection of brightly coloured shirts and jumpers were more suited to a pop festival than a wildlife course. For three days she sulked and grumbled to herself in spite of the generous attempts to cheer her made by the whole group. On the third evening Richard met me after a long day in the hills. He was jubilant with success. They had climbed three summits each with mind-blowing views over tumbling hills and glens. They had seen a wide selection of mountain birds and animals, and the alpine flowers had been unforgettable. Then his face clouded. 'But Joy,' he sighed, 'would have done better to have stayed at home.'

'Oh dear,' I said. 'What happened this time?'

'She slipped and slithered in those silly shoes and grumbled and moaned the whole day long. She was not an asset.' Richard is a master in the art of under-statement.

The following day was my responsibility and, since it was that precise moment in the year when most of the red deer calves are born, I decided to venture into the hills to find some, newborn and immobile in the heather. I had been watching several groups of pregnant hinds gathering in high secluded places over the previous few weeks and I had a fair idea where we would find them without too much difficulty. The party, including Joy, was enthusiastic about this expedition and we drove off in the morning in a bubble of excitement and expectation.

In the great wide sweep of Glen Cluanie I pulled off the road and parked the van in a lay-by beside the river. After the long spell of warm weather the river, although some thirty yards wide, was a gentle flow without urgency or flourish, a quicksilver ribbon threading its way between boulders and stones, flashing and winking in the sun. We paused at its edge to watch a dipper with three fat fledgeling young, replete after their morning feed of succulent larvae from the river bed, flit anxiously from stone to stone as it tried to urge its sun-and-food-sleepy young away from our approach. The three fat fledgelings, plonked rather than perched on their warm stones, blinked unintelligently at their parent. Finally, the mother abandoned her insensible brood and flew away downstream chirping agitation and scorn at them and us together. We crossed among them, as it were, hopping from stone to stone and passing them, unperturbed, a few feet on either side.

All morning we climbed up the gentle soggy foothills of Ben Loine. We passed through a belt of cool birchwood where redstarts flashed their scarlet tails and tree pipits, vibrant with song, gave the place an ethereal quality so that we had to drag ourselves out into the sunlight again and press on up the slope to the moor beyond.

We ate our lunch high on a knoll of moorland before the mountain itself rose steeply to a summit a thousand feet above us. But that was not our destination. Before we settled for lunch I had spotted, still a long way off, a group of hinds lying in the sun on the south-eastern face of a corrie no higher than we were at that moment. There was a gentle breeze which had shifted once or twice with the contours of the hill as we climbed and, before closing in on the deer, I wanted to sit awhile to see in which quarter the wind was constant.

The spiritless Joy had so far been no more dispirited than expected but had stomped along in her inadequate footwear complaining only a little and being largely ignored by the rest of the party who, by now, were determined not to allow her to spoil their holiday. Over lunch, however, the unfortunate girl was bitten on the forearm by a horse-fly. At this she remonstrated loudly saying that if she had known there were going to be horse-flies she wouldn't have come, and adding, as if to make quite sure that I understood that the horse-fly bite had been my fault, that she was not particularly interested in deer anyway. Perhaps, fortunately I had at that moment a mouthful of sandwich on which I studiously chewed for about ten times more than was necessary.

At that point an eagle appeared on the horizon flying low over the ground, quartering back and forth in the process of hunting or searching. Even our fly-bitten friend couldn't pretend lack of interest in an eagle, and there was a flurry of sandwich wrappers and spilt thermoses as people grabbed for their binoculars. I was grateful for the appearance of the eagle, not just for its added benefit to the day, nor because it over-shadowed our taut moment with the horse-fly, but because I had begun to wonder whether the red deer hinds sleeping distantly in the sun had, in fact, given birth to their calves or whether we had happened upon a group of non-breeding hinds. Golden eagles are particularly partial to red deer calf, or a juicy afterbirth, and there is no doubt that weakling and still-born calves contribute substantially to their diet at a time of year when grouse and hares, the two other important items of food, are both behaving secretively in protection of their own young and are especially hard to find. There was no doubt in my mind that our eagle was quartering that particular corrie for red deer calves.

Red deer hinds

Instead of watching the eagle I focused on the hinds, and, even as I thought it, I saw two or three jump nervously up and stand anxiously watching the great predatory bird as it passed by them and up the side of the corrie beyond. For several minutes they stood nervously pawing the ground and staring at the horizon where the eagle had disappeared. Then, one by one they moved a few cautious paces and bent their elegant heads to the ground. That was exactly what I had wanted to see and I was confident that each hind had been checking its calf in the heather before returning to settle again in the sun.

My group was now excited and discussing the relationship of the eagles and the deer, we hurriedly finished our lunches and made ready to set off. We moved cautiously up through the hollows of the moor until we were about five hundred yards away from the deer. Then, after lying and studying them and the ground around them closely for some minutes, I stood up and coughed loudly. In an instant the hinds were on their feet staring sharply at me, ears forward, nostrils flared, each a statue of rigid flesh and bone solid as the rock beneath them. In ten seconds, despite the absence of scent, they had assessed me as predator and chosen to flee. Many mothers in the wild will attempt to lead a predator away from their young and hinds are no exception. They sped at full gallop up and away to the left of the corrie until they were a clear three hundred yards from where they had been lying. Then they paused, inviting us to change direction and follow them. When we didn't, but carried gently on towards their young still lying inert and hidden in the heather, they turned back and came on towards us in little halting rushes, stamping their feet and snorting and coughing angrily. Then, seeing our numbers, they left us, deserting their young and relying instinctively on the brilliant camouflage of the calves to foil us.

Without taking my eyes off the place where the hinds had been lying, I walked slowly on until I was in the middle of the little sheltered arena they had chosen. For a moment I thought I had been fooled. All round me was the flattened grass of their beds, and fresh steaming droppings only minutes old. But nowhere was a calf to be seen. One by one the group arrived, looking bleakly around in disbelief at the emptiness of the place. The corrie was totally silent; all seven of us standing, speechless with expectation, and on the brink of disappointment. Flies buzzed loudly round the glistening droppings beside me. Quite suddenly a gentle, measured voice spoke.

'Well I'm buggered!'

A middle-aged vet from Wales, very much the character of

the group, was standing pointing at the ground six feet from his boots. Carefully we moved in towards him and, staring hard at the ground, several of us saw it simultaneously. As stifled cries of delight broke from almost every lip, a pair of large, wet, brown eyes blinked open and regarded us coolly. Against a tuft of grass, not hidden, but just lying there, was the half-moon shape of a newborn deer calf. Its domed and wrinkled head lay cradled between its front legs, and its fawn and buff, white-spotted back arched round in a crescent to its hind legs tucked neatly beneath it. It was at once perfection and the epitome of innocence. Although I have found hundreds over the years, I never fail to be moved by the human desire to sentimentalize, to caress and protect. The illogicalities of the human make-up perpetually floor me. As predators only recently removed from the hunting scene, we should smack our lips at the prospect of a succulent deer calf and yet we want to protect it. I personally find a newborn human infant almost too repellent to touch, just as I do the unfledged young of some types of birds.

Once everyone had seen what to look for it took only minutes to find a dozen more. Eventually we stopped looking. We had been in the calving corrie long enough, and the hinds were reappearing on the skyline, dark silhouettes against the silver sky, clearly anxious to return. There must have been fifteen or twenty calves lying hidden in that corrie. They were spaced at twenty or thirty foot intervals, in no pattern or design, but just where there was a tuft of grass or heather to snuggle up to. Many were very newborn, their umbilical cords wet and bloody; others perhaps a day or two old at most. Some of my group spent long minutes on their knees photographing the calves inches from their twitching noses, which can be done without any fear of disturbing the calf or upsetting the parent when she returns. Many sporting estates catch up their deer calves and ear-tag them to help with census and control, and the business of tagging and weighing is accepted by the hind, often within her vision.

We retreated quickly for about a mile downhill and lay and

watched the hinds come back down into the sheltered hollow. They came cautiously at first, craning their necks forward and testing the air with each step, just as a walker in winter tests the ice before stepping out to cross a frozen lake. Then they began to trot and finally run as their anxiety got the better of them. Each ran to its own calf and bent over, nuzzling it with its nose. We saw one or two calves stand to suckle, legs askew to keep its balance and wobbling like a broken chair.

In the afternoon we climbed the final thrust to the summit of Ben Loine. From beside the cairn the world seemed a far distant thing, below and beneath us, quite apart from the scaly alpine roof where we stood perched like roosting starlings. To the west the hills stretched away dim and green to Kintail and Skye, with the jagged Cuillin ridge sharp against the endlessness beyond. Below us the great blue eye of Loch Cluanie winked and sparkled, curtailed artificially at its eastern end by the hard line of the Hydro dam bisecting the valley; and from it the tinsel ribbon of the river winding its way along the moraine and boulder strewn valley floor. It was a rare hill day; a day when the moment assumes gigantic proportions. I have often noticed how these mountain views silence even the most garrulous climber, and whole parties stand about oblivious of each other. Just as a small child stands dumbfounded before the first image of itself in a mirror, so, I believe, is the climber dumbfounded. In any normal day-to-day environment a scene is made up of a multitude of familiar features of everyday life in which one can find total reflection and identification. But the high mountain panorama is purified by its removal from daily life and stands empty of mirrors for the human eye. Endless billowing hills or clouds; an orb of sky; a foreground of wind- and frost-sculpted ridges and crags; an upland desert of sky and stone. For the first few moments the individual is lost, swallowed up, consumed by the totality of the experience. I stand back and observe little signs of nervousness or insecurity. A man reaches for his car keys or fiddles with money in his pocket. Mouths drop open, eyes glaze. A couple together reach out to hold hands having not been near each other all day. That day was remarkable for the total absorption of our group. I think we remained on that summit for twenty minutes and no one spoke a word until I rounded them up and started to move them downhill.

By half-past five we were back in sight of the river and the van, a tiny speck reflecting fire from its windows as the sun sank towards the mountains in the west. It had been a long, exciting and tiring day and we were all pleased to be going home to supper. Some of the group had pressed on ahead while I stayed back with one or two of the less agile ladies who had difficulty coming downhill – always the hardest part. As we reached the river valley I saw the small group of figures ahead standing by the river and thought they were waiting there for us to catch them up. Slowly I became aware of a new sound, a low roar that I hadn't heard before. I stopped and listened but couldn't explain it and imagined it must be a very high aircraft out of sight. Five minutes later the horror of the situation dawned on me. The roar was louder now, and with it an angry crashing of boulders. I sprinted forward to join the figures standing by the river bank. To my absolute disbelief the stone-studded river of the morning, where our dippers had sat asleep in the sun, was now an angry torrent swirling and slashing at the banks and the vegetation, and rolling great boulders along its bed. It was brown with debris and flotsam, and driftwood of every kind bobbed urgently past as we stood open mouthed in amazement.

The dam had been opened for perhaps the first time in months. Even as we stood watching, the water was rising. I got out the map and did a quick calculation.

'It's two miles to a bridge downstream and two to the dam upstream,' I announced bleakly. The van, not a hundred yards from us glinted tantalizingly on the opposite bank. 'That means a walk of another four miles to get round,' I concluded.

'I can't walk another step,' said Joy testily.

'Can you swim?' I asked, intending to be facetious. It was

an unfortunate joke. 'There's nothing for it,' I said, 'we'll just have to get wet. I'll go across first to see if it's possible.' I stepped out into the stream and was almost knocked off my feet. Somebody handed me a walking stick, and, like Friar Tuck, I set out to cross the torrent. I had chosen a point where the crossing could be done in three stages, two large boulders protruding at separate points in mid-stream. I reached the first all right and set out for the second. The swirling water came up to my waist and dragged savagely at me, but by taking each step carefully and making sure I had a good foothold, I made it relatively safely. Beyond the second boulder was much slacker water so I didn't bother to cross that, but turned back to encourage the others across.

I suggested they form a chain alternating man and woman, with a man at each end so that each woman had a man on either side. Inevitably, because the numbers were wrong, Joy was the odd girl out.

'Don't worry,' I said, 'I'll come back across for you as soon as I have gone over with the chain.' She looked utterly dejected.

Slowly the seven of us edged out into the stream, taking it firmly and purposefully, the leader getting a firm footing and then the second coming up to him, and so on, until we had reached the first boulder. There we rested and, as I leant against the rock I noticed that the water was still inching higher. I thought it better to say nothing. The next leg was pretty hazardous, and one girl, who was shorter than everyone else stepped into a hole and gasped as the water surged to her armpits. The two men on either side quickly hauled her out and a few minutes later we were all ashore on the other side.

As I turned to re-cross for Joy one of the men offered to come with me, but I declined saying that I was sure I could manage. They all looked pretty tired and a bit frightened, so I thought it better to try alone. Little did I know what I was letting myself in for.

Joy greeted me coldly as I waded ashore for the fourth time. 'I don't think I can do it,' she said.

'Oh, yes you can!' I assured her. 'You've seen us all do it and we're all alive.'

'I'm frightened,' she announced.

'So was I,' I said, 'but it only lasts a few moments. Now hurry, because the water is still rising.' That was a mistake and she began to cry.

'Come on, now. It's not that bad. And I'm here to take you across.'

Taking her hand I stepped back into the stream. But I had overlooked her shoes. We had all had climbing boots with heavy treads which could get a grip on the rocky bottom, but her flimsy plimsolls offered no such help and within two paces she had slipped and fallen. The water took her immediately and swung her away downstream. It was all I could do to hold on to her hand. With a desperate heave I hauled her up and returned her to the bank. She was completely wet and very frightened. I saw no alternative but to carry her.

'I'm going to take you across on my back,' I said. 'But you must keep absolutely still, or I'll lose my balance. Do you understand?'

'Yes. But I don't like it.'

'Nor do I, but we've little choice,' I muttered as I hitched her up on to my back. She was a small girl, but not light, and I wondered if I was going to be able to manage. I stepped out into the river for the last time.

About ten yards out, after painfully slow progress, she said I was hurting her legs and she didn't feel safe. I ignored her and struggled on to the first boulder. I set her down on it and rested. After a few moments I moved round to the main-stream side of the rock and told her to climb on to my back again. She complained, saying that it was too difficult, but nevertheless managed it. I hitched her up firmly and stepped out again. Immediately I trod on a stone which moved and I lurched horribly to one side. Joy screamed.

'Shut up and keep still,' I said, struggling to hold my balance, but she had other ideas. She swivelled round and tried to make a grab for the boulder we had just left. I was quite unprepared for this sudden shift of weight and I went over like a skittle, the river snatching my feet from under me and the current dashing me downstream. I remember trying not to struggle but letting the current take me until I saw a boulder coming up that I could grab. It was a big one with very smooth surfaces, but I found an edge and hung on until my feet found the bottom and I was able to stand up. I was up to my armpits and in mid-stream, the position of the fastest flow. Suddenly I was aware of people running down the bank towards me shouting and pointing. Then I saw Joy. Her head bobbed momentarily above the water and then disappeared again, heading for the gap past my boulder. It was too late to change my position and so, as the body swirled past, I lashed out and grabbed her by the hair. For a moment I thought either I was going to be plucked out into the stream with her, or her hair was going to come out in my hand. But it held. A hand came up and grabbed my arm and I was able to transfer my grip to hers. I pulled wildly and got her up on to her feet. But she was much shorter than I and almost out of her depth.

By bracing ourselves against the rock we were, with a struggle, able to get back into the pick-aback position. We set out again towards the bank and I was relieved to see two of the men wading out to help us ashore.

We drove home in total silence. No one had anything much to say. We were all completely wet and the water dripping from us sloshed about on the floor of the van. I delivered them to the guest-house and scuttled off for a bath myself.

Two hours later at nine o'clock I arrived back at the guest-house to inquire after everyone's well-being. I was told that they had all gone to the hotel to drown their misfortune in drink. I hurried after them in the hope of being able to buy them a round by way of amends for the day. As I entered, they were all sitting at the bar. Joy appeared to be the centre of attraction, surrounded by locals and tourists alike. I stood and listened.

'And suddenly,' she was saying, with exaggerated suspense, 'he tripped and fell full length into the river, and before I knew what was happening he was dashed away downstream. I immediately jumped off the rock and struck out after him . . . only just managed to grab him in time . . . he clung on to me and I on to him . . . and we made it ashore together.'

'Have another drink, Joy?' I said from the wings. She spun round looking momentarily aghast.

'Oh, hello!' she said. 'I was just telling them about our day.'

'I missed that,' I said. 'Perhaps you'd better start again.' Riotous laughter came from the assembled crowd.

For the remaining two days of her week Joy did nothing but talk of her adventure and how exciting it had all been. She was a transformed person, gay and laughing all the time. As Richard astutely remarked later, 'Perhaps we should include a calculated hazard in every week's course.'

These dramas were and have remained the exception. That first year our excitements lay in exploration and discovery for much of the ground we were covering was new to me. Sometimes the days we planned turned out so differently that we had to abandon the original ploy and focus on some unexpected element, so absorbing that it took up all our time and sapped our interest for what we had originally intended. On one such occasion we were sitting quietly beside a loch in the shade of an old stone wall, watching a pair of common sandpipers hysterically piping and screaming at their tiny, unbelievably delicate young which scuttled and sprinted from stone to stone, bobbing their preposterous stump-tails in emulation of their parents. These chicks, when they first emerge from the egg are so small, so minute, that they resemble fluffy bumble bees with less-than-match-stick legs and tin-tack bills. When they bob down into a posture of instinctive camouflage they become pebbles, tiny insignificant pebbles in a sea of shingle which is their habitat. Every stone is to them a castle and every boulder a mountain as they scramble and dart, snatching flies and other small insects from invisible cracks and crevices. Even as we sat watching this side-show the hysteria of the parent sandpipers re-doubled to a frenzy of ear-piercing anxiety as the scimitar shadow of a bird of prey slid across the water in front of us. With a scarcely audible rustle of pinions and scrape of talons, a huge bird pitched on the uppermost silver branch of a dead pine tree at the water's edge not thirty yards from us. It shook itself parrot-like from the fan of its golden tail to the crest on its creamy head; it tipped forward on its perch pointing its tail irreverently skywards and ejaculated a long white trail of fishy ordure which splatted onto the shingle below like the spoor of an incontinent tennis-court marker.

Ospreys occur throughout the Central Highlands regularly even though their breeding numbers are still very low. Every year we see one or two, usually solitary immatures over-summering on one of our fish-abundant lochs, and, rarely, a pair passing through in search of a breeding site. They are among the finest of birds and that day we sat spell-bound as it perched and preened, cocked its predatory eye at the flash of a rising trout and then, launching headlong at the gleaming water, snatched the invisible fish and winged leisurely back to its pine with the flash of silver immobile in a clenched talon.

For several hours we watched it fish and feed, the debris dropping to the stony floor and the white line streaking out behind. It slept, it preened and finally it elbowed off across the loch and up, over the hill, perhaps to some high and lonely lochan where pink-fleshed char, the mountain salmon, are found by a few who carefully guard their secret. The last we saw of our fish-hawk was a dark silhouette rowing upwards, a speck against the eggshell sky.

In these early days I found that I had much to learn and I read avidly from Seton Gordon and Fraser Darling in an effort to build up a supply of information and opinion to help inform the groups. I struggled to learn bird song, spending any spare time sitting in birch glades listening and document-ing. In that first spring I found that to sleep outside was the only way to reach real familiarity with the sounds of every habitat and, before the summer midges drove me back to human habitation, I spent many nights beside a stream or small loch, in a pinewood on the dry needle floor, beside a marsh, or somewhere in the vast and lonely moor. After a while I slept well in the open air, waking only to a new sound or animal presence so close that I seemed to awake intuitively, knowing that I was no longer alone.

In May and June in the Highlands the hours of darkness are reduced to almost nothing. As the year draws towards the longest day so the light leaves the sky for little less than an hour. For the wildlife watcher it is the most excellent opportunity. Birds and mammals, normally strictly nocturnal, are forced to hunt and move in broad daylight, and, to those people prepared to sacrifice or alter their normal sleeping routine, the whole world of nocturnal activity is open. Many times I woke to find myself being studied quietly by inquisitive roe deer unable to believe their noses. Hedgehogs bumped into me; a stoat once ran over me, chattered angrily at my presence and ran on; just once a slit-eyed wildcat met me face to face in the early dawn. It was a tom-cat so lynx-like, so huge seen from my prostrate position, that my heart jumped and a snatch of fear travelled over me. I had to force myself to hold its gaze. I am not sure how close it was: I know I could have touched it with a long reach and I was obviously the unexpected obstacle in its path. Our encounter lasted seconds which seemed like minutes and left an impression it would have taken hours for any lesser creature to inflict on my sleep-clouded brain. But the eyes and the frown on that broad tiger mask, and the implacable flicking tail, remained with me long after he had turned aside and disappeared into the tangle of dead bracken from where he came.

Perhaps the most astonished of the varied assortment of beings I met during my star-counting nights were the humans. Early morning shepherds, with their sticks and skirmish of black and white collies, must have been astonished to find a sleeping tramp so far from human habitation with his bits of sack and his binoculars and his boots beside him, or on his knees cleaning his teeth in a bubbling burn. Speechless and wide-eyed, they staggered away into the heather oathing at bristling dogs as they disappeared from view. Or the poacher who, working so hard to drag the snared carcase of a young red deer stag through the heather by its stumpy velvet antlers, dropped it and ran, never looking back at the wraith-like figure, dew and cob-web laced, which had arisen as from the grave beside him. If that poacher ever returned for his booty he would have found the two haunches of the stag neatly amputated with clean knife strokes through the hip joints, and the slots severed at the hocks, because I went home that morning with a venison ham over each shoulder and my bed-roll under my arm.

I found, too, that there were limits to which other people were prepared to extend their interest. A young couple came to me early in our existence and declared a passionate pre-occupation with otters. They had read Gavin Maxwell's books and many others and had seen otters in zoos and wild-life parks, but never in the wild. Now they had come to the Highlands and, more than anything else, this was their ambition. I happened at that time to know of the whereabouts of a pair of otters whose webbed footprints I had seen regularly on a sand spit in the river Glass. I told them where to go and how to position themselves; to spread their sleeping bags on the sand with a scoop for hip and shoulder and to sleep there, every night for a week. Then they might see their otter. They looked at each other in amazement, even horror.

'Couldn't we go there at dawn?' they queried.

'Not if you want to see and know otters,' I said. 'There is no other way.' They left the following day, disillusioned, and not convinced in their hearts that I had been serious.

Chapter Eight

By midsummer I was beginning to experience some difficulties with the running of the enterprise. Returning tired from the hill each evening left me only enough energy to bath and change and cook myself a meal. Afterwards I felt disinclined to tackle the pile of correspondence or deal with the bookings and inquiries in the mail that day. My only day off was Saturday and that was always consumed by farewells and arrivals and last-minute arrangements for the week ahead. The two or three days in the week when Richard was in charge of the group were fast becoming inadequate for the office work; and anyway, in very busy weeks we were forced to run two groups and so the correspondence accumulated, like bank interest, into a suddenly alarming bulk. It became clear that I should have to employ some secretarial aid.

One way in which I did manage to reduce the load effectively was to hand the enterprise advertising over to my remarkably helpful telephone acquaintance, Sorrel Bentinck. We became reliant upon her copywriting for a large proportion of our bookings and, by making just one telephone call each week, I could shelve that duty entirely. But in a curious way things sometimes fall into place, as when doing a job about the house one suddenly needs a screw of particular dimension, and without having to think or search, one comes to hand. Or as one winter when Richard, completely snowbound in his large and un-centrally heated house, ran out of firewood. Searching round in desperation for fuel he pounced upon the ten or a dozen stout timbers which covered a deep inspection pit in his garage. Weeks later, I arrived to find his household in a state of crisis following the mysterious disappearance of the Frere dalmation. Remembering the open pit Richard and I rescued the poor dog which had luckily suffered no harm. As we did so Richard swore to replace the burned timbers at the next opportunity.

'What about that door?' I said, pointing to an old door stored inconspicuously at the back of the garage. Together we dropped it gently into the groove around the rim of the pit. It fitted so perfectly, so completely to within a centimetre of clearance on the length, breadth and the thickness, that we stared at each other in amazement. So it was that, one afternoon in July as I got up wearily from my desk after several hours of laborious two-finger typing, and even as I said to myself 'What I need is a secretary,' there was a knock on my cottage door. The girl who stood there asking if I needed a part-time secretary had appeared so suddenly, so completely out of the blue, that I stood there staring at her as if she might as suddenly vanish again.

'Who sent you?' I asked incredulously.

'No one. I saw one of your advertisements and liked the sound of your enterprise and, since I was living nearby for a few weeks, I thought I'd come and ask for a job.'

It would have been appropriate if Susan Walton had disappeared one day without trace, thereby securing her mysterious image, but it was not the case. She worked enthusiastically for the five short weeks of her stay in Scotland, sometimes bringing in her boyfriend to help compile brochures during his time off from the local hotel where he worked. Then they departed, unobtrusively as they had arrived, to marry and emigrate to an outdoor life of their own in New Zealand. I have never heard from them since but I remain grateful to them for their help. By the time Susan left, the season was drawing to a close and I was not really in need of help any more.

August was humid, and with its cloying stickiness came two serious problems. Firstly the Highland midge, unequalled in number or ferocity by any other gnat in Britain, set upon us in its millions; and secondly the bird life of the Highlands, the life form with which we were most deeply involved, sneakily disappeared. I knew this was going to happen, and, throughout July I had watched the decline in the numbers of birds as each species reared its young and moved in their seasonal way to new feeding grounds.

The Highlands has relatively few resident birds because of its latitude. The further north one goes the fewer there are which are sufficiently well adapted to find food in the semi-arctic conditions of winter. But in contrast, in spring and summer the insect life of the north is so prolific that it can supply the needs of almost unlimited quantities, sizes, and shapes of birds. Consequently, tremendous migrations take place between the Arctic and the more temperate climatic zones of Europe. In early spring, while there is as yet no green on the hills, the sky is raucous with the cries of geese moving north to their Icelandic, Scandinavian or Siberian breeding grounds. Our east coast estuaries and firths are full of wildfowl waiting for the cold in the north to recede so that they can return to breed. There are huge flotillas of long-tailed duck, as majestic a bird as one could wish for, thousands of scoter and eider, and goldeneye, greylag and pinkfooted geese and whooper swans in lesser number, none or very few of which stay to breed in Scotland.

At about this time the glens and forests are full of hysterical thrushes all making their way north, many to Scandinavia and beyond, redwing and fieldfares among them. And even as they are moving on and the wild bugle music of whoopers has passed over the house every day for a fortnight, so their places are being filled by the small perching birds, passerines, which have arrived, some from the far south, to breed with us. They arrive suddenly, one day absent, the next in position as it were, setting up shop for a mate and a family. Wheatears, wagtails, stonechats and whinchats, willow warblers and fly-catchers, redstarts, pipits, finches and buntings, and many others.

From the beaches and estuaries there is a massive movement

too. Those wildfowl not going north to breed, the mergansers and goosanders, wigeon, teal, mallard and a few rare others, are moving up the rivers into the hills and forests to their own particular nesting sites. With them come even greater numbers of waders, curlew and redshank, greenshank and sandpipers, oystercatchers, golden plover and lapwings by

Lapwing in flight

the thousand. The shingley burns ring with piping calls, and the moors with the shriek and mew of lapwings and the liquid bubble of the curlew.

To the high hills and to secluded lochs and mountain tarns come some of the rarer and more exciting migrants: Slavonian grebes and red and black-throated divers with their eerie laughing calls; ospreys; golden plover and, on the very mountain tops, the handsome snow bunting and the delicately beautiful dotterel. All these, and many more, form the kaleidoscopic pattern of the Highland spring migration. For a while, for a few short weeks during April, May and June, the landscape is dominated by the chatter and bustle of a myriad breeding birds. Then, quite suddenly, as the evenings begin to draw in from the nightless days of June and the bracken is wide fronded and waist-high, the bird song begins to diminish. The ground is littered with discarded fragments of eggshell and every bush and fence wire holds a chirruping, dumpy-tailed youngster. The mallard chicks on the river are now as big as their mothers, and on reedy lochans the cries of common gulls are not those of nesting colonies but of glossy white chicks in their first plumage screaming to their parents for food.

By mid-July many of those young have flown, with their parents, to the coast or down the rivers and out of the hills. When the grouse-shooter arrives with Land Rover and dogs, and lines of beaters in the heather, no curlew rise from beneath their feet and the greenshank have gone. The moors are strangely silent.

At a lower altitude in the birchwoods and forests of the glens, where a week or two before there had been redstarts and flycatchers and troops of rowdy siskins working over the conifer tops, there are now only the thin whistle and trill of coal-tits or the clatter of falling debris from the cone-cracking crossbills. The August woods are silent but for the residents, the ubiquitous wren and robin and the relict pinewood species who have no reason to move on.

But it was by no means impossible to fulfil our function during August. There were peregrine falcons to watch, the eyasses trying their still-growing wings, stooping in practice at pigeons and rooks and even at each other, pulling out clumsily – if a peregrine can ever, even in youth, be clumsy – and avoiding contact perhaps because it is a game young falcons play, or perhaps because they really aren't up to killing just yet. There are eagles capitalizing on the mammals so abundant now in hot, sticky weather, their young learning the extent of their soaring wings, with the heather in such radiant purple bloom below that, even if the observer is unlucky enough to find no eagles, the scenery is splendid compensation. That first year we worked our way through August without a halt. We had to walk further to find the birds we wanted to see, and access was not always possible because of sporting interests. But we coped with the midges and the other difficulties bravely and enjoyed many successful expeditions. I made a mental note, however, to think hard about August for the future. There was a further problem which, that year, was not so serious, but I could see that it was going to loom much larger in the years ahead.

The myth has always existed in Britain that icebergs abound in every loch north of the Edinburgh-Glasgow line throughout the Highland winter and well on into the spring. A visit to the far north in any month other than high summer means icy rain and devastating winds. The snows barely recede in time for the heather to bloom before winter sets in again with Gaelic vengeance. When I first left England to live on Skye, friends asked me incredulously 'and where do you go for the winter?' as if one had to get out or perish.

While this myth persists the visitor to Scotland will continue to miss the best months in the north, and the two which are currently so favoured, half of July, August and half of September, will continue to become more and more overcrowded. For me the combination of humid weather, merciless midges, no birds and hundreds and thousands of tourists, makes the high season a short nightmare. Added to this, the problems of hill access, because of grouse-shooting and stalking, made it clear that the successful operation of our venture during this period would require a fair degree of luck. By far the worst facet of this problem was the unpredictability of the tourist. Where last week had been a quiet lonely lochan with an interesting bird, our next visit a few days later would reveal two caravans and several tents in position around its shores and several canoes and rubber dinghies bobbing about its surface. If the bird was there it was lurking deeply in a reed bed, but more likely would be that it had moved on. There was no telling where the bird had gone nor, for that matter, where the tourist would get to next.

Ideally, for our members to get the most out of their time in the Highland area, they were somehow to be persuaded to abandon the high tourist season. Many Highland hotels don't even bother to open until June; and March, April and May were unquestionably our three best and most stimulating months. It was going to be difficult to persuade any guest-house or hotel to provide the accommodation and food we needed at this early time of year. Even as early as that first season I knew that the enterprise could never really develop properly as long as we were dependent upon someone else for the essential domestic side of the operation. Although we discussed it thoroughly, Richard and I could find no solution in the near or distant future. Besides, there were other more pressing needs like that for a permanent office and a base. I felt sure that I could manage a second season somehow with the excellent guest-house we had used from the start, so I shelved the problem until our future became more clear. But I knew, in my heart of hearts, what I really wanted. I wanted a Field Study Centre based on an old country house like one or two of those exemplary establishments run by the Field Studies Council in England, to which I had been in the past. There was no such thing in the Highland area, and I knew that of all the settings in Britain the Central Highlands was the most appropriate and among the best. It was a dream and one which gnawed at me whenever I saw a large and picturesque country house for sale.

Towards the middle of August I had to make a fleeting visit to London to discuss the illustrations for my book with the publishers. As I travelled down by train overnight I lay awake in my sleeper wondering what it would be like to be in a city again. It had been over a year since I had been near a town larger than Inverness, and two years since I left the hubbub of industrial South Wales. In the event I found the change refreshing for twenty-four hours, after which I began to find the constant noise and movement unnerving. After two days I had had enough, and fled. The following day, sitting in the quiet solitude of my cottage-office in Glenurquhart I had occasion to telephone Sorrel Bentinck in London. After discussing our current advertisement she asked me what the weather was like in Scotland.

'A bit humid,' I said, 'but otherwise it's fine.'

'Yes, it's hot and sticky here,' she replied dolefully, 'hellish for office work.'

'Yes, I know. I was in London yesterday and I found it thoroughly uncomfortable.' There was a short pause.

'You were in London yesterday?' came the indignant rejoinder. 'For how long?'

'Only a couple of days,' I said. 'I had some business to sort out.'

'You were in town for two days and you never came and took me out to dinner? After all the work I've done for you all these months!' The voice was unforgiving, touched with anger, and I began to hope she was joking.

'It was a very rushed visit,' I said, 'and I was terribly busy, I hardly had a moment to myself.' I hoped it sounded convincing.

'Well . . . I suppose I shall have to forgive you this time.' A tremor of humour edged its way back into her voice, and then she added as gruffly as before, 'But don't let it happen again. And I shall want at least two weeks warning!'

I laughed. 'All right, I promise. But the adverts had better be knockouts in the meantime.' We said good-bye and rang off. It was strange, I thought to myself, that I had been talking to this girl every week for five months and still had no idea who she was or what she looked like.

The season had ended. We had closed our books and taken stock. It had worked. We had travailed and brought forth a minibus. Such profit as there was permitted me to pay for the wretched vehicle completely. Even in that short season our use of it had proved to be too much for the shoddy manufacture of the vehicle. The engine had given constant trouble and now, after only a few thousand miles, the doors and windows no longer fitted properly, the suspension was flagging, and the van had become unpleasantly noisy to drive. But it was our only asset, I could sell it only at a heavy loss, so I was stuck with it. At least it was now paid for. Somehow that achievement made its faults less glaring and its shortcomings more tolerable.

I now knew for certain that we were to continue with our venture in 1972. I could go ahead and plan new publicity material and advertising, and make arrangements for accommodation and food. So it was to London I went with a light heart, and full of enthusiasm for the future. My publishers, too, were enthusiastic. *The White Island* was in proof now, and I and they were pleased with it. I was taken to lunch at the Travellers' Club and afterwards we sat in leather armchairs and discussed the literary world as if I were Oscar Wilde or Bernard Shaw. It was a long way, I thought, from the moor and the loch and the greylag geese I knew were now moving back into Braelundie Bay for the winter. I listened to my companions only half-attentively, and my eyes roamed over their clothing and shoes. My own flimsy town shoes felt strange on my feet, like slippers, after the heavy-soled walking shoes of my life in the north. And the suit, and white cuffs, and the constriction about my neck felt unfamiliar and strange. Again, for the second time in two years, I felt the powerful conviction come over me that I must never allow myself to lose contact with man's natural environment. If it never did anything else, I thought, my little Highland enterprise would help a few people, caught up in city-existence, to re-find their contact with nature and their origins.

That afternoon on an impulse I phoned the *Sunday Times* and asked for the Classified Ads department. It came through. 'Could I speak to Sorrel Bentinck please?' I asked.

'One moment please.'

'Can I help you?' The same calm voice I now knew so well. I disguised my voice.

'Good afternoon,' I said. 'I should like to place an advertisement in your travel section please.' I gave a fictitious name and address and continued with the copy. 'Single gent travelling from Wild Highlands of Scotland seeks female companion for dinner tonight.' There was a pause and I heard her take a deep breath. 'I see, and where might this gentleman be met?'

'At the National Liberal Club,' I replied as calmly as I could, 'at 8.00 p.m.'

'Right, I think I've got that, thank you very much.' Click . . . Purr . . .

I stood wondering if I had imagined it or not. This lady was a cool customer indeed and I was not at all sure whether I would now ever get to meet her.

When I returned to my club the porter greeted me and said, 'There was a telephone call for you a little while back, Sir. At least, not for you exactly, but a lady inquiring whether you had booked in for tonight. She didn't seem to want to speak to you, Sir. I thought you might like to know.'

'Thank you, thank you, yes,' I stammered. 'That is exactly what I wanted to know.'

So there was now no doubt. She had identified me straight away and had checked with the club to make sure her visit was not part of an unkind joke. I retired to my room and wondered what I had let myself in for. I had no idea of her age, nationality or race. I could not really know less. I had committed myself to a blind date with a stranger. After a few minutes I returned to the hall to solicit the help of the porter.

'Sidney,' I said, 'you may not believe this, but because the lady who phoned earlier on is a total stranger and is coming here at 8 o'clock, I want to book a table at two separate restaurants, one good and the other ordinary, and then cancel one once we know what this lady is like.'

'Oh, I see Sir, I think,' Sid replied shaking his head to

indicate that he didn't. 'I'll do that for you, Sir. Where had you in mind?'

'Well, we could make one the Savoy Grill, that's always good, and the other perhaps somewhere round the corner here?'

'I know a place in Greek Street might suit very well, Sir, nice little restaurant, nice and cheap, where you could be in and out again in ninety minutes.'

'That sounds ideal,' I said. 'Perhaps you'd fix that for me, would you?'

'Certainly, Sir, right away. I've been asked to do some funny things in my time, but I ain't never booked two tables for the same gentleman before, Sir.' He went off still shaking his head. I called after him:

'When I come down to meet this lady, Sid, I'll tip you the wink and you cancel the Greek Street place. But if I do nothing you'd better cancel the Savoy and wish me luck. O.K.?'

'Oh! I see, Sir. A bit of a plot is it, Sir? Right you are, Sir. It's all in a day's work ain't it?' And he disappeared into his porter's office with a wink and a laugh.

For me this was the most bizarre situation. I had never had a blind date in my life and anyway I secretly disapproved of the idea, justifying it to myself by the quick familiarity we had both found it possible to adopt over the telephone at six hundred miles range. Now that the range was reduced to yards and the moment was pressing I felt strangely ill at ease. There was nothing for it but to pitch in and make the best of whatever sort of a situation it turned out to be. I bathed and changed, dressing unusually carefully and surprising myself at it. I became sharply aware that I had not had any sort of a social life for many months and I was quite unused to dressing up. Even after my most painstaking effort to look relaxed I saw myself as a farm labourer at a wedding. My collar would not lie flat and my hands, brown and calloused from outdoor life, felt awkward with no implement to swing and no rough walking stick to guide me. I returned to the mirror a dozen times but achieved nothing better. I *did* look wind-burned and rudely healthy, and that was that. I gave up and turned to the bar for comfort.

At eight o'clock a waiter came to my table and told me a lady was waiting for me in the hall. As I went out on to the landing I winked at a large statue of Mr Gladstone and said 'Wish me luck!' I think he did. From the top of the marble stairs I could see a figure standing in the lobby below. The stairs seemed to take an age to curve their way down to the ground floor.

An elegant girl of medium height stood watching me approach. She was dressed in a full length cloak of fine blue cloth with a fur collar and a large and heavily ornate silver clasp at the throat. She had long golden hair falling in ringlets to her shoulders and the eyes which were scrutinizing mine were piercing and vividly blue. An hour later, infinitely relaxed, we curved our way down the same marble stairs and across the hall to a waiting taxi. I winked almost audibly to Sidney the porter and said to the cabbie 'Savoy Hotel, please'.

I now remember all too little of that evening. That it was 14 October is clear enough, and I know that my blue-eyed companion ate steak tartare, but the rest of the evening, our conversation, the cabaret and the dancing girls are lost to me in a blur of well-being. I can remember, however, with absolute clarity, the intense disappointment when the Savoy band leader finally stopped playing and asked us if his band could go home to bed. It was 4.15 a.m. and we had been the only couple dancing since 3 o'clock. Reluctantly we agreed, and a few minutes later stood on the street in the chill autumn air. A top-hatted and tailcoated doorman was suddenly ushering Sorrel into her taxi. With a wave and a flick of her ringlets she was in and the taxi had pulled away. My own cab was beside me and the tall doorman was holding the door. We swung into the near-empty streets of the West End and away into the night.

Chapter Nine

The long rest I had looked forward to that winter never happened. Any vision I had harboured of long cosy days by the fireside in my little cottage, while the wind roared outside and snow built up thickly on the window-sills, was rudely cut short by two unfortunate events. Firstly Sheila Cox had sold her large Victorian house beside the loch and secondly, and not surprisingly, she wanted to move into my cottage at some point towards the end of the winter. Both moves were sad. The loss of the big house was doubly agonizing because it held happy memories for me and had seemed impervious to time and the outside world. As mansions go it was not beautiful, but it was very comfortable and, with its wide drawing-room windows opening out on to the spreading loch with the brown hills and forests beyond, it was in a most enviable position. One never likes to see one's friends relinquish an enviable position. But this wound was considerably deepened by the certain knowledge in my own mind that the house was the ideal, even perfect, situation for a field-study centre. It was being sold with just less than twenty acres of interesting land which included loch-side, bog and marsh, alderwood, water-meadow and birchwood, and formal garden and plantation. A remarkable diversity of habitat within so small a compass. The house would comfortably accommodate up to thirty people without much alteration and there were good outbuildings. In a flash I had it all worked out and could think of no better place. But it was out of the question. Our little venture was scarcely eight months old. We had only made enough money to pay for a vehicle, let alone a

Highland mansion. I did every sort of sum every possible way and even cheated to make the projections justify the capital borrowing. But it was useless. And the time factor was against me too. The prospective purchaser was pressing for a contract and I would have had to move like lightning to secure it.

Alongside this disappointment the business of having to find a new cottage for myself was a trifle and I accepted it philosophically from the first. What I had not realized was how difficult the actuality was to prove. Not only had I to find a new base, but I had to set up office there, get a telephone organized and make myself some sort of a home all before our new season got under way in April. I started searching.

The early 1970s saw a property boom in the Highlands which became an angry political sore. As well as the general inflation of property prices, small cottages, even ruins and old Highland crofts in dire need of modernization became suddenly valuable. The demand seemed endless and folk were selling off what they had hitherto considered to be worthless sheep-shelters for many thousands of pounds. When I started investigating the market I was appalled at what I found. Cottages which I knew for certain had been for sale a few years previously for a few hundred pounds were now way beyond reach of the working man. They were the status symbols of the middle-rich; a Highland holiday cottage to be used for a month or less during the year and costing a merry fortune. But then status symbols have to be expensive to be effective, and so the crazier the prices became the more the demand increased.

The Highlands has had a depopulation problem for many years due to the young people migrating away to work in the cities and industrial areas. Now even those who wanted to stay were being forced out by the impossibility of buying a house. In many instances it was a sad story. Highland folk who had been a knit community for centuries were being forced apart by holiday cottages. Some small villages became ghost villages overnight; cottage after cottage locked and deserted for the long winter months.

To add to this sad state of affairs, I immediately fell foul of another stroke of bureaucratic genius which showed no thought for the community. To my delight I found a cottage in a singularly attractive forest area, and was promptly disheartened to learn that the method of sale was by concealed bid. This iniquitous system requires the prospective buyers to send in their offers in a sealed envelope. The highest bidder gets the place. There is no opportunity to increase an offer and often no guideline beyond a minimum asking price. The effect of this was to force prices only higher. City tycoons grasping to secure a holiday cottage for their families were bidding wildly in excess of their worth to be sure of getting one. In the first attempt I made I learned later that I had lost the forest cottage by as little as £150. It is well known to me now and, ironically, it has been on the market for many months. The family who bought it came from Kent for two weeks some years, and not at all during others. I don't suppose the place has been lived in for six months in the seven years since they bought it. And now, in a property slump, it is temporarily unsaleable and anyway worth no more than they originally paid for it, even after seven years of inflation.

But in the long run I had the better of any city tycoon. I had the great advantage of being there, permanently, with my ear to the ground. My needs were widely known among my friends in Glenurquhart and the word was quickly passed round. Where there was a chance of a private sale I could be first there and bargain with the seller face to face. As it happened there was no such need. By the New Year 1972 an offer had been made to me which was impossible to refuse. A large cottage in the high, secluded Guisachan valley at the head of Strathglass, with an ornate Victorian addition to the rear forming kennels for the sporting dogs at one time kept on Guisachan estate, was offered to me exclusively to help me out of my dilemma and to be a base for Highland Wildlife Enterprises. No bargaining, no concealed bids, no fuss.

Furthermore I was given immediate entry which meant that I could start work on the place straight away.

My move was taking me twelve miles further west from my loch-side cottage in Glenurquhart, twelve miles into what must be one of the most dramatic blocks of mountain scenery in Britain. From Inverness on the east coast a rough circle is inscribed across the Central Highlands by the two roads to the west. The northerly route going from the Beauly Firth through Muir of Ord, Garve and Achnasheen, and dropping down to Loch Alsh on the opposite coast; and the southerly route passing straight down the Great Glen and Loch Ness and branching off at Invermoriston to take you through the spectacular sweep of the mountains which form Glens Cluanie and Shiel. This great circle, some two hundred miles in circumference completely encloses five main glens: Conon, Orrin, Strathfarrar, Cannich and Affric. Access by vehicle into each glen is only from the east, and within the circle there is no exit through to the west coast. Thereby the whole area is saved the oppressive feature of through traffic. The roads are used by those who live or have work there, and by the occasional tourist. This feature alone makes the area especially valuable and attractive. Our road systems have so regularly dissected natural blocks of countryside in this crowded island that it is refreshing to experience an area of this nature. It is possible to stand on a mountain in any of the five enclosed glens and to escape the nerve-shattering noise and vibration of our daily lives. No trains, no heavy lorries roaring and gear-changing their way along mountain roads such as is hard to avoid in the Cairngorms or the Lake District; and what traffic there is inches almost invisibly along the winding single-track roads in the bottom of the glens several thousand feet below.

In the western section of the circle the land is extremely mountainous, many peaks rising to over three and a half thousand feet and a mass of high moorland with fine glacial scenery covering the centre section; it is only in the extreme eastern corner, where the circle clips Inverness and the Black

Isle, that the land drops to the flat agricultural soils for which the Black Isle is famous.

The three southerly glens in the circle drain east into Strathglass and thence to the Beauly Firth. It was this drainage system that I had chosen when I first moved to Glenurquhart as the most potentially interesting to a naturalist, and on which I had started a small personal study. Now, fortuitously, I was moving to a new home beside the source of that whole system. The site could not have been more appropriate or more exciting and I was anxious to make the move as quickly as possible.

The Kennels (for as such it had always been known) itself was a unique building. Originally it appeared to have been a traditional Highland cottage with two rooms up and two down with a front like a face, a central porch and windows either side, but it had been altered at some period probably contemporary with the arrival on the scene of Lord Tweedmouth in the 1840s when he created the now defunct Guisachan Estate, a showpiece of aristocratic self-indulgence in the Victorian era. The great Georgian mansion and its magnificent parkland with exotic species of trees from all over the globe; the farm and its unique dairy and the largest enclosed steading in Scotland with a central clock tower dominating the valley; the village of Tomich, now protected as a monument to estate architecture, where the scores of workers were housed; its ladies' walks and rides of which paved remnants are still to be found radiating up to a mile and a half away from the house, and little bridges over burns or beside crashing waterfalls, their structure absurdly ornate with cast-iron ramifications quite out of place in the tangle of undergrowth which has long since overtaken the painstaking labours of three generations of groundsmen and gardeners. And, if you know where to look, there is an old power plant beneath a waterfall, probably one of the first private hydro-electricity installations in Britain. There is a mill and a ruined butchery and an underground wine cellar; a laundry and a bakery.

All this grandeur is now in total decay. The great house is a ruin, roofless and with small trees sprouting from the broad wall-heads. The property, once tens of thousands of acres, is now fragmented into small units by far the largest of which is in the hands of the Forestry Commission. Those buildings which are still in good repair are owned by many private

Old Guisachan house

individuals, and the unity which must once have been paramount is now completely missing. Very few people in the village remember the old days, and it is difficult to piece together the confused scraps of history I have gleaned over the years. It compares unfavourably with the great estates of England, or even the Border country, because it was *so* remote. The whole valley must have been regularly cut off in winter, sometimes for weeks on end and, even in high summer, it was a full day's coach ride from the Highland capital thirty miles away. The estate must have been almost totally self-sufficient for basic everyday needs, and the importation of luxuries and other supplies must have been essentially a seasonal operation. When buying some tweed from a well-known tweed merchant and tailor in Beauly one day I mentioned that I lived at Guisachan.

'I have a small amount of Guisachan tweed left, if you are interested,' he remarked. I was, and he produced from a top shelf a dusty bolt of heavy houndstooth check. He explained that this had been the Tweedmouth livery for the game-keepers, stalkers and groundsmen, and the old man remembered as a small boy riding with his father in a pony and trap up the long valley to Guisachan. In those days, he told me, it was beautifully kept, and the drive down the avenue was of fine gravel. They were travelling to the estate to measure and supply the suits of long, heavy plus-fours for the men. As they trotted up the long drive the trap cut and lined the surface of the gravel, and, as it passed, men with rakes appeared as if from nowhere and smoothed the gravel over again. On their return journey, when they left the house, he told me the gravel was perfect, not a stone out of place. I bought a good length of the old tweed and it has served me well.

Despite all the extravagance and grandeur of the house and its surroundings, the great attraction of the Highlands to the many wealthy English who came north in the Victorian period was the sport. The red deer stag and the grouse were paramount among British sporting quarry, and the land around Guisachan was given over solely to the natural propagation of these two game species. As on all other sporting estates the gun dog was as important as the gun itself, and kennels and kennelmen were essential. Perhaps for this reason Lord Tweedmouth had ordered the extension to the old cottage providing at one go a better standard of accommodation for his kennelman and luxury for his dogs.

The dog-kennels themselves were built on to the rear of the cottage and were lavish to a degree. The floors to the runs were paved in glazed terracotta and black tiles with a worked sandstone surround from which fine interlooped railings rose to a height of six feet to contain the powerful dogs. Inside the dog-houses each kennel had a paved floor, pine-panelled sides to five feet, and a central heating duct beneath the floor which contained large cast-iron water pipes. This installation ran the full length of the kennels and was operated from a boiler house at the far end. There were no windows as such for the dogs, but louvred panels in the doors to the outside provided draught-free ventilation, and along the apex of the slated roof ran a full-length ventilation shaft which in turn was roofed in slate, giving a double-roofed pagoda effect to the whole structure. As well as all this there was a cold water supply to cast-iron drinking bowls in each run, and a central drain so that the whole area could be scrubbed and hosed out. There were three runs and three kennels in a row beneath the one roof, and it must have been designed to accommodate a minimum of twelve large dogs.

At the west gable of the cottage a two storey extension had been added, probably at the same time. Part of this provided the extra accommodation for the kennelman, but by far the largest area, almost equal to that of the rest of the cottage, was a large stone-floored room rising the full height of the two-storey cottage. This was pine-panelled to five feet with plaster and lath above, but its most remarkable feature was a large central boiler which dominated the whole room. It was a coal burner with a huge cauldron above and a stove pipe rising vertically through the roof. Around this moloch ran a gutter in the flag floor leading to two large drains. On the walls were a variety of hooks and pulleys which indicated that this room had been built as a kennel kitchen in which the dogs' food was daily prepared. On a sporting estate there was clearly a fair amount of offal from deer carcases and it seems likely that heads and feet, hearts and lungs and a good deal else besides went into the great cast cauldron to be boiled up for the baying multitude outside.

These appendages, then, the dog-kennels and the big

kitchen, were bonuses. They were not what I had been looking for, but together with the cottage they presented such unlimited possibilities for conversion that it was impossible to assess the cottage between them on its own. The whole property is so radically altered now, after four years of constant activity and change, that it is hard, even with the help of photographs, to remember what the little house was like to begin with.

It had been empty for a long spell and bore the marks of neglect. But latterly someone had paid a little attention to it and had covered up, if not repaired, some of the defects, and it had been let for a few summers as a holiday house. There had been a fire, too, at some stage, and on my first inspection of the roof space I emerged completely black, better than any commando preparing for a night exercise, from the charred rafters and beams. The roof had a wobble in its ridge as the result of amateur repairs after this fire.

The house had woodworm. More woodworm than I had ever seen anywhere in my entire life. And it leaked in a dozen places. Never seriously, or enough to warrant a bucket or a mop, but just enough to allow one to lift and peel, one by one, the incredible display of wallpapers which had collected over its fascinating span of history.

But none of these features was remarkable in old Highland cottages. I had seen better and I had seen worse in my search for a home, and I was certainly not perturbed by anything I found. In fact I was elated. The place was magical and possessed features I had certainly never seen anywhere else and which gave the cottage an air of distinction. There was a door which separated the main front room from the passage which led to the stairs. Unlike any other cottage door I have seen it was a panelled door made, I think, of pine. I can only imagine that it might have been made for Guisachan House and have been surplus to requirements; or it came from somewhere else altogether. It was neither square in its frame, nor were its panels truly symmetrical, but it had been made by hand and by the hands of a man who had made a lot of doors and to whom the work was a joy. It was exceptionally thick, as if the craftsman had said 'Today we will make a thick door,' because by implication, the thicker the frame, the deeper and more ornate the inset panels can be. These panels were deep and contrived with extra fluting to make them look deeper still. Above all it was a successful door. It not only looked and felt good but it closed with a clunk like the doors in churches and cathedrals. Whatever else I might do to the house it must clearly be done around that door.

The house had a corridor. Very few cottages have corridors. They are a luxury of space reserved mainly for houses of grander station and design. But this cottage, thanks almost certainly to Lord Tweedmouth, had a corridor. It led from the remarkable door to the stairs and the bathroom which was an impromptu affair put in, I think, for the holiday tenants in the most recent epoch of the house's history. The corridor was disproportionately wide for the size of the cottage and on entering from the back door it gave, as well as an air of uncrampedness to the whole house, sufficient space for two people to pass freely, to carry a bag, or struggle into an overcoat.

These old houses were built, probably at the end of the eighteenth century, from the only local materials available to country folk building for themselves. There is very little building stone in the central Highlands and the houses had to be built of schist boulders gathered from river beds and morraines. Dressed down, the schist made a good rough face and, provided the stones were packed together tightly with a rubble and lime fill, they made a very stout wall. But of necessity the absence of mortar required the wall to be thick. Commonly these old stone walls are three feet thick at foundation level tapering to an even two feet higher up. In the Kennels the walls varied between two and three feet thick, which, with a plaster lining on the inside and a wet cement harl on the outside, made the place a veritable fortress. Because the house had been added to, there were places inside where one passed through old gables and external walls to reach the new area. Again it was like entering a church crypt or a castle basement. One did not simply open a door into another room, one had to walk through an entrance in which the door was only a start. It gave those rooms a great feeling of separateness as if one were going into another house when passing through a wall. Obvious advantages of sound insulation presented themselves, and even after conversion there remained rooms where one could scream oneself hoarse and not be heard anywhere else in the house.

The rest of the inside of the cottage was no more or less remarkable than any other in the Highlands. It had all the similarities of design and manufacture I had become used to: low ceilings upstairs; tiny dormer windows in the roof; bedrooms tent-shaped by the steep combe of the roof clipping a quarter of the ceiling away on either side; and, perhaps most typical of all, floor joists on the ground floor laid unceremoniously on the bare earth so that after a hundred and more years the floorboards were held together by habit more than anything else. The only joist I troubled to inspect before buying the place was of the consistency of plum pudding and was growing an exciting variety of fungus in several shades of umber and pink. I was never under any illusion that there was no work to be done.

Closing the porch door and stepping outside again on that first winter day of inspection, I was met with a flurry of wind and stinging rain spitting from the north-west. For a few moments I took shelter in the lee of the building and found myself looking up under deep cavernous eaves. This was far from being a Highland feature. Scottish houses in general are eaveless, often completely so; the roof comes to a sudden and abrupt end at the wall-head both along the length of the building and at the gables. In windy areas, notably the west and east coasts, houses habitually have their gables built up beyond the height of the roof, providing a low barrier to the wind and preventing it from getting underneath the slates. But here there was no necessity for that. The inland districts of the Highlands, even in the extreme north, are not plagued by the badgering, worrying wind which tans the outer isleman's face into lined leather in advance of his years and is perhaps responsible for the Aberdonian's dry humour. Here, in the sheltered valley, Lord Tweedmouth's estate architect had licence to create his own distinctive style of Highland home and he had done so with flair and skill. Much more than the Kennels, the houses in Tomich village are remarkable for their intricate roof design and gable ornamentation, but all his houses share in common the gift of long over-hanging eaves.

What you do with eaves once you've got them is an arbitrary point. Clearly in Mediterranean countries they provide shade for the walls and help keep the house cool. Perhaps even in very wet climates exaggerated eaves afford some measure of protection to the walls and occupants, but such conditions did not apply at Guisachan. The fact remains that eaves are an extravagance of design and a luxury – if you happen to like them. I do, and I equally dislike the stark unprotruding roofs of the truly indigenous architecture; for me they were a relief and a pleasure, a place for swallows and house martins to nest in summer, and under which a pram could be parked during a shower and where my dogs could find shade on a grilling June day. And at the end of winter when the snow thawed it could come roaring down the roof to be thrown out fully five feet from the wall by the eaves above, forming a rampart of snow ringing the house – a source of constant delight to small children spellbound by the winter mystery.

A little way off stood another house, a holiday cottage lost in the jungle of its overgrown garden. When I first saw it, it was alive with redwings and fieldfares, a dozen in every bush bickering and arguing over the booty of rose-hips and holly berries and the seed heads of currant bushes which dominated the whole jungle. The house stood silent and empty and posed no threat to the great valley; as far as I was concerned it was not there. There was a sound of water away to the east, and only because I had crossed its little bridge on my way in did I know the exact whereabouts of the torrent which had served the Tweedmouth saw-mill. The extant buildings of this old industry were visible against the fine beeches and oaks of the avenue; and although the mill had been out of service for many decades, the Forestry Commission used these old barns for the storage of their sweet-smelling larch posts and other fencing paraphernalia.

Distantly there was a more insistent roar from the river – at that moment in a mini-spate after heavy rain – two hundred yards away behind the Kennels and hidden by a line of wet-footed alders and planted poplar. Between the river and the house lay a low, wet meadow which, I later learned, belonged firmly to the river and became a broad extension of it at least twice a year. The Kennels was built, it seems, at exactly that point beyond which the river had never been known to flood. Often the grey waters have risen to the garden fence, entered beneath its rails, stopped ten feet from the house and slunk away again in the night.

Larch

To the south the land rose dramatically in terraces to the moorland one and a half thousand feet above the house. The first five hundred feet had been heavily planted with conifer by the Tweedmouth silviculturalist, and the trees, largely

Scots pine and larch with some fine stands of Noble fir, were now in maturity, stretching into the sky and hiding the moorland mass behind. There were deer in these woods, and I could see from the slot-marks in the broad grass parkland in front of the house that they regularly came there to graze. On a windy day the trees swayed back and forth like yachts at anchor and their supple crowns made a rhythmic swishing like a lullaby. To lie awake at night and hear wind in trees belongs so profoundly to our distant origins that it has a sedative effect akin to a mother's heartbeat to the child in the womb.

This, then, was to be my home. The base I had sought and dreamed about, where I would live and move and have my being modelled by the forces of nature about me. I hurried away to complete the purchase arrangements and to beg my neighbour at the farm, who was selling me the property, to let me move in and start work straight away. No one could have been kinder or more helpful, and his enthusiasm made the whole business flow easily and painlessly forward. The conveyancing of property is a sort of exclusive chess game lawyers play largely to their own advantage. If permitted they can keep it up for years; but if the sponsors are worldly and know some of the rules of the game it can be little more than a brief exchange. So it was with the Kennels and what brief intervening period there was we covered properly and justly by a flexible lease. Within a week the key was mine. A big, old, slightly rusty, heavy key with a tatty label. It felt good in the hand and was cold and hard in the trouser pocket. To own a key which turned a lock which opened a door into a house like the Kennels was as good as any lawyer's deed and I drove away proudly with it, back to Glenurquhart and the loch and the past. All that had gone before was suddenly unimportant and I could scarcely pack my possessions into boxes fast enough.

Book Two

Chapter One

Sorrel Bentinck and I were married in June 1972 in a tiny Hertfordshire church by an elderly and distinguished Highland minister. It had been a crazy courtship conducted largely over the telephone, punctuated by infrequent perilous winter dashes seven hundred miles from snow-locked northern Inverness-shire to the home counties where fog and the freezing slurry thrown up by heavy traffic were an added hazard. I had spent a happy relaxed Christmas in her Hertfordshire family home of which I remember only an amalgam of well-being – heavy William Morris wallpapers, the chink of glasses and perpetually flowing Burgundy.

Sorrel returned briefly to Scotland with me for the New Year and we celebrated that essentially Scottish festival in an absurd forty-eight hour reverie of first-footing with a gallon bottle of whisky. It returned, I seem to remember after visiting some twenty houses, with more whisky in it than when we set out. Such was the hospitality of those we visited, we were not allowed to drink from it ourselves; and lacking the Highlander's ability to go on drinking whisky for ever, I took to furtively emptying my glass into the gallon bottle in an effort not to offend our over-generous hosts. A crofter friend later remarked that only an Englishman could steal whisky from a Highlander in his own home at Hogmanay!

That whole spring was a flurry of preparation and I was reconciled to the knowledge that the season would suffer for it. I was unable to snatch even the odd week-end away, and from the time of our engagement at Easter we were forcibly separated until the day before the wedding. I worked out one day that we had been in each other's company for less than a month. But, if for no other reason, it was essential for our little business not to delay. I desperately needed help with it, and for every trip south to pursue the delights of courtship something was neglected in the north.

Sorrel brought excellent qualifications to the enterprise. Although still in her twenties, she had a wide experience of commercial life, had worked successfully in television and the media, and had made the communications industry a career. She had planned to combine child education with her career and was working at the *Sunday Times* as a stop-gap before taking a place at a teachers' training college. She was well into this course when we married and I am guilty of having forced her to abandon it.

Living and working at the Kennels while the winter receded and the Highland spring emerged had been exhilarating. The first indication had come one morning when I awoke to hear the shrill excited cries of lapwings around the house. The valley had been empty of bird song all winter and now, literally overnight, a troop of these pied tumblers had arrived. The meadow behind the house was good rough pasture with dips and hollows and tussocks of rush and grass. The lapwings came here every spring to nest amongst the grass. They spun and swooped and shrieked to each other, flashing their terra-cotta tails and the green gloss of their backs. What I did not know then was that these twenty or thirty birds were the remnant of a greater number which had nested in the valley since Tweedmouth's day. They were the last of the generation to be born there before the farm changed hands and, in the name of necessity and an improved agriculture, the field had been drained and rolled and transformed into better grazing and for the vital growth of silage. Fewer and fewer lapwings had returned each year until only this handful remained behind the Kennels. That was the last year they nested there; they came again in our second spring and danced and performed before us with all their previous panache; but it was a gesture only, and within a few days they had begun to move away in search of rougher pasture more to their liking.

Alongside the lapwings that April came the gulls. I cannot now enjoy herring gulls and black-backed gulls beside the sea. I had begun to dislike both during my sojourn on Kyleakin Island where I had the tedious task of keeping these rapacious scavengers away from our eider duck colony. Their repeated attempts to annihilate the fluffy eider chicks as soon as they were hatched, or to steal the eggs before they even had a chance, had kept us in constant battle warding them off and destroying the bolder and more persistent of their number.

Gulls

But for all their unpleasant character I had a sustained regard for their grace in flight and their aerobatic skill. Now, however, I was living in daily contact with new and different gulls. These were land-gulls, common and black-headed gulls, and as far removed from the raucous scavengers of the coast as the salt spray itself. Common gulls are badly misnamed. They are one of Britain's rarer breeding gulls and are restricted largely to the Highland area. Black-headed gulls are far more common in that they occur evenly throughout the country.

Those which came up the river with the spring at Guisachan were largely common gulls. The others were hangers on, opportunists, loitering on the edge of the troop. And in comparison with the Kyleakin gulls they were refined, delicate and elegant, like a dove beside a crow, or a ballerina beside a boxer. They came, following the water course uphill to the high desolate lochans, where they would nest on islands and promontories out of reach of the passing fox or other resourceful predator. Often the process of getting to the final breeding site was a long one of working upstream through farmland and staying to make best use of whatever food was available. It is a common sight throughout the Highlands in the spring to see a tractor smothered in a cloud of reeling and diving common and black-headed gulls as it drags a furrow through last year's stubble or pasture. As each sod is turned a wealth of worms and grubs are revealed and the gulls pitch in exactly as they would to bubbling fry in the crest of a wave. They were about us at Guisachan for two weeks that year, waiting around the river-fields for some new activity on the farm. When there was no treasure to be picked from the turning soil they wheeled and circled above us arguing and bickering among themselves, and pitched on the roof and the fence-posts to sun themselves in the bright spring air.

Sorrel came to live at the Kennels having never seen a Highland spring and without any knowledge, first or second-hand, of its natural history or the wildlife which moved constantly around us. The scenery she accepted as being dramatic and exciting; but beyond that, she was removed from any personal experience of the countryside by her city career and by an upbringing largely indifferent to country life. I was interested to discover what facet of the abundant mystery would attract her first, or whether the essential interest was not a part of her make up at all. I remain impressed by her objectivity. To this day she is as moved by a beetle, electric-blue carapace and gyrating antennae, as by a peregrine falcon with all its dash and fire. When I presented her with a bulging handful of goldfinch chicks fallen from their nest, her reaction was never 'I must rush out and study them and become the world expert on goldfinch chicks'; but simply 'How beautiful they are. How refined, how precise and complete they are.' She had no desire to extract information from them for herself or anyone else, no concept of personal gain occluded her own special style of interest and involvement. 'You be the naturalist,' she would insist. 'I don't need to know the name of everything to enjoy it.' And when a tree pipit moved into the large oak tree beside the house that summer and set up territory there, Sorrel came running in to tell me. 'There is a wonderful bird in the oak tree,' she called. 'Do come and listen to it.' I hurried outside and we stared up into the twig-latticed sky. There he was, on an upper branch, whistling away better than the proverbial (and actually disappointing) nightingale. 'What a lovely song,' Sorrel observed. 'I could listen to that all day.'

'You will have to,' I said. 'That chap is here to stay now and will be letting us know he's there until his wife has laid some eggs.' Sorrel peered unfamiliarly through binoculars to see this musician more closely. The richness of his notes were, it is true, remarkable and I found myself listening more intently than I ever had before to a tree pipit. If I had been asked to list my favourite songsters I don't think I should have included the tree pipit until that summer. I had known it well enough; it is a common summer visitor, and I could identify it positively by its descending song without bothering to look for the bird. But I had never really listened to it before, and I was faintly cross that my novice birdwatching wife should have opened my ears to its very individual quality.

'Aren't you going to ask what it is?' I said after some moments.

'I know what it is,' came the unabashed reply, 'it's a minstrel bird or a honeymoon whistler, it doesn't much matter which name you use.'

'Thank you,' I said, 'I shall try to remember. But you may

find difficulty in communicating its identity to other people with those names. Tree pipit you will find is universally more acceptable.'

'A *tree* pipit!' She exclaimed. 'How boring.' And I had to agree.

In those early days Sorrel was able to come out with me from time to time and join in the activities of the enterprise. One day we sat beside a lonely loch watching a red-throated diver asleep on the water a hundred yards out. The group were keen birdwatchers and this highly specialized bird is a feature of the Highlands many come specifically to see. Only in the north, in its breeding grounds, can it be seen in its full plumage with silver slate head and neck and pyjama stripes mimicking the ripple of light on the surface of the loch, and with a gorget of fiery brick-red.

Suddenly the bird awoke and looked around. For the first time the patient watchers saw the colour and form of that elegant head and throat side lit by the strong morning sun. We watched in busy silence for some moments and then, without warning, it dived. A startled cry broke from Sorrel sitting beside me. 'Oh God!' she said, 'it's sunk!'

But moments of embarrassment were rare, and for the most part Sorrel joined our activities with such infectious enthusiasm that any shortage of technical knowledge was amply repaid by the high morale she created. Perhaps the only facet of our daily life she found hard to adapt to at first was the hills. Some groups were unsuited to climbing, so Richard and I would prepare a programme which carefully avoided much uphill walking. If we had to achieve a high altitude to see some particular alpine inhabitant, we would choose a hill with a very high start, taking the vehicle to the highest point and following well demarcated mountain paths which zig-zagged gently upwards. On other occasions, however, an obviously competent group would arrive with high demands for long uphill walks and roof-top scenery. These were Richard's delight, and he would handle them majestically so that even the fittest and most demanding returned weary and exhilarated. But it was not always possible for Richard to take a complete week of such enthusiasts and I often had to take over for alternate days.

It was on one of these weeks that summer, when the weather was so upliftingly glorious without being sultry or too hot, that Sorrel could not bear to be left behind. 'It'll be hard going,' I warned her, but she was insistent and we set off. We had chosen a mountain with a steep rocky face which rose sharply through scree and gulleys beyond a flat, wet moor. Our plan was to cross the moor and climb the far shoulder where a series of steep, grassy terraces led to the summit, rather than struggle to find a way up the rocky face. We set out in high sunshine and high spirits. But within a mile or two of the mountain the moor became hot and oppressive. In the lee of that peak the weather changed, and the evaporating bog-water seemed to hang in the air about us producing clouds of midges and causing us to sweat profusely. In their anxiety to get up above the moor and the deep dragging heather, my energetic party strode doggedly on at a savage pace. Sorrel, already falling behind, was clearly in trouble. I went back to her and found her in a worse state than I had imagined.

'Oh! I do hate this,' she said meaningfully, knowing that she was out of earshot from the rest of the group.

'Well never mind,' I said; 'it's not far to go now and you mustn't hold them up, they're so keen to get climbing.' That was the wrong thing to have said and I saw the colour rising in her cheeks.

'I mustn't hold them up, eh!' she snapped back. 'So that's how you feel, is it?'

'Well you did choose to come on an energetic day, and I did warn you it would be tough going.' The 'I told you so' line was the worst possible tack I could have adopted. Sorrel exploded. Not loudly, but a low shaking explosion which was much more alarming. 'I think you should know that I hate mountains, and heather, and this stinking bog and its lousy midges more than anything else God created except perhaps the idea of hauling myself up that wretched hill on a filthy hot day like this. I was, it may have escaped you, doing it for you and that rabble of frustrated antelope up ahead. If all you can find to say is 'I told you so', then you can climb your lousy mountain by yourself and fall over the edge when you get there for all I care. I shall be at home, sunbathing!' With which she turned and began to walk back the way we had come. I was stuck. It was clearly going to take a long time to conciliate this little tempest, and I could not wait for it to abate. My frustrated antelope were already half a mile ahead and I dared not let them get any further unescorted. I was hurt, too, and it got the better of me.

'Go home then,' I shouted after her, 'and it won't bother me if you do get stuck in a bog with no one to haul you out.' Remembering suddenly that I had the van keys in my pocket, I felt that the war had swayed in my favour somewhat, and I strode off across that sweltering bogland with self-righteous smugness.

I quickly caught up with the group and explained lightly that Sorrel was not feeling too well and had decided to turn back. We laboured on up the toiling landscape like ants crossing a ploughed field until we were at the foot of the great shoulder ahead of us. By now I was regretting the whole incident, and was worrying not a little about the many hazards which can befall an inexperienced walker in such hostile country. Supposing Sorrel fell and twisted an ankle, or got bitten by an adder. Or just got lost, as it was maddeningly easy to do in moorland where every feature looks the same. As we rested for a moment before starting the ascent, I lay and scoured the ground behind us with my field glasses. Sorrel was nowhere to be seen in the great empty expanse below us. Now I was worried. Perhaps she had fallen already. I sat up and worked over the land, systematically quartering every dip and hollow. She was nowhere to be seen.

Suddenly, out of the corner of my eye, in the extreme left-hand sweep of my glasses, a mile from the route Sorrel was supposed to be taking, I saw a movement. I quickly focused in on it and a weird apparition took shape before my eyes. A figure, apparently naked, but of most curious shape, was rapidly approaching the foot of the mountain face. I glared intently through the binoculars to identify this remarkable creature. To my horror I saw that it was, indeed, my wife. She was not as I had at first thought, naked, but almost. She had stripped to a bra and panties which, I observed, were of a bright red tartan. Her clothes were apparently stuffed into her shirt which was somehow tied around her neck so that the bundle hung down her back like an indian papoose. And so, in climbing boots, a bra and tartan knickers, with her shoulder-length hair streaming out behind her and a papoose on her back, my new and lovely wife was running and scrambling like a frightened goat up the scree slope and on to the steep angry face of the mountain. I felt suddenly relieved that we were not in earshot, because I had the uneasy feeling that she was probably screaming like a dervish as well. I looked away, not so much in confusion as in concern lest any of the party should follow my direction of sight for themselves. But happily they were busy together and agitating to go on. Since there was nothing I could do anyway, I agreed and we moved upward once again. Periodically I stopped to check the progress of the apparition, but it had now disappeared into a gully and I never saw it again.

Clearly the girl had gone mad. It was as well that I should find out now, in the early days, before life's commitments made escape too difficult. The Highland life was obviously too much for her and perhaps, after all, she was more suited to a city career where physical exertion was unknown.

My group were now in their element. We were clear of the heather, and the steep grassy slopes and rocky outcrops made brisk, exciting climbing, even in that heat. I was hard put to it to keep pace with them, and had little time or strength to worry about Sorrel. I had formulated a rough plan to sweep round in her direction after we had reached the summit and, by leaving the group to have lunch, I could go off and make my search in private. I had no idea what I should really expect to find, but resigned myself to reacting as calmly as I could.

I don't think I have ever climbed that or any other mountain as fast as I did with that little party of athletes. We almost ran to the top and, out of pride only, to prove that my chosen way of life had given me stronger legs than the others, I reached the summit cairn first, knees trembling, thighs quivering uncontrollably, and my heart ramming like a piston inside my chest.

To my complete astonishment, there, sitting at the foot of the cairn, fully clothed, with impeccably groomed hair, sunning herself and munching contentedly at her packed lunch, was Sorrel. I was speechless, as were the two or three others of the party who panted up seconds behind me.

'Oh there you are!' she said coolly. 'I was beginning to wonder what had happened to you.'

'John told us you had gone back,' exclaimed one of the others in badly disguised astonishment.

'You weren't feeling very well,' stammered another.

'How the hell did you get here?' Questioned a third with more than a touch of indignation.

'I'm afraid I'm not up to all this long distance stuff,' she said modestly, 'I had to give up and come up the easy way.'

'The easy way?' one demanded. 'Which easy way?'

'The short way,' she said with a smile, 'up the face.'

'Up the face?' echoed two or three together, and they peered disbelievingly out over the 1,500-foot void from the summit to the torpid moor below. I have climbed that face, up the chock-stone gully, both before Sorrel and since, but always painfully slowly because it is steep and frightening and there are places where one has to cut laterally out of the gulley to traverse an impasse and then return to it higher up. It always drips with water, except in winter when it is frozen, and the walls and boulders in it are green with algae and moss, and as treacherous as ice. I would never have allowed Sorrel to do it alone for the first time and I was so thankful that no disaster had overtaken her in her mad rush that all the anger and indignation went out of me.

For ten minutes her gang of admirers drew her into exaggerated descriptions of her climb, and I saw the twinkle in her eye more than once. A little later when the others had gone away to extol the view I approached her alone.

'Well, well!' I said. 'You certainly won that round. And in tartan knickers too!'

'Oh God!' she exclaimed. 'You didn't see.'

'I certainly did,' I replied. 'The whole bizarre performance.'

'And the others too?' she demanded anxiously. 'Did they see?'

I couldn't lie, although I badly wanted to.

'No, don't worry, but I watched you until you went out of sight in the gulley, and I quite thought you had lost your senses.'

'I couldn't possibly climb in all those clothes,' she explained, 'it was far too hot, and I only just made it to the top before you, you know.'

'You looked as though you'd been here half an hour.'

'As I came up over the brow of the summit over there, still in my tartan knicks, I saw a mountain hare running towards me across the summit and I knew enough natural history to know it couldn't have been me who'd disturbed it. So I stopped there and then, and dressed as fast as I could and ran to the cairn and sat down. I only just had time to comb my hair and jam a sandwich in my mouth before you came storming up. There was only twenty seconds in it.'

Sorrel was invincible in the estimation of the group for the rest of that week; and although she continued flatly to deny it, they departed certain in their own minds that she was an experienced climber of overdeveloped modesty, and that it was really no disgrace at all to be beaten to the summit by a mountaineer of such obvious international standing.

As the summer sped by and the days began to shorten again the van, cursed implement, became a constant source of nuisance to us. Its latest trick was to boil at the least suggestion of a hill and fill the interior with clouds of evil-smelling steam from the heater vent. At great expense I had a new radiator fitted and for a week or two the problem seemed to be solved, but sure enough, the first time it was put severely to the test it started its turkish bath trick all over again. It became a daily chore to drain and wash out the radiator and by doing so it was possible to reduce the likelihood of occurrence for that day, given, of course, that I studiously avoided steep hills and heavy loads. In the end, there was nothing for it but to sell it.

When it had finally gone for good we bought a safari Land Rover, second-hand, from a local dealer, and that old vehicle and others like it have laboured for us ever since. While four-wheel drive is not essential for our purposes it has been endlessly useful to us and to others we have helped in sticky moments.

That week-end, the week-end of the new purchase, we had no bookings and we were free to take it where we liked. It was September, the weather was fine and there were hundreds of square miles of the north-west Highlands Sorrel and I had never explored. We drove to Gairloch, I remember, perhaps one of the most picturesque fishing villages of the Highlands, and one which is paying, inevitably, for its beauty by the heavy toll of tourism for four months of the year. From Gairloch we drove out along the incredibly convoluted coast for many miles until we came to a tiny settlement. There the road turned back, away from the coast, and inland to the mountains and the main roads once again. It was late afternoon and we were loath to drive on. We looked longingly out across the sea to headlands and coves which were out of reach.

'There's a track!' said Sorrel. 'Let's take it.' We did. Over stone and rock, over timber laid on peat, into sand and threading through dunes where it was scarcely discernible this old track was pulling us roughly away from civilization and out to the wild headlands beyond. It wound and twisted and dipped into soft oozing hollows where I feared we would certainly stick; then up again, over marram and new shingle along a rabbit-and sheep-cropped sward on the land's rim where a black line of seaweed told us the sea came right over our little road and flung debris into the dunes beyond.

Here and there the track was invisible for long stretches at a time and we were forced to take the least line of resistance for fifty yards or more before stumbling across it again and jogging on. We passed a ruined cottage, fully six or seven miles from the little settlement, no doubt where a shepherd or salmon-netter had once lived. We passed the rotting hull of an ancient boat, a fine old vessel, now high in the dunes and picked clean of its clinker boards by the wind and the sea. Its ribs and spine stood against the sky like the bleached skeleton of some great sea monster.

At last, and quite unexpectedly, we rose abruptly to a rocky ridge, mounted it, and tipped steeply down its southern side in the full-blooded glory of a Hebridean sunset on to a magnificent white beach. It was a long, broad crescent, a mile or more in length, and was one of the most hauntingly wild places I have ever been to. It has a name, of course, this Xanadu, like all others in the Highlands, and I sought it out on the ordnance survey map on my return home; but to name it here would be to sell it heartlessly to a world to which it does not belong. We have never been back, Sorrel and I, and, if we never do, it will be for fear that it has gone, like so many others before it, trampled under the material demands of too many people.

And so we found ourselves, entirely by chance, on this spreading crescent of white and yellow sand edged by the tighter crescent of pure white foam at the water's edge. We walked along it barefoot in a little wind which spun the sand past us in wisps and coils and picked up Max's velvet ears so that he looked strange and unfamiliar to us. Ringed plover and dunlin in scurrying packs broke from the water's edge and flicked away from us on humming bird-wings to pitch again a little further on and continue their game of tag with each tumbling wavelet. Gulls rowed overhead in the darkening sky, moving out to feeding grounds offshore; and invisible eider duck cooed softly on the gentle wind somewhere out beyond the curling waves, invisible in a counterpane of crimson and gold.

On our way back to the Land Rover in the semi-darkness we stopped to examine flotsam in the tide-wrack at the head of the beach. There was little rubbish, and what there was revealed more of an island existence than one dominated by modern mainland ways. There were corks and sections of damaged net, broken oars and the ubiquitous fish boxes. And then I found a distress flare from a vessel, a long waxed cylinder which had somehow come ashore unused. We read the instructions carefully and, not expecting for one moment that it would work after weeks in the sea and perhaps months in a soggy pile of wrack, I pulled the canvas tab and struck the phosphorous panel revealed beneath.

To my surprise, it burst into a fountain of angry orange flame and ochreous smoke. I stuck it in the sand like a beacon and retreated quickly. A quick look round showed for certain that it was invisible to the land behind us, which was a relief, but open to the expanse of sea to the west. I had a fearful vision of some Christian skipper turning his vessel to the signal and impaling his boat on the reefs and rocks which litter that coastline. We heaped sand and debris on the dragon, but it was unquenchable. It roared six foot into the night in a cone of dazzling heat, and the bank of vile smoke, spread now by the wind into a thick horizontal column, hid the land completely from view. Finally, in despair, we abandoned it to burn itself out. Happily, to the best of our knowledge, no vessel ran aground and no coastguard died in the dunes in search of a phantom shipwreck. Hours later, in the middle of the night, feeling strangely restless in that beautiful place, and while Sorrel was asleep in the Land Rover, I walked back along the beach to examine the flare. It was still burning; deep in its hollow, charred tube a little flame spluttered and winked sending a final wisp of hope curling up into the chill salty wind. I had not the heart to douse it.

In the dawn we sat together huddled around a small drift-wood fire and cooked bacon on a wire strung between two sticks. Water we boiled in an aluminium cannister scavenged from the tideline, and with our last tea-bags and a drop of milk from a thermos we brewed our tea. Our blackened bacon, laid on wood-smoke toast dripping with butter, was a feast. The new day was grey and promised rain later, so we put on extra clothing before walking along the firm sand to the rocks at the northern end of the beach.

As we neared them we realized we were no longer alone. Two large oceanic eyes watched us from the nearest rock. We stopped and stared back. A grey seal cow lay stretched across the rock, head seawards but turned towards us, her tail flippers raised in an upward curve behind her. Her wide nostrils flared, exhaled deeply in a long weary sigh, and snapped shut with the habit of several million years in the sea. We stood watching each other for some moments before she struggled her way forward and slipped gently into the shallow pool beneath. For a full minute, or perhaps two, she lay submerged until we thought she must have rounded the headland to peace and quiet on the other side. But then, there she was again. Straight out from us this time, heading in through the waves to the shelving beach beside us.

I had recently read a magical book by David Thomson called *The People of the Sea*, a journey in search of the seal legend, about which Gavin Maxwell had written, 'this book recalls some splendid cave drawing, telling as much of man as of beast, and leaving us in awe of each.' Since reading it and becoming absorbed in seal legend, this was actually the first selchie or grey seal I had met face to face. The book says much about seal song, the music of seals and the wind and the sea, when all that is desolate and Hebridean can be sensed rising and falling on the air at any of the grey seal colonies off our coasts. Out of this haunting music has arisen the tradition that seals respond to human music and song, and I was anxious to try it. We stood by the sea that day and sang to our wet-eyed selchie, ballad after ballad, hymns and carols, psalms and anthems and pop songs with great hummed gaps where we didn't know the words, until we could find no more to sing.

The seal, whether in enjoyment or astonishment, stayed with us, its glossy head bobbing only a few yards away, intent with concentration on this remarkable performance. To our delight, in the middle of the forty-sixth psalm, somewhere around '. . . though the mountains be moved into the midst of the sea . . .', a second seal, with a worried expression, appeared from nowhere and bobbed up beside our friend. We renewed our efforts with vigour and sang on lustily, but no more appeared and after a while they ducked away beneath the tide. Exhausted but not disappointed by our experiment, we gave up and went back to our smouldering fire and the last of the stewed tea.

Chapter Two

The enterprise had made no progress in its second season. The employees now numbered three against a badly curtailed season and, largely through neglect back in the winter of our courtship, there were too few bookings in the weeks we were able to work. By September the thing had ground to a halt. No more bookings, no future bookings, no inquiries coming in and no money to pay the handful of outstanding bills. The house was, it is true, ours, but that was little consolation. Every time I looked closely at it I found something else which needed replacing and I had long since given up mending, repairing and painting fabric which had only to be ripped out in the not far distant future.

Sorrel and I sat at a table and considered our future. If we went on with the enterprise it was going to be a long hard struggle, virtually starting all over again. If we wrote it off I would be able to survive, I knew, by free-lance writing, but only just and there would be little hope of funding the renovation of the Kennels from that source.

Carefully we worked out our loss for the year. At least, I say we worked it out, but it would be truer to report that we worked a bit of it out, sublimely ignoring a devastating petrol bill at the local garage and an account from the G.P.O., the size of which I almost couldn't believe. We had had to have the telephone installed and it had meant bringing it from the village anew, erecting poles and cables all the way. I had asked for an estimate and glimpsed at it before casting it quickly into the fire. If your existence requires bread, and bread is the price of gold, the price ceases to mean anything, the acquisition only being important. So it was with the telephone. The poles marched towards us and men with leather belts and coils of wire ensnared our tumble-down house in a web of telephonics. Once or twice I pretended not to notice a man purple with frustration trying to attach his vital box of tricks to woodwork rotten with worm. Finally it was tethered and rang, limply, from our window-sill. There was, apparently, a shortage of signal, but all that would be altered when the S.T.D. came – as it happened, five years later. I resisted the desire to inform the engineer that there was also a shortage of funds, all of which would be altered, too – when my ship came in. Unfortunately my expectations were not to be allowed to take five years to fulfil. There is a man with a whip who lives in Aberdeen and works for the G.P.O. who periodically visits outlying districts, like the wolf of Badenoch, and wreaks not dissimilar havoc amongst his selected victims. Hearing of this man in advance of a visitation I contacted him on his own machine, in his own den, as it were, and assuming a super humility I told him that we would continue to pay promptly for telephone calls, if only we could have a little more time to pay for the capital cost of the installation. He replied with a twist of bureaucratic bayonetry unlike any other:

'What a shame you could not have delayed this installation for another month because we're standardizing installation costs for the whole country to £25 regardless of distance or materials.' There was an empty pause and then he continued 'We couldn't announce it before, because everyone would have cancelled expensive installations until the new rules came in and then we would have been flooded out with demands.'

'Yes, yes, what a shame,' I jibbered, and replaced the suddenly very heavy receiver. Although he had agreed to my repayment plan, the thousand per cent difference in cost that one month meant to us made it one of the hardest bills I have ever had to pay.

There was only one possible recourse after a year like that, and that was a holiday. We packed a few possessions together and defected for a delayed honeymoon to southern Spain and Morocco.

On the morning we left we stopped at the garage to fill our tank for the long journey south. Don Cameron, our friend and saviour on many disastrous occasions, was there to serve us himself. I had foreseen this eventuality and had written him a short note explaining that we were going away for a while but would give his account high priority when we returned.

After filling the tank he came to the window.

'I take it you'll want this on the account?' He asked with a wry smile.

'Er – yes please, Don,' I said.

'You couldn't manage a small advance one of these days, could you?' he inquired. I was ready with my note.

'Ah, well! Funny you should say that,' I said. 'I've got a note for you here.' I thrust the envelope at him. His eyes lit up.

'A ten-pound note is it?' He asked with a laugh.

'Er – no, I'm afraid it's not. It's an – er – explanatory note.'

'Oho, yes. An explanatory note is it? Yes, yes, I've seen one or two of these before. Ah, well, you can't win all the time I suppose,' he sighed and turned away. 'Have a good holiday,' he said as an afterthought, and then turning back to face us he waved cheerily calling:

'And for the explanatory note, I thank you from the heart of my bottom!'

If one is feeling particularly beggarly it is always a very humbling exercise to go and sit amongst the real beggars of the third world. Sorrel and I sat in the rat-infested, disease-ridden alleyways of the old city in Tetuan, the Khasba, and watched those ageless living carcases hobble by. Some, not expecting to see European tourists in that quarter of the city, passed by uncertain of our purpose; others shambled up to beg the meanest coin, supplicating as only those whose existence depends on it knew how.

When we arrived in Morocco it was Ramadan, the Moslem daylight fast which continues throughout the ninth month of their calendar. Nowhere in the Arab quarters was there food to be seen during the day, and we were forced to eat in the modern European sector of Tetuan. Here, the beggars were markedly healthy and sham, like the modern prostitutes of Naples or Milan, working for an overseer, working to hours and rules, and not the real thing at all. Many of these beggars were even bad actors, dropping their act immediately they saw that one was not fooled, and walking quickly away without the limp which brought them.

As we sat outside one restaurant quietly eating breakfast in the early morning, one such beggar laboured up to us with much shuffling and moaning. His rags were real enough, and he appeared to be permanently bent over a meagre stick with which he turned bits of rubbish in the gutter in search of something to eat. This in itself, since it was Ramadan, was a give-away, and we watched with amusement. After a long performance which culminated at our table, the actor stood huddled before us. Sorrel, having bought a salami which was so powerfully loaded with spice as to disguise any decay as it hung in the hot North-African sun, offered a large chunk to the beggar. He pretended not to notice and continued to whine for alms. Sorrel placed the sausage in his dirty hand as he extended it to me. The result was electric. He screwed up his face in disgust and flung the salami into the gutter, demanding as he did so: 'Money!'

'You old charlatan!' shouted Sorrel in genuine anger. 'How dare you!' And she caught him a sharp crack across the fingers with a spoon.

The man looked as though he had been struck by Allah himself. His hitherto creased and diseased eyes opened wide to reveal strong healthy whites and, picking up his skirts, he ran like a gazelle down the street.

That evening at sundown bells tolled throughout the city. It was the end of Ramadan and the end of the fast. Suddenly the streets and alleyways were full of people, talking and laughing, lighting fires and carrying out cauldrons of soup to mark the end of the festival. We queued with scores of

Arabs and children, all jibbering happily and incomprehensibly, for the magical soup which was ladled out by a grinning, toothless old man into rough earthenware bowls. The soup was excellent, thick with vegetables and spices. We drank from the rough lip of the bowls until they were empty and then, following the example of the children, ran back to the queue and waited for more. The sick and crippled, the halt, lame and aged were brought out to partake in the celebration, and it was touching to see the pleasure it gave these human wrecks to join in.

The old man with the ladle smiled at us again, calling as he did so to his companion at the cauldron.

'Look at these infidels,' he seemed to be saying, 'they are back for more soup!' I thanked him profusely in French of which most understand something, a legacy from the days of the Protectorate, and he gave us more so that our bowls overflowed, and the children laughed and danced around us.

From the aridity of North Africa the stark beauty of the frost gripped north was dramatically refreshing. Inverness-shire was under snow and in the clear sunlit air the Cairngorms and the Grampians shone like celestial cities on far horizons. It was late November and we were returning home elated both by our holiday and by the life-saving news which had greeted our return to London. My publishers had revealed astonishing sales figures for *The White Island* and supported their news with a large royalty cheque. It was immensely gratifying, and only just in time.

Quite regardless of this transfusion we had decided, in Morocco, to continue with Highland Wildlife Enterprises for one last season, with all the stops pulled out, to see if it would pick up again. Jokingly we said it wouldn't really matter if the house fell down around us since it was a summer exercise and if need be we could sleep in a tent. We had little idea that we would have to. Now we had enough money to pay all the bills, launch a badly needed advertising campaign, and start renovation work on the Kennels.

All that winter we drew up plans, locked in our frost-bound hideaway, our days spent around the old range which glowed red through the casting and which cooked most of our meals. Sorrel tapped at the typewriter incessantly, sending out advertisements, answering inquiries, planning new brochures and publicity material. I lived beside the telephone constantly chasing architects, builders and tradesmen, and, most frustrating of all, the department in Edinburgh which was approving our alteration plans. Because the Kennels is a listed building the local planning authority were unable to pass the drawings on their own authority, and had to send them to the Secretary of State for Scotland. It seemed that he was either away or on leave, missing or dead, because the plans sat desolately on his or someone else's desk for weeks on end. At last they were approved with pernickity reservations to which we merrily appeared to agree rather than risk a further span of hold ups while we appealed against them. Frosted glass, they said, was essential in the bathroom windows in case people should look in. The fact that the windows concerned looked out from an upper storey across boggy fields, forest and mountain without the remotest possibility of oversight by anything except a buzzard or a lost helicopter, made no difference to them. Rules were rules, and since the principle was unquestionably sound they could not be departed from under any circumstances.

Our only recreation that long winter, in which days and weeks merged so effectively that we arrived for church one Monday morning to find that we had lost Sunday altogether, was an opportunity which presented itself to us quite unsolicited and which gave us disproportionate pleasure. Our kind neighbours at the farm had two strong Highland garron horses which were growing fat through lack of exercise, and we were asked if we would take them on for the winter. Sorrel, who had ridden extensively in Tasmania as a child, liked the idea; and I had been reared in an equestrian tradition by my father who is a fine horseman and who had trained cavalry horses as a young man.

We agreed quickly to the offer and the horses were moved to the field beside the Kennels. From then on, every morning, at dawn, unless the weather was so foul that no one in their right minds would have gone out, we caught the horses, rubbed them down, and took off up the stony paths and tracks which Tweedmouth had generously laid for that very

Sgurr na Lapaich, Glen Affric

purpose. From Guisachan they radiate far into the hills and moors and we tried them all, five miles up to the lonely stalker's cottage at Cougie, seven miles over the mountain to Glen Moriston, and two miles down into Glen Affric. When the frost was hard and the sun slanted strongly into that little valley we met it, face to face, spreading across the high moorland like molten steel spilling from the crucible. Such dawns and sunrises were among the most exhilarating experiences I can remember, and the soft crunch of hooves on snow, and hot, sweet breath in clouds about us from horse and man alike are stirring to recall.

As if it was not luck enough that *The White Island* should

have done well so quickly, and just in time, a second stroke of good fortune arrived. I received an extraordinary request. Sorrel's father, being one of those people who never really has a career, but rather wafts through life trying this and that and doing each one successfully until a greater temptation presents itself, has been variously an author, playwright and broadcaster, a radio-talks producer, jackaroo and farmer; but at that particular moment he was trying his hand at film production. He was working for an advertising agency producing 'commercials', and happened at that time to be working on one for Spiller's dog food.

Professional dog trainers had been summoned from far and wide with their groomed charges, and interviewed without success. Whatever it was Spillers required of their dogs, these unhappy hounds were not able to do it. Henry Bentinck telephoned me in exasperation.

Max had featured prominently in *The White Island* and was known, to a degree, to my father-in-law. Max had walked away with the grand championship of a Field Trial as a young dog, and, wishing him to remain a champion for life, I vowed never to enter him for anything again. I had spent long and painstaking hours with the dog and he was, by anybody's standards, an excellent gun dog in the field. Knowing this, Henry quizzed me penetratively:

'Are you sure you can work him indoors?'

'I think so,' I said, 'provided his interest is keen.'

'Will he mind the lights or be distracted by all the cameras and crew?'

'No, I'm sure he won't, as long as I am there to instruct him.'

'Righto! You're on – or rather Max is.'

Two days later Max and I were hurtling down country aboard the Royal Highlander from Inverness to London, all expenses paid. We had a first-class sleeper and Max snored all the way to Euston. From Euston we took a taxi to the studio in Soho and presented ourselves to the team.

The job, as it turned out, was a complicated one and it was

not surprising that other dogs had failed to meet up to the heavy demands of it. Max was not the star of the advertisement, he was the co-star. The leading role was played by Basil Brush, the highly successful television puppet owned and worked by Ivan Owen. One of the main problems with other dogs had been that their owners had not been able to give a cast-iron guarantee that during filming, when Basil Brush was fully animated, their dogs would not attack, bite or otherwise damage the priceless puppet. Max had never been aggressive. Even the principles of self-defence had been omitted from his gentle make-up and I was quite confident that he would never harm Basil. But when I was asked if he would allow Basil to lean his head against him in a moment of melodramatic endearment, I was not at all sure what his reaction would be.

The set was a country kitchen with pine furniture, dresser and sideboard, miniature table and chairs, all dog size and manufactured to a clever and special perspective. In the foreground stood a dog-bowl and a box of the biscuits Max was to eat. Next to these stood the dapper puppet in his hunting coat and stock. At the rear of the set was a panelled kitchen door outside which Max sat awaiting command. The action was filmed 'wild' which is producer's jargon for without soundtrack, and the end result was dubbed later. This allowed me to shout, whistle and talk constantly to Max so that he moved to the right position and acted in the right time sequence for the script.

Basil Brush is a glove puppet operated from beneath the stage by his owner who watches his own performance on a close-circuit television. It is a skilful act and is carried out with great professionalism which was a help to me. I talked to Ivan Owen at length and we decided on an interpretation of the script which would remain satisfactory to the producer and which would be most likely to stimulate the right reaction from Max.

Clapper boards snapped in front of the camera and the first shoot was on. I whistled Max to enter through the pine door. He came in, pushing the door open with his nose. I then shouted the command for him to close the door behind him. He pushed it shut and walked forward, ears up and tail wagging merrily at the sight of the fox – to whom he had been introduced earlier in the proceedings – who was producing a constant stream of dog-biscuit monologue punctuated by lame jokes at which Basil roared with laughter in his own distinctive manner.

There were chalked positions on the stage for where Max was to sit and stand, and I directed him to these without difficulty. I had to keep myself in direct line with the camera so that it never appeared that the dog was interested in any outside distraction. Like all good T.V. personalities he looked straight into the camera or at Basil Brush.

The two of them were now sitting round the bowl of food and the packet of Spillers shapes. Basil was making another crass pun about the biscuits keeping him ship-shape, and I then gave Max the instruction to eat. Max obediently buried his nose in the bowl and ate enthusiastically from it. Basil kept up the commentary. Having consumed the contents of the bowl Max sat there grinning and wagging his tail while Basil leant his head against Max's shoulder in the silly endearing gesture which was supposed to have ended the scene. Max, however, being of star quality, had other ideas and, to show that he was suitably moved by Basil's approaches, turned and licked the fox across the nose with a long exaggerated stage-lick.

Clapper boards snapped and the cameras stopped. There was a long and ominous silence. I saw the director and the producer turn away together. I heard an expletive break from the director and I feared that it had all gone wrong, although I couldn't see how or why. I walked over to join them.

'How was that?' I inquired. The director turned sharply to me and put his hand on my shoulder, saying 'That was what is known as bloody fantastic. We normally allow three days to shoot pet commercials, and we've done it in seven minutes. Magic, dear boy, that's what it is, bloody magic.'

Max was excessively congratulated during the next quarter

of an hour, so much so that I suspected Basil Brush's nose might have been put slightly out of joint. It was necessary to go on shooting the sequence several times more because there is, of course, no guarantee that the client will like the first shoot, or that the film was of perfect quality, or any one of a dozen imponderables. The agency had to have sufficient film at the end of the day to be able to piece together several different commercials from which to choose the final one for broadcasting.

We carried on throughout the day and the studio became hot and unpleasant with cigarette smoke. By about the fifth shoot Max had become acutely bored and it was no longer possible to get him to do the whole sequence straight through; it had to be done in pieces and edited together later. The first attempt remained the best and was the one eventually used, on national release, for several months.

Max and I returned to the north jubilant. Our forty-eight hours' work had earned more money than I had paid myself in the whole previous year, and we had a huge supply of biscuits to boot.

By the spring of 1973 the Kennels' improvement was in some measure under way. I had decided to do all the demolition work myself and to employ professional help only with the main re-building and with the wiring and plumbing. The ground plan was to completely modernize the cottage, raising ceilings upstairs and putting in large windows looking out over the river-fields behind, creating two new bathrooms and an extra bedroom, and bringing the huge kennel kitchen with its high ceiling and fine proportions into the house as a large drawing-room and dining-room combined. The dog-kennels behind the cottage were a great disappointment. All that fine Victorian woodwork and panelling was so badly worm-eaten that it had to be destroyed. The roof and all the features which made it unique had to go and so it was decided to dismantle the building altogether and rebuild it as an accommodation extension to the cottage. We designed this as two self-contained flats, one above the other each with its own entrance, large kitchen and living-room, two double bed-rooms and a bathroom and hallway.

We wanted to be able to accommodate our friends and family in style when they had made the great trek north to see us, and so we gave high priority to the appointment of these two flats. We also knew that if the business picked up and gathered strength we would need accommodation for a helper. It seemed to be the most sensible use of the space available.

The demolition work to the dog-kennels was easy. It did not affect our daily living in any way and I was able to work unhindered, stripping the diseased woodwork and burning it in huge stacks outside. I became agile on the roof and taught myself to strip Ballachulish slates for re-use. By the time the first lapwings appeared behind the house the dog-kennels had gone. The roof was off, the slates stacked neatly by the fence, the timbers burnt and the walls a bare shell ready for re-building. Only the cottage remained inviolate and it looked small and humble without its proud Victorian extension. Even the railings were gone. With a heavy heart I had dis-mantled them and sold them to a sporting estate owner in a glen further north. At least they were to be re-erected as kennel railings and are back in long deserved service.

The results of Sorrel's labours were dramatic almost beyond belief. Every mail brought a heavy bundle of inquiries, and the bookings were piling up at such a rate that I began to worry whether I was going to be able to fulfil them without further help. Her little room now looked like an office with wall charts and calendars heavily ringed and marked with the fast-filling courses. The typewriter was never still and boxes of hurriedly opened stationery and brochures from the printers lay about the floor in an ordered confusion. But as well as all this planning for the year ahead, there was a new project about to be launched. A large and unfamiliar map was spread across the wall, strangely marked with red lines and circles, and by the end of March every delivery of mail held letters and packets with brightly coloured foreign stamps and unpronounceable names. There were books, too, lying about the house left purposefully open or marked with tabs of paper protruding from the pages, coded for easy reference, and the compilation of a greater mass of information.

We had decided to take an expedition to Arctic Lapland to look at the taiga, the great forest belt of the north. We wanted to do it at the beginning of the Arctic winter to experience that great wilderness under ice and snow. I had given the task of organization largely to Sorrel and she had lost herself in it. As she sat at the typewriter tapping out replies to our routine inquiries, a record-player droned away beside her in Swedish. She had bought a record language course and was determined that if we ever got there she would have the means of basic communication to hand.

We hoped that by mid-September that year the re-modernization of our home would be complete and that we could leave for the eight-week expedition with clear consciences. We would go straight from the last course of the year into the expedition, returning to the Highlands for Christmas. It seemed a fool-proof plan and we worked hard at setting it up. I found a builder who agreed to our time schedule, and was optimistic within it. Secure in the knowledge that that part of the year was well tied up, we began to advertise our expedition. It needed cost-sharing members who were prepared to tolerate hardship and extreme cold, and who would join in with the spirit of the thing without question.

We were already four in number. Besides Sorrel and myself we had invited our close friend and neighbour Simon Fraser to come with us. Simon was a young painter who lived and worked in Tomich. His treatment of the Highland scene had such integrity of observation that we were compulsively drawn to him and to his work. We had come to know him well since we moved to Guisachan and it cheered our day to see his diminutive figure meandering across the fields towards us. Sometimes he arrived so exhausted from a long walk into the mountains, not having eaten for many hours, or so white and cold after sitting all day in a snowdrift watching and drawing deer, that we forced food and drink on him, making him spend more time with us than a passing visit might have allowed. And sometimes, after the first hot food for too many hours of driving himself insensible with overwork and exposure, he would sink a life-giving whisky and crawl away upstairs to sleep beneath a pile of blankets on our spare bed.

For many reasons Simon was a natural choice and he agreed keenly to coming with us. It was his idea, too, to ask his sister, Jean, who had just finished a *cordon bleu* cooking course and whose cheerful presence would be a constant bonus if conditions became burdensome. It was essential that Sorrel should have help with the catering for the expedition and we enthusiastically added Jean to the list. But the cost was as yet still far too great for even four of us to share so we needed at least two more. It was personally essential to me to have a professional botanist on the expedition. While I felt sure I could cope with recording all the mammal and bird life we might see, I was a bad botanist and therefore not prepared to launch myself into an entirely new Arctic flora with all its mosses and lichens without help. There was nothing for it but to advertise for the last two members.

Applicants came and went. Some were bizarre, some colourfully impracticable, and others one felt had provided no good reason why they should join an expedition, and at the same time there was no good reason why they should not. One of these, who was a botanist, we chose. As we know him now, Peter Wortham could not have been more undersold. If we had cast him aside like the others the whole shape of our future would have been different. He was the definitive shy graduate, unassuming, hyper-modest, quiet and gentle and never any trouble to anyone. I shall never know why we did eventually pick him, unless perhaps the very fact that we did, and that we still don't know why, is the greatest testimony of all.

Number six chose himself. We had known Roy Jonas for some time as a friend who had made use of our courses for walking the Inverness-shire hills. He was a middle-aged bachelor whose one abiding passion was Land Rovers. He spent his daily life converting Land Rovers into fire tenders and armoured jeeps for warring Arabs, and his own tried vehicle had taken him over ground which Land Rovers had no business on. The front-mounted winch with its neatly coiled cable and hook gave the vehicle a business-like demeanour which I came to respect and be thankful for.

I had once driven the wretched van into a peat bog so foul that Richard and I foundered up to our knees vainly digging to raise it from its stagnant grave. Roy had arrived the following day by which time the van had sunk to its floor so that it sat, flatly, on a mud-pack of semi-liquid peat. The wheels were invisible and there was no means of levering it up because there was nothing against which to lever it. From a far-off vantage point Roy bedded his Rover into the stony track I had originally left. Ground anchors and deep-driven stakes had to be secured, tried and driven deeper before the great pull.

At last we had done everything possible to secure Roy's vehicle, and the cable peeled stickily off its drum and snaked out to the sunken van. We hooked it on. The result was an impasse. At maximum pull neither vehicle budged an inch. We stopped and scratched our midge bites in silence. Richard's resourceful and endlessly practical mind ticked audibly.

'If we can effect a pulley on the van and double the cable back on to the Land Rover, we can double the pull!' He announced triumphantly.

Roy dragged that miserable vehicle through sixty feet of mire, Richard and I digging as fast as we could in front of it to reduce resistance, and the foul black liquid filling each shovelful as we heaved it out.

So when Roy telephoned and asked us to accept him and his Land Rover and equipment, we had no need of testimonials. But by accepting Roy's vehicle our costs had sharply risen and, correspondingly, so had our carrying capacity. We decided that between the two Land Rovers we could take eight, and we made ready to advertise the two remaining places straight away.

In the curious way that these things sometimes happen – synchronisity Jung has called it – and even before we had had time to place our advertisements, I received a letter from John Willett. John was at that time chairman of the British Deer Society and had steered it from inception to the important scientific body it had become. He was an amateur wildlife film maker, but an amateur with a professional record of success and achievement. He was keen to make a film of the moose rut, the mating season, in Lapland and was writing to suggest that we joined forces. He would need space to carry all his equipment and would be bringing a sound recordist with him.

So many of our plans overlapped that it was a *fait accompli* from the start. It was a simple matter to designate Roy Jonas's Land Rover as the film unit while ours carried everyone and everything else.

From that moment on all the organization for eight people and two Land Rovers to spend eight weeks inside the Arctic Circle in winter was left to Sorrel. I had my hands entirely full with the busy courses we had managed to fill throughout the spring and summer, and with the Kennels' conversion. In June the builder arrived and opened the roof into the old cottage to start preparing for the new dormers. Then he went away again. I worried and telephoned him constantly. A few weeks later a huge load of timber arrived. Now I felt sure we were under way. But it was late July and we wanted the job finished by October at the latest.

One by one the summer weeks slipped by. I suppose it was inevitable that I should have to find out about Highland builders the hard way. It appeared there was nothing I could do to pierce the armour of that implacable nature, the aura of unconcerned timelessness which sets life on a different scale of priority and understanding. It is no good blaming one man because the fault is a composite affair, belonging to many similar men steeped in the same inherited attitudes to time and work. With each one depending upon the next for the supply of labour and materials, the effect is compounded beyond the wildest nightmares of innocent southerners such as myself. There are no yardsticks for the measure of time in that great scenery of desolation of rock and wind. Time is as lost in the wind and rain. It is an attitude apparent in the Highlander's speech, his clothing and his architecture, and in his dignity in old age. It will go, in time, I have no doubt, with interbreeding and improved communications, until the nation possesses a uniform colourless people who will talk of the old Highlander as we now talk of the Viking.

Like all the best experiences in life, one has to lose by them to assimilate their full worth. At the time, when the summer weather was running out far faster than I knew the roof could be rebuilt, I thought it the meanest trick of fate; but in retrospect, years later, I can see the personal importance of the whole episode, to Sorrel and myself.

By the time our little expedition left Scotland for Scandinavia on 25 September not one nail had been struck on the Kennels' job. We departed to high promises that it would all be done by the time we returned. But by then we didn't care. We were departing on a great adventure.

Chapter Three

It was no mere whim that was taking us inside the Arctic Circle in winter when there was apparently so much to do at home. My own reasons, as well as wanting to establish a pattern of winter expeditions as a part of Highland Wildlife Enterprises' normal routine, were personal and urgent.

Those remnant stretches of Scots pine forest beside me in Glen Affric and in the other glens in the Strathglass watershed area are among the last of what Fraser Darling has called the Great Wood of Caledon. It is more commonly known as the Caledonian Pine Forest and history books tell us of its destruction under the axes of iron-smelters, the scorched earth policy of the Hanoverian oppression after the battle of Culloden, and the clearance of hill land for sheep and deer in the nineteenth century. It is held as a unique and remarkable forest which, as little as three hundred years ago covered three million acres and stretched from Ullapool to the Trossachs on the west, and from Inverness to Perth on the east. It is romanticized along with the clans who roamed its needle-strewn floors and the red deer they hunted. Highland folklore, song and fable tell of the great predatory animals of the forest, the wolf and the bear and the lynx, and of the prey species they required in large numbers around them: reindeer and boar, moose and wild cattle, now all extinct largely because of man.

As an immigrant from the south of England and as a naturalist, I was sceptical about some of the legend, and able to be far more objective about it. I was certain enough there had been a great forest, and that animals existed there is also beyond question; but I was not so sure that it was unique, and least of all was I certain that the literature which existed and some of those connected with it had really any concept of what it was like three hundred years ago, let alone when man first appeared on the Highland scene, on the west coast, perhaps as little as six thousand years ago. Geographically, it is clear that just as the south of England belongs to the French mainland, so the Highlands are the outlying tip of the same mountains which corrugate Norway and Sweden. What is unique about Britain is that she has been cut off from the rest of Europe for a sufficiently long time to allow her to adapt to, and cope with, the more maritime climate that her surrounding waters have forced on her. This is especially true of the far north where the land is narrow and the latitude stormier and more inclement than further south. The climate is still shaping the Highlands away from her Scandinavian parent.

I figured there must therefore be areas where the forests and mountains were very similar to the Highlands as they were during the first few thousand years after glaciation and the retreat of the ice-cap. It did not require much research to discover that there were vast areas of virgin Scots pine wilderness in Lapland, a part of the great taiga, the pine forest belt which girds the northern hemisphere from Norway to the Bering Sea. It was clear that I must go there and see for myself.

It was also the case that in running these courses on Highland wildlife, which were becoming more and more technical and scientific in the depth of knowledge they required, I was by implication setting myself up as an authority on an environment in which I had lived for barely five years. It began to matter enormously to me that the birds and animals we saw and spoke about should be seen as an integral part of that environment, and without a wider and more profound understanding of what the environment had been like in its original state, I could not be expected to fully understand its much more complicated position today. I had to do time, as it were, in a great pine forest, day and night, like an archetypal Highlander, until I really understood what it was all about.

Information began to assemble in our own little pine-forest home. Two fine Scots pines stood outside my study window, on the edge of the forest behind, and they were strongly symbolic of my quest as the preparations took shape all through that summer. Friends and contacts in Swedish universities and the Forest Service sent detailed descriptions of the places we were to visit. The picture that was unfolding from these thick packets, with such exciting postmarks as Lulea and

Scots pine

Jokkmok, Uppsala and Umea, were so remarkably 'Highland', so precisely relevant to my own doorstep and the wet forests all round me, that I could scarcely believe it to be true. Slowly we narrowed the territory open to us down to one dramatic patch of Swedish Lapland which, very much to our advantage, was national park. It was to our advantage because it was documented, heavily researched, and unquestionably wilderness. When the Swedes use the term 'national park' they do so with precision, unlike the limp description we bandy about in Britain, and their administration is exemplary to the world. Only by courting the Royal Swedish Forest Service could we gain entry to these areas, and, having satisfied them that our purpose was bona fide, restrictions were lifted and a super-efficient world of courteous and high powered assistance was pressed upon us.

Sweden possesses more wilderness than any other European country outside Russia. The areas I wanted to see were the main block of national parks in Lapland: Sarek, Stora Sjofallet and Pajelanta, which, with Muddus, constitutes the largest preserved wilderness area in Europe. Together they cover a breath-taking three thousand square miles of mountain, lake, heath and forest, about half the size of Wales.

Yet with this stirring information arriving daily at the Kennels came hard warnings. 'Do not underestimate the Arctic winter,' said one. 'Communications are bad or non-existent in these areas,' said another; and a third, a famous ecologist, wrote in his description of the whole area: 'Visitors must be prepared to undertake a real expedition. There are no facilities except a few bridges and trails in this wild area where one is obliged to rely on one's own psychic and physical ability. Never go out alone ... People inexperienced with Scandinavian mountain wilderness should entirely avoid visiting these national parks.' It was clear that it was not going to be a jaunt, and Sorrel and I spent many hours planning equipment and supplies to ensure that we had not failed to heed these warnings.

We travelled by car ferry to Gothenburg and drove straight to Lake Vanern in southern Sweden. John Willett had made contact with the King of Sweden's chief game warden and he had directed us to a small private forest park on the top of a table mountain, called Halle-Hunneberg. Here we pitched our first camp in golden autumnal woods and spent a week familiarizing ourselves with each other, our equipment and the moose.

For the King's pleasure Halle-Hunneberg was maintained as a private hunting forest and possessed at that time some two hundred wild moose in ten thousand acres of forest, heath, bog and lake. It was the greatest concentration of free ranging wild moose in the world. If we were to help John Willett shoot good moose film when we got to the far north we had to work hard at getting to know the animal and how it operated, here, in the comfort and ease of a temperate climate and warm autumn sun.

We had been given the freedom of the royal forest. A bunch of keys permitted us to take the Land Rovers into the interior where we hoped to be able to film from the top of the vehicles. The machinery of excessive Swedish hospitality and generosity had begun to turn.

We had chosen Nyrud, our first forest camp-site, quite fortuitously. Knowing nothing of the terrain at Hunneberg we had pitched into the first convenient clearing. As forest sites go it could hardly have been better. We erected our tents on three sides of a square and made our fire in the centre. The forest around us was dense pine and spruce, dark and dominant, with the hardy northern birch invading every space where sunlight flickered on the needle-strewn floor. It was both practical and picturesque; sheltered and far enough from the forest track for us to feel the full intensity of the forest atmosphere.

Our map showed six large lakes in the interior and a further nine smaller swamps and ponds. Knowing the moose's like of damp places we split up into pairs and chose to explore four of the largest lakes and their marshes first. John Willett and I felt sure there would be signs of moose activity somewhere in one of these areas, and from the first reports we could begin to piece together a map of their movements. We had no idea of what we were to find. We ate our supper in high expectation and slept soundly.

It was a good thing that we did. An eyeball to eyeball confrontation with a large bull moose at the doorway of one's tent on the first night in a strange Swedish forest might have been enough to keep one from sleeping for the rest of the expedition.

What hour we were invaded we shall never know, but

when we emerged from our cocoons rubbing our eyes in the grey morning we were aghast to find the clearing traversed and encircled by the great round imprints of moose-slots, and the inevitable bile-green mounds of droppings, scarcely cold, scattered liberally round about us. It seemed incredible that this huge and cumbersome beast could have staggered clumsily about our camp without any of us hearing even the snap of a twig. But our ignorance was as yet complete. We knew our quarry only from photographs and the printed page. We knew his dimensions and his distribution; the food he ate, and the time of year he chose to take a mate – a scientific curriculum vitae complete from the length of his sexual organs to the colour of his eyes, and yet we knew nothing of the nature of the beast. On our first night in his territory he had scattered the pages of our text-book information like the yellow leaves of the Nyrud clearing, and left us only the cleft of his hoof and the dung from his bowels to feed our conceit. It was a profound lesson and one which ran deep in the early morning.

As I split white birch splinters to kindle our fire, the full humiliation of the event closed in on me. I think some of the others felt it too, for we were curiously silent as we sat around our thin spiral of smoke and caressed our mugs of tea.

I believe that all forms of involvement with the natural world are the manifestation of a need in us all to look back and retain some contact with our beginnings and the soil. Unfortunately we have come too far, and it is fatuous to imagine that we could now return to being an integral part of the biocommunity like the ancient Lap or the North American Indian. So we dream up a fashionable compromise, a sort of foot in both camps, which allows us a comfortable degree of involvement and an opportunity to proceed sanely through life at the same time. But there are limitations to this dilettante philosophy and from time to time they emerge, bluntly, before us, barring our progress and returning us, literally to earth with a bump.

The moose at Nyrud was symbolic for me of just such limitations. He is an anachronism, belonging more properly to our pre-history, to the spirit of cave paintings rather than to the Domänverket, the state forests of Sweden, her largest and most profitable industry. Their mysterious presence in our camp that night was a warning. We had blundered into our own past, drunk with the data of a scientific approach and with our senses dulled by the sophistication of our equipment, and by doing so we stood to negate the very spirit of the beast and its existence. Humiliated, we were to learn more in a few hours than in six months' research.

Now that we knew the moose were close at hand, we re-formed our plans to quarter the belt of dense forest between Nyrud and the chain of lakes to the north. We disappeared into the forest, pair by pair, each one of us certain that the first moose would be idly grazing behind the next bush, ready to be photographed, assessed and plotted in the log, like landmarks in a tourist guide. But we had a lot to learn yet.

Two days later we felt as though the moose were playing a game with us. It was perfectly clear they were all round the camp and that they not irregularly passed through it. As each pair of observers returned we could tell from their long faces that they had seen nothing.

My diary entry for Tuesday, 2 October, breaks the pattern:

The alarm went off at 4.00 a.m. and I rose quickly to kindle the fire and boil some water for tea. I shook Simon and Sorrel from their sleeping bags and they emerged to sit silently around the fire and clasp mugs of hot tea in an effort to wake up. We left the camp in complete darkness before 4.30 a.m. We followed the hunter's trail up through the forest to the north-west to the lake-side at Grinnsjön. It was painful going. This part of the forest was very old and many fallen trunks lay about making free movement through very difficult. Even out of the forest and crossing the swamp towards the lake, it was too dark not to use our torches and we floundered into many bogs and hollows so that we were wet to the knees. At last we reached a chosen bluff above the lake and we sat in the heather for an hour while dawn broke up the night sky around us. All we saw was a red squirrel in a pine beside us and the waking birds of the forest emerge and busy about their day. I had never seen a wren stretch before. As the light spread across the lake we scoured its long sweeping marsh and swampland for any sign of moose feeding there. It was entirely empty. At eight o'clock we picked our way slowly back to camp. John Willett and Joan, his sound-recordist, were still out – filming, we hoped – and the others were finishing breakfast around a huge fire. Jean Fraser gave us bacon and eggs and delicate chanterelle picked from the edge of the Nyrud clearing. A bonus to our carefully planned rations.

After lunch John Willett and Joan elected to return to their lake at the west end of Grinnsjön where they had mounted the cameras and dug themselves in. Sorrel and I decided to take the Land Rover off round some of the rough interior tracks, to explore some of the area we had not already covered on foot. This proved to be a very good plan. At 4.30 p.m., just as the sun was going down, we saw our first moose. It was a lone bull. A young one, we thought, standing in open scrub about eighty yards from the vehicle. He was quite undisturbed and continued to browse delicately at the willow thicket.

The bull grazed slowly across our vision, from right to left, picking at each bush, carefully plucking the softest and uppermost foliage. Quite suddenly there was a loud, sharp grunt from somewhere out of sight away to our right, and our bull, as if whipped, threw up his head, spun round and made off at a high stepping trot. We heard the grunt again and a third time, and by now our moose was running quickly towards the source of the sound, still out of sight to us.

We were amazed at the speed with which it covered the ground.

Within seconds it was gone, and our first moose watch was over. We had been speechless and enthralled for half an hour. Now it was clear to us how these huge animals moved about our camp without a sound. Their long thin legs were cunningly designed to enable the animal to pick its way daintily through the thickest tangle of under-growth, its great cloven hoof spreading to form a perfect grip in any terrain, and its height permitting the huge bulk of its body to move along through the space between scrub layer and the browse line of the trees above. With a stride as huge as we had just witnessed it was clear that even at a slow walk the animal could cover the roughest ground quickly and with ease. At a long leg-stretching run the animal was as graceful as a racehorse.

Our second sighting, only ten minutes later, was again a solitary bull and may have been the source of the loud grunting. This beast was enormous and had a pair of well-developed antlers heavily branched and perched across the crown of its huge elongated head like a tangle of driftwood from a Hebridean beach. Again we were speechless as it nimbly crossed our front and vanished into the thicket to our left. The bushes seemed to part for it, its grey body merging completely with the dense twiggery and its antlers instantly becoming living branches lost in the growing wood.

I was compulsively drawn to compare this most striking animal with the cave paintings of Lascaux and Altemira and the hump-shouldered bison depicted there. It is the shape which is so essentially paleolithic with the long prehensile nose and massive head, the mountainous shoulders tapering to more graceful and streamlined rear-quarters.

This time we drove on for only two hundred yards before our third sighting which was a sequence probably so close to mating that the animals appeared to be quite unconscious of our vehicle only twenty feet away. A large bull and two cows were standing together beside the lonely track. The bull was at first inactive, watching us and blinking his large wet eyes gently. The cows were obviously sexually excited and moved about restlessly, nuzzling the bull around the neck and shoulders and passing close beneath his chin so that their rear ends were perpetually under his nose. There was no response for a while as the bull watched us, probably because we were so close, but, slowly, the tantalizing behaviour of his cows drew his whole attention back to them and he began to sniff delicately at their genitals. At this point one of the cows knelt down on her forelegs and made as if to suckle the bull, nuzzling softly up underneath his belly and scrotum. We were unable to see whether she was licking him, but it is possible that she was. She rose to her feet again and continued to circle the bull with the other cow. This level of provocation had excited him and he now followed them round in a full circle with his nose firmly located on one cow's rump.

At this crucial point there was a loud grunt from a challenging bull further back in the forest behind them. Instantly the bull's concentration was broken and the trio moved off out of sight behind a clump of birches. Throughout the entire episode, which lasted some fifteen minutes, the cows kept up a perpetual soft winnowing sound – an intimate muted whine as they nuzzled each other and their bull, which was scarcely audible even as close as we were.

It is so prehistoric, this animal, that we are still very much in awe of it. Having seen it close to and observed its most intimate behaviour we find ourselves unable to come to terms with it. It appears as such an anachronism beside us and our Land Rover, so unlike the red and roe deer we are familiar with in Scotland. It has a facial expression which seems to belong to quite another age, one in which it had time to evolve these great velvet ears and the soft nostril flanges which curve downward like the folds of an Elizabethan courtier's costume. And yet, for all his size and density of body I have not seen a beast move with such dignity, nobility almost, and grace, across what must be the most difficult terrain.

We have been struck, ever since we first arrived at Hunneberg, with the silence of the beast. Now, seeing it close to and watching it about its business, we can understand its noiselessness. Each great foot is placed with a million years of practice. Even when alarmed it moves off without a sound. The first bull we saw disappeared, running across all that broken scrub as if in a silent film. Our own efforts to walk silently in the forest are ludicrous by comparison. Little wonder that we had such ill-luck in seeing them when we first arrived. We must have passed them by in the forest time and again, each moose moving gently away unseen and unheard.

Our time at Nyrud had been well spent. We had learned a great deal and compiled a considerable log of information on what the moose was eating at that time of the year, as well as on a great many aspects of his habitat. In one day I had seen six different species of woodpecker and a gyr falcon, a bird

I had always wanted to see in the wild, which obliged me with a long rewarding view. But perhaps most important of all was that we had learned to get on with each other, discovered each other's needs and expectations, and formulated a plan for the main section of the expedition. It was quite clear that filming was not going to be easy. John and Joan would have to work alone much of the time, building themselves hides where they would have to lie up and wait if need be for days at a time. Filming from the roof of the Land Rover had been all right at Hunneberg, but in the far north we were going to be operating largely on foot and there would not always be the opportunity of taking a vehicle.

As we prepared to leave Nyrud we were blessed with the most perfect Indian summer weather. We had walked in shirt sleeves about the forest for two days and on both evenings there had been extravagant sunsets which spread the whole of the western sky with orange and ochre. Now, with a horizon not of sea and distant mountains, but of silhouetted coral shapes of pine and spruce, it appeared as though we were witnessing some great forest fire in the distance. Once in this light we had seen moose. John was mounted on the Land Rover roof behind his cine-camera and the sound recording equipment was housed inside, microphones and parabolic reflectors bristling from the windows. We were driving gently along a track with open scrub stretching into the distance on either side. This expanse was broken occasionally by a birch or group of pines like oases in a desert. To our right the sky was aflame with a spreading sunset, the vegetation burning with the sky behind it. Just as John passed down the message that the light was too poor for filming we saw our moose. I stopped the Land Rover and turned the engine off. Only twenty yards from us stood a large cow, in the centre of a small birch thicket already yellow with the season, now gold in that weird light. She stood watching us with wide unblinking eyes. Her huge laurel ears were up and nostrils gently dilating. She was quite pink. Her thick charcoal fur reflected the western light in full and she stood transfixed

17

▽ 18

Red deer hinds fording the river below the Kennels

Glen Affric, truly arctic with Caledonian pines and frozen loch

The Kennels job at its most daunting moment

In winter red deer stags came down around us at the Kennels

'Not one nail had been struck in our absence and our home was in ruins'

22 Glen Affric. Luxuriant in summer . . .

23 . . . and a shimmering, fairytale wilderness in winter

24 'The ducks came winging in from the river fields to haggle and bicker for a handful of gr

25 Sorrel and Warwick with the dogs by the river in the autumn of 1975

26 Sometimes grey seal cows are aggressive in defence of their pups

27 'Daffodil examined us passively . . . quite without any sign of fear or aggression'

28 ' "There's a big house standing empty down near my cottage," Paul Johnson casually announced'

29 'Aigas it is called, and its pink sandstone silhouette gives a little indication of the work to be done'

as if caught in a footlight while taking a last curtain call.

Despite the poor light the camera whirred above us and we saw her ears stir to catch the sound. Only then did we realize that her calf was standing beside her. Previously hidden by the scrub, it moved forward and continued to graze, less guarded than its parent. We watched it stripping the leaves from birch suckers with the long soft flange of its muzzle curling round the stem like a velvet hand. But the mother was jealous of her child and spoke to it in firm muted utterances so that they turned and slipped silently away. Suddenly it was dusk and a wine-red sky was turning purple at the edges as the night closed in around us.

That must have been the proverbial calm. Next day brought blizzard and impacting sleet as we drove north up the main highway. At times we were reduced to a crawl and it was necessary to stop every few miles to clear headlamps and windscreens of packed snow. We travelled in convoy, not daring to let the other vehicle out of sight for fear of being separated in that awful whiteness. All day we forged on passing Swedish traffic abandoned or immobilized by the weather. In four-wheel drive we could keep going even where the regular snow ploughs had not been, but it was wretchedly slow and the vehicles drank fuel so that the gauge needles dropped almost visibly.

After twelve hours we had had enough and we pulled off the highway and made camp. We were exhausted and it took a great effort to unpack the tents and equipment, light a fire and bed ourselves in. After food and a warming drink we slunk away to bed. As I damped down the fire the moon appeared through the cloud barrier and the snow stopped. I knew we were in for a frost.

This cold weather was unexpected. We had been given to believe that we should comfortably cross the Arctic Circle without bad weather, provided we did so before 15 October. We were a week in advance of that date and we were nowhere near Lapland. But we were fully equipped for the cold since we knew the greater part of our journey would be under winter conditions, so I went to sleep unworried that it would affect us too seriously.

During the night my air-bed collapsed and I was awoken by a deep numbing cold rising through my hip-bone. I lay there for some minutes thinking about it and then came fully awake with the realization that when we had gone to bed there had been snow on the ground, but no frost or ice. For the ground to have got this cold beneath a sleeping figure inside a tent, there must have been a pretty dramatic freeze. I sat up and promptly grazed my head on the tent; clearly there had been a dramatic frost. The soft cotton of the inner tent was as stiff as a sheet of corrugated iron where the condensation had been gripped by the frozen air. I shook Sorrel awake. She agreed to share her air-bed, and as we shuffled to reorganize ourselves we became aware of a strong light shining through the tent. I parted the entrance and we stared out on to a moonlit land as light as some English winter days. We were beside a large lake. We knew there was water there because our headlamps had revealed it on arrival, but we had no idea how big it was. We were in a forest of tall pines which went right to the water's edge and there were two moons and two forests each one so perfect that a photograph would not have been able to reveal which was the reflection. I reached for my camera but Sorrel stopped me saying, 'Don't bother. You'll be wasting your time. No photograph can ever do justice to that. Let's keep it for ourselves.'

At dawn everything was frozen. The axe frozen to the ground, the kettle solid, the white kindling prepared the night before solid once again so that it had to be broken apart with the axe. After some time I managed to get a small fire going, but the heat was so small and the cold so heavy upon it that the smoke drifted out from the fire sideways. The thin layers broadened out across the camp so that I stood in a sea of smoke, my body and the ground invisible from the waist down; to pick something up from the ground I had to duck beneath the canopy of smoke to locate it.

By the time the others emerged from their tents, the smoke

had risen to about eight feet from the ground and had spread right through the surrounding forest so that it gave the appearance of early morning mist. Jean Fraser would not at first believe that it was smoke, and she wandered around the camp jumping up and down trying to sniff at pockets of it to satisfy herself.

We all stood and watched the sun rise across that lake before pulling out and taking to the highway once again. It was majestically beautiful in all that gripping cold and none of us had anything to say about it. Weeks later, back at home, I was going through a sheaf of sketches Simon had made during the expedition and I came across one of a forest lake with two full, round moons. I recognized it instantly and quizzed him on it.

Yes, he too had awoken and seen it and had chosen to say nothing to anyone about it.

We arrived at Muddus, the great virgin pine forest of central Lapland a hundred miles north of the Arctic Circle, after a few more days of arduous travel. And it was here, in this huge forest wilderness we had driven a thousand miles through the snow to see, that for me the important part of the journey began. The drive north had been uneventful save for one near accident when my vehicle skidded off the road and hung precariously over a deep ditch with its front wheels rearing high in the air. We calmly unloaded it and winched it back on to the horizontal with Roy Jonas's expert help, and drove on. It had been no more than a good exercise in testing our extraction gear. Each night we had camped a little way off the deserted highway and the business of setting it all up soon became streamlined and efficient. There was no question of anyone shirking their duty because if you were inactive for more than a few seconds you began to freeze. One night we were late and overtired after an unusually hard day's drive. As we pulled off the road in search of a camp-site the headlights of my Rover picked out a low barn nestling snuggly in the edge of a wood. Secretly dreading having to get out of the warm vehicle and begin the struggle with frozen gear, I suggested camping in the barn for a change. Everyone readily agreed.

It was a pine-log barn built to house some sixteen reindeer, eight on each side, in crude stalls. The floor was deep in dung, but it was so old and dry as to be completely inoffensive. There was a cutting wind outside and the building provided such a welcome release from it that we needed no second thoughts. The girls cooked an evening meal at the door while we laid out our bed-rolls, one to a stall, to the cheerful accompaniment of Simon singing Gaelic folk songs. It was one of the cosiest nights we spent during the whole trip. The gas cooker and the hurricane lamps quickly got a fug-up in the barn and we each did two minutes' running on the spot to get our blood circulating to the furthest extremities. Simon sang us to sleep with lilting ballads in his clear tenor voice, and we all slept unusually soundly.

At Muddus, where we met the virgin pine belt, we abandoned the Land Rovers for the first time. We were glad to. Conditions were cramped for travelling and after such a long haul we were only too pleased to be able to stretch our legs. We had reported to our Swedish Forest Service contact in Jokkmok, the only town in the area, and he had made us most welcome. Our first surprise was to be given a guide. We had hoped for maps, certainly, and references, and even points of contact out in the wilderness, but never had we dared hope for a full-time guide.

We drove to a point on the edge of the forest so like Scotland that I felt entirely at home. I plucked a sprig of familiar green from a low pine branch and examined it closely. It was the same. Good old Scots pine, *Pinus sylvestris*, without any noticeable variation. The trees were shaped with exactly the same rounded crowns as Glen Affric trees and the spacing between them was identical too. I felt completely relaxed. Here were all the ingredients of my own home. The same plants on the forest floor, that unmistakable quilt of *vaccinium* and heather and great cushions of sphagnum moss. Even the lichens, the *cladonias*, hanging in wisps from the bark and branches of the trees, were identical. The birches and the willows stood in precisely similar juxtaposition to the pines and the light fell among them casting the full deep Highland shadows we knew so well.

It was ten days since we had left our own pine forest at Guisachan where it had been autumn. In ten days we had travelled back five thousand years in Scottish history to a point before the influence of man, even if he was present at that time in the Northern-Central Highlands, and when the forests themselves were in their infancy. The precise chronology of the retreat of the ice from the Highlands after the last period of glaciation is difficult to establish for any one position. Certainly the Highlands was subjected to the many advances and retreats of ice from Finno-Scandinavia until the end of the Scandinavian period some ten thousand years ago. Much of what is known has been established from the analysis of varves taken from lake-bottom clays, but to sort out a more exact chronology extensive work on foraminifera and deep-sea cores must yet be done. However, the picture seems to be that by ten thousand years ago most of the ice had gone from the Highlands, having retreated up the sides first, giving access to colonizing plants and animals up the west coast and from Perth up the Spey valley towards Inverness. After the ice, came a period of tundra exactly similar to that found in the sub-Arctic today. This lasted for a little less than a thousand years before birch forests emerged preparing the way for pine. During the period known as Boreal Time, roughly eight and a half to seven thousand years ago, the pine became dominant over the whole of the Central Highlands while, incidentally, oak, elm and hazel began to dominate over the pine in southern England which was then still very much attached to the Continent.

For comparison with the Highlands, Lapland, and in particular the central area where we were, was relieved of the ice-cap only seven thousand years ago, being some 760 miles further north than Scotland. It then took an exactly similar period of time for the various stages of vegetation to produce the climax pine forest of today, calling on the same stock of animals, birds and plants as the Highlands, from further south in Europe, with the notable exception of man, who in the case of the Highlands seems to have come indirectly from the Mediterranean, and to Lapland from ancient Finno-Ugrian stock. So it can be seen that to stand in the Lapland pine belt today is in many ways very comparable to the situation in the Central Highlands some five thousand years ago. The Lap has only recently ceased to be a true part of the biocommunity, within living memory, and his old style of existence, hunting and herding his reindeer, are well known and documented. It was of particular interest to me to attempt to make some rough visual gauge of his impact on the forest itself since it was at about this comparable period five thousand years ago that man reappeared in the Central Highlands as Mesolithic man after being either forced out or exterminated by the last re-advance of the dying era of glaciation some four to five thousand years before. The only remains known to us of this early period stone-age man are bones and implements found in the famous Inchnadamph cave in Sutherland. There lay the bones of bear, Arctic fox, reindeer and man, side by side, giving us a glimpse of what the northern fauna contained during that cold and twilit period.

Mesolithic man had the Highlands to himself for possibly as long as three thousand years, and in most areas must be looked upon as the original inhabitants of the Highlands. They were a simple stone-age culture living by fishing, fowling and hunting in forests. They lived particularly on coastal fringes and in river valleys, a tribal existence with few needs and no husbandry or agriculture. They built primitive huts and had dugout canoes which almost certainly accounted for their quick and probably accidental dispersal throughout the Western Isles. They also had fire and may, like the Lap, have used it for hunting.

We know for certain that the Mesolithic Highlander was well provided for by way of game. There were red and roe deer, as there are today, reindeer in the mountains and upper margins of the forests, wild pig and moose as well as wild ox and goats, and a complimentary array of predators too. Bear, lynx, wolf, Arctic fox, red fox, wildcat, wolverine, otter, badger, European mink, pine-marten, polecat, weasel and stoat were all there, roaming the forested uplands. Little wonder that out of this great beginning has sprung the depth of myth and fable which surrounds the old wood of Caledon today. Little wonder that the remnant stretches like those beside us in Glen Affric and Guisachan should harbour that aura of great age and history which has moved ecologists to write of them with reverence, departing from their scientific text in lyrical and spiritual recognition of their own human origins.

Here we were, then, face to face with the thing we had

come to see. There was a marked trail, we had been told, along which we should walk to meet our guide. Such strange instructions in any other land might have caused concern or doubt, but here in the frozen north men spoke little and meaningfully. We never questioned that he would appear, as of course he did, a little later, as we followed the narrow path into the forest ahead. The boggy forest floor was frozen and a light covering of snow made the going easy and firm. Now and then capercaillie rose from the ground with a flurry of huge

Crested tit

black wings and powdery snow. And there were crested tits, too, of the northern race, in abundance in these pines like those at home. We stopped along the trail to watch troops of these tiny familiar birds in the dense green crowns of the trees, and it was as we were engaged in this that we saw a figure striding towards us through the forest.

Lennart Arvidsson was a Swede but his work and his way of life brought him regularly into contact with Laps and their remote wilderness settlements; and he was an authority on them. But essentially Lennart was a naturalist of the back-woodsman-type whose knowledge was built up from years of first-hand experience of one type of environment. He was a tall heavily-built man in his mid-forties and he spoke clearly understandable English in a broken Scandinavian accent. His job was and had always been, it seemed, that of warden to this particular national park, Muddus, and the adjacent nature reserves of the Sjaunja Bird Sanctuary and the Tjnoltavnobme Forest Reserve. It was an impressive area of roadless forest, bog and lake in which the only means of transport was on foot. He told us he could comfortably cover forty miles a day in winter on skis and snowshoes, and even over the impossible wet terrain of taiga swamp he could cover twenty miles during the long hours of daylight in an arctic summer's day.

We liked Lennart straight away. He was warm and friendly and interested in our journey. He was fascinated to learn about our virgin forest in Scotland, the warring history and fine stone castles of which he had read in history books at school. (It was interesting that the Scandinavians appeared to hold the Highlander in similar warrior regard as we do the Vikings.) He also had a homely look about him which we liked immediately. He wore no special clothes for his arctic outdoor work, an old khaki jacket over a home knitted jersey, a woolly hat, old corduroy trousers tucked into thick socks, and heavy leather boots of the sort issued to the armed forces. Into the soles of these he had nailed stout half-inch spikes which, he insisted, were vital for crossing frozen rivers. Three items of his equipment, however, were special. On his hands he wore reindeer-fur gloves with a cord connecting each one through the sleeves of his jacket, and in the right hand he held a long pole. One end of this pole was plain-ended, but from the other protruded the most savage looking four-sided spearhead I have ever seen. It was ground to wicked sharpness on each of the four angles and the point was long and keen. He walked with the pole pointing its spearhead to the sky. It was not, as we had imagined, for repelling the advances of angry bears and wolves, but a vital tool for the testing of ice. In winter the best route to take through this very uneven country is along a watercourse and over frozen lakes, but because some fast-moving water remains unfrozen, or perhaps only thinly so, it is essential to have a tool with which to stab at the ice every few yards to test its thickness. The spear was so designed to penetrate several inches of ice with one thrust so that if, first time, it cut through to water the user knew it to be unsafe. If however the ice withstood two or even three sharp jabs, then it was certain to be firm enough.

Before long we came to a small river and Lennart demonstrated the pole. He stood on the bank and jabbed sharply down. The ice was thick and a spurt of white crystals rose from the hole it made. He stepped confidently on to the ice and strode out over its rough surface stabbing in front of him with every other step. Out in the middle he stopped and stabbed two, three, four times into the same hole, twisting the spear as he did so. Ice chips flew from the hole and with the fourth stab he was through. He held up the wet end of the spear triumphantly for us to see. 'This ice is wery deep,' he said reassuringly – 'It is safe to cross this place.'

The third item of equipment which was strange to us was a light wooden frame which he wore on his back exactly as we wear modern aluminium back-packs for mountaineering and hiking at home. But this one differed in the unusual feature of a complicated harness system coming together in a broad strap which passed up the side of his neck and head and on to his forehead in a wide, padded band. Most of the weight of the load strapped to the frame – in this instance a bedding roll and a wooden box – was taken by his head and the shoulder straps served only as locating harness. He explained that all Laps carried their loads in this way, and when on skis it was by far the best method for perfect balance and control. Simon immediately modified his own heavy pack to be worn in this way. Several of us tried it but found it wickedly uncomfortable after a while. But Simon doggedly stuck to it throughout the rest of the trip. We discovered later that Simon possessed a rare and worrying determination to shut out pain and discomfort to the extent of considerable bodily risk.

Lennart led us through that forest for many miles on trails, sometimes on animal paths and sometimes just through the forest in any direction he chose. We were carrying food and supplies for one week, but we had no idea where he was taking us. As the day wore on and the sun went down below the tops of the trees, I began to worry about where we would camp. Suddenly we came to the edge of the forest. In front of us stretched the huge expanse of a frozen lake. Lennart stepped out firmly, his steel studs crunching crisply on the white surface. He pointed with his spear to the dim forest edge on the other side. 'There we will camp,' he announced as he strode forward. Perhaps it was two miles, or only a mile across that huge lake. We never measured it. To our unaccustomed eyes and feet the great ice expanse seemed endless, and even when the trees on the far side became clearly discernible in the dimming light it seemed as far again to reach them. When, in virtual twilight we arrived at the other side, Lennart strode off into the forest anew as if there was no reason to stop. Our hearts sank. We were all near to dropping, having found it hard going with our heavy packs, but now it seemed we must press on further.

Suddenly we were in a forest clearing beside the lake. Lennart was banging the ice and snow from his boots against the steps of a log cabin. It was the most unexpected and welcome sight our eyes could possibly have seen. In minutes oil lamps blazed and a curl of smoke snaked upwards through the trees into the starlit sky above. Lennart produced an axe and swung it sharply into sections of dead pine stacked neatly alongside the cabin. Half an hour later we were sitting round a crackling fire each with a mug of steaming soup and our kit stowed in bunks round the walls. This cabin was Lennart's personal retreat where he lived out long periods of storm and blizzard and to which he could return from any part of the forest if in need of shelter. It was a cabin built from pines felled in the clearing outside, and the bricks for the hearth and chimney and a few other items of equipment had been dropped in by helicopter. Other than these, all the furniture and fittings were fashioned from the native pine, most of which Lennart had made himself. It just happened that there were eight bunks as well as his own and a few visitors, like ourselves, had been permitted to visit the hut. For seven days the hut at Muddus Fjallets was our home. We left it at dawn to trudge through the frozen forest in Lennart's firm footsteps, and we returned to it after dark to sit round the fire and listen to tales of old Lapland and its wildlife while he whittled and carved animals and ornaments from the gleaming white pine and mended the nets with which he fished the lake in summer.

For me they were days of total absorption. It was a living experience not of modern and changing Lapland but of the old Scotland of the past. Glen Affric and Guisachan were there, somewhere beyond the frozen lake and the crystalline forest, an extension of Muddus shared if not by Lennart on his skis then certainly by the crested tits and the moose whose footprints on the ice approached the hut that night and veered away again at the heavy taint of new and strange humans. Moreover I was a part of the living forest myself; something I had never felt at home. Here, through the taut senses of Lennart and his Lapland ancestry, I was as much a part of the forest as the pines themselves and the frozen sphagnum underfoot. It was huge and awesome and dominant, about and above me, like a cathedral to a small child and I whispered for the same unquestioning reasons. There was no chance to be objective and to superimpose a trained intellect over the exigent needs for survival. Impressions, like sights and sounds, were crisp and clear and intense in that ringing ice-garden, and to abstract and meddle with them was to negate the gift of sensibility the great forest had forced upon me. I was glad that I had no other purpose there, no film to make, no specimen to collect. I was there to see and to listen and to accept, and I felt, perhaps quite wrongly, that I came away with a more resonant image for it.

'Here has stood a big bull moose,' says Lennart pointing to the deep slots in the ice, 'a rutting bull, and he cries here,' and we see where the front feet are slightly spread. 'The moose makes a very strange cry like a swan,' he says, 'or like a fast train.' His father was told by an old Lap that the moose put back his head like a wolf to utter this sound, but he has never seen it. But his father can call a moose, he tells us, and he did once in the evening and the old bull came on towards him thinking he was another bull. Lennart was afraid. It was dark and in spruce and birch scrub with no big trees to hide behind. When the scent is bad it is possible to call a moose very easily. We walk on through the forest.

As we move quietly along behind him he stops and cocks an ear to a flock of small birds calling in the pine tops far above our heads. 'Pine grosbeaks,' he announces and walks on. Later, as a bird rises from our feet in a cloud of snow he turns and comments, 'you do not know the hazelhen in Scotland I think.' He turns and walks on again without waiting for confirmation.

'Here,' he says as we cross a frozen pool to a swamp clump of dwarf birch in the middle, 'a whooper swan nests always.' Even snow-covered it is easy to see the great concave of many years' nests made and remade on top of each other. 'This year she has made five babies.'

Back in the forest we stop at a tall tree beside the moose path. The bark of this pine is heavily clawed up to seven feet and more. 'The bear has been here since many years.' We finger the deep gashes in astonishment.

'How does he reach up here?' We ask, staring at the marks high above our heads. 'Does he climb the tree?'

'No,' Lennart replies, with surprise in his voice. 'This is the marks of a big bear.' There is no arguing with that. The brute must have been enormous. We walk on.

'Here,' he says, pointing to a small clearing in the pines, 'last spring I find a big bull moose who is killed by the bear. In spring when he comes awake the bear is wery hungry. Berries is not good for him then. He returns many weeks to the moose to eat from him. The foxes and the jays come here too. Now there is no moose to see.' We stand gazing at the small clearing, each one of us re-enacting in our mind's eye the drama of the killing. Before this moment the adult moose had seemed to us to be invincible. All that huge body, those massive hooves lashing wildly. The great beam in those antlers Lennart had shown us at the hut. Only the claw gashes in the pine tree were greater than these.

Now we were standing among a group of pines all with strange square scars in their bark. 'The Laps have cut these when capercaillie is scarce.' He tells us. The soft white bark layer beneath the outer flakes was removed and ground up after being roasted on a fire, and was eaten as bread or porridge. 'When I am a boy I remember old Laps who shoot capercaillie with the bow and arrow,' he adds for our information. 'The gun is new to Lapland.'

A mile on we came to a huge boulder standing in the centre of a clearing. Around its edges the stone sloped inwards leaving small caves beneath it. The pine forest around was dark and thick, ringing us round like a great fence. 'An old Lap tells me,' Lennart starts, pointing to the caves round the edge of the boulder, 'he comes here to sleep in the shelter of the stone. Here he tries to light his fire. But always the ghosts come and put the fire out. Soon he gives up and tries here.' Lennart moves round the boulder to a cave on the other side. Pointing at this shelter he continues, 'Here there is no ghost and the fire burns well. He can sleep here.' All round us the pines are marked with the square wounds of old Lap bark cuts. Pointing to one long deep cut Lennart says, 'This man has many children.' He grins broadly, chuckling to himself.

'Do you know the hawk owl,' asks Lennart, 'who lives here in the forest always?' We do not know the hawk owl. Our book, well thumbed now as we have searched for new and unfamiliar birds tells us briefly of its habits. 'He is here always and you must see him now.' Lennart starts off down the trail towards the ridge which separates the lake from the huge marshes to the north. The trees are mainly spruces here, the great Christmas trees of the north, quite unlike the pines, thick in canopy and closely bunched together. Suddenly Lennart stops and stares up through the dark sea of green around us, into a patch of blue sky above. The hawk owl is there, a dumpy silhouette perched on the apex of a tall spruce. Lennart whispers to us, 'He is living here in these spruces and sits always on the highest one.' We move gently round so that the light catches his feathers.

This owl is one of the few diurnal owls. It lives by hawking birds and small mammals like a sparrow hawk, which it is very like, and which it is often mistaken for. It is significant that like hawks and some other birds of prey the hawk owl chooses a high perch from which to view the hunting field. The owl saw our movement immediately and extended its neck to peer down at us. I noticed for the first time its tail. Quite unlike any owl I have ever seen it had a long straight tail, another parallel with the sparrow hawk.

Siberian tits and crossbills sat around us in the nearby spruces and pines ticking and chattering their dislike of the owl. It struck me that we must have looked strangely owl-like ourselves with our binoculars protruding from our eyes, which, seen straight on from the owl's end, would appear round and spectacled like the bird itself; a feature which when directed at small birds of any sort might add to the generally hostile shape of man. I made a mental note to experiment at a later date.

Another day Lennart says we must walk far and so we start early. We are few now because the film team have gone off with Roy to work near the lake and Jean stays behind to cook. Lennart walks at a tremendous pace. 'It is good to walk fast in the morning,' he announces without any room for suggestion that it might not be. 'We are going to a wery old pines place three thousand feet above the sea.'

We race through the frozen woods zig-zagging upwards on to the forest mountain. As we climb higher the pines become thinner and wider spaced. On the top of this mountain is a stand of very old, gnarled pine. Here the frost has been so intense that every twig and needle is encased in ice. Slowly we walk through this magical frozen grove high in the sky. We come to a huge pine tree. It has been struck by lightning and is hollow. We ask how old the tree is. Lennart shakes his head. 'We cannot know,' he says sadly, 'because his heart is burned out. But I have taken drills all round and he is four hundred and sixty years up to the hollow. He is an old tree.'

From beside this tree there was a view out over the coniferous belt. I cannot calculate how many miles of gently undulating forest lay below us. Maybe it was a hundred, or perhaps one could see two hundred miles from that great height and in that crisp sharp air. In any event it was apparently endless. Looking at the map one sees that it is, of course, endless. It is a ring of wild coniferous woodland encircling the globe with only one real break and that is the North Atlantic. From the Western Highlands of Scotland to the Bering Sea it is a pine belt – Scots pine, we call it in the west, and rightly so because it seems to begin there, although the race and type slowly change from our familiar short-needled, rufous-barked form the further east you travel through Russia. This then was the Taiga, the dominant pine and swamp vegetation which at some time or other had covered most of Europe and certainly the whole of Britain. It is what botanists call climax vegetation; it is a good word, climax, and profoundly fitting for such an awe-inspiring sight as what lay below us now. This was pure wilderness. No animal, man or beast, had been the shaping factor here, and while both man and beast belonged to it they were there because of it. They had relied upon it for their survival and for their own evolution. It was the primaeval forest, shaped by the wind and the rain and the spin of the earth, as essential in being as a mountain or an ocean and arousing in us the same elemental emotions.

I don't know how long we stood and looked at its vastness. After a while I heard Peter Wortham, the quiet botanist, click the shutter of his camera four, five or six times, compulsively almost, as if it were some rare animal about to spring away forever. To my right I could hear the busy pencil scratch of Simon Fraser at work on his pad. How do you draw a thousand square miles of forest? And there was Sorrel standing beside me, her breath clouding our vision like mine. We stood, all four, and wondered each in his own way, at it. It was, after all, what we had come to see.

That night around the hut fire we talk of the pressures on

our forest land at home and its wildlife. Lennart listens intently with his wind- and cold-scarred face sad in the firelight. 'These things are the same here, too,' he says, 'and I cannot see the end of them.' He tells us of the break up of the Lap way of life, the advent of the rifle and the snowscooter and how the rare animals are hunted for their valuable skins. He tells us that falconers come from Germany and ask him for gyr falcons – 10,000 krona he was offered last spring for gyr falcons. He talks of the hydro-electricity schemes damming the great rivers and breaking the flow of life through the wilderness. It was a sad evening and our last with Lennart and at Muddus, but these things must be said.

When we left Muddus, some of us by helicopter provided by the Domänverket, and the rest of us bringing the Land Rovers the long and laborious route to Kivikkjokk and walking in across the barren Arctic landscape to join our skyborne companions in the mountains, our Lapland adventure had just begun. John Willett had exposed next to no film and the hard, long night and dawn watches for moose were yet to come. We were to meet Lapps and reindeer; come close to the last wolves in Scandinavia; meet on common ground across the mountain snow wastes of Sarek, lynx and wolverine, pine-marten and mink, and wild and beautiful birds like the great white-tailed eagle and the ubiquitous Siberian jay. We were to follow herds of reindeer back through the dark pine belt, sleeping out with them under the forest roof. We were to experience breakdown and accident, and worry about Simon who went missing for forty-eight hours, returning, blue with cold, and with a pad full of moose sketches, no whit abashed and quite unconcerned; and we were all to be drawn outside from a farewell party in our last cabin, in shirt sleeves and clutching food in our hands, eight of us, mesmerized, speechless and unconscious of the gripping cold, to witness the heavens above us split open and reveal the northern lights raiding the night sky at full soundless tilt. Huge curtains of wild and mystical light folded and unfolded above us, spreading and crumpling in floods of wine and purple and pale ice-green. Wild rockets of coloured light soared and arched across the star-dotted dome and fell away in cascades of dazzling rainbow brilliance. We stood for an hour unable to move, transfixed by the celestial magic, and when we returned inside, the show over, the party spirit had died and each of us slunk away to our bunks and our own thoughts with no comment to make.

But these things, memorable though they are, are no part of this story. They would need a book in themselves to tell. The fun and the adventure apart, my own purpose was fulfilled in those few days at Muddus. I had located the old Scottish forest, intact, bountiful and replete in a few square miles of that winter land. Through Lennart Arvidsson and my own broad footprints in the virgin snow I had glimpsed its wholeness and its unity – perhaps, after all, *spirit* is the right word. That was enough, for now, and in my mind I hurried through the rest of the journey to get back to Guisa-chan which, translated from the gentle Gaelic tongue, means 'place of pines'.

Chapter Four

It was as well that we had become hardened by the Arctic winter and accustomed to the sight of the clouds and the stars above us, because when we returned along the bumpy track to Guisachan, along through the sleeping village in the early morning after driving all night from England, up the avenue of oaks and beeches and along the forest edge where the two tall pines marked the position of our home in that grey dawn it was well that our spirits were soaring high with the sheer pleasure of arriving, for we found our house in utter desolation.

No one had been near it, even once, since we had left at the beginning of winter, two and a half months before. The tarpaulins stretched over the open roof at the back of the house had long since been torn to shreds in weeks of violent Atlantic gales, and the constant torrential rain had driven in from the ridge to the rotten floor for thirty or forty days.

As we picked our way through the rubble of smashed and dissolved plaster covering our few stored pieces of furniture, it seemed easier to walk away and leave it all than to begin the cruel task of renewal. If Sorrel cried then I could not see it for the rain streaming down her face. We were speechless and thankfully alone.

It had been a great build up, all along the wet road from England, and we had discussed it constantly: what the new roof looked like, whether the glass would be in the windows, whether the flats had been started yet or not. We had talked of interior decoration and furnishing, planned trips to Edinburgh to choose wallpapers, and our minds had been busy with the trivia of completion and the creation of a home. Now there was no prospect of any of these things that winter, nor for months to come. There was no one room dry enough to live in; and except where we had had the foresight to cover them in polythene, all our possessions were sodden and ruined under a rubble of plaster and grey slime which the rain had washed from burnt timbers of the roof. Back in the summer, the summer lost behind us in memories of travel and adventure, I had bought an old caravan, so old that we had had to tow it gingerly, scarcely daring to look behind us to see if it was still there. We had used it to accommodate two schoolboys who had wanted to join in our activities, and it was, just, waterproof. Now it seemed a haven of dryness and windlessness beside the dark ruin of our house.

It is always those most desperate situations which can be improved upon the most. It was only two or three days before we were back living, if not sleeping, in the house. We cleared the main rooms we needed, secured new tarpaulins to the skeleton of the roof and rescued what we could of our possessions. We had a table to sit at and chairs to sit on, and if a blind eye could be turned to the dozens of pots and buckets scattered about the floor and passages to collect drops from the not entirely effective tarpaulins, we succeeded in regaining a semblance of normality.

The builder said the weather had been too bad to do any work on the house. If that was a lie there was no point in challenging it; and if not, it was a measure of his concern that he had never even been to look. It was also the first of the serious blows I learnt to absorb from the Highlands that winter. I don't regret it now, but at the time it hurt so that I wanted to collect my wife and my dog and a few possessions and drive away into the rain and the mist to seek another kinder and more practical idyll. But I did manage to extract a promise from the builder that he would start to put things right straight away, regardless of the weather; and far from ostracizing myself from him by being angry I offered him every assistance I could dream up, including my own services as a labourer to work beside him. To my surprise he came.

Guisachan winters come in three disguises. Atlantic and wet, when the airstream is solidly west and south-westerly and comes straight off the North Atlantic Drift, the current which brings warm water and air from the Gulf of Mexico, up the east coast of the United States, and across the North Atlantic to the west coast of the Highlands where, because of it, it is possible to grow palm trees and tropical gardens, and may never know a frost in the span of a man's memory. It also brings the highest rainfall and humidity recorded in the British Isles.

The reverse of that situation is Siberian and cold. Some winters are dominated by north-easterly winds which sweep the Atlantic influence away to the west and chill the Central and Eastern Highlands to a static icy desert. It brings snow with it when it comes in, and then the cold drops far too low for precipitation of any kind. The clear short days produce a piercing low-angled sunlight which dramatizes the mountain scenery and makes it, like Lapland, a place of icicle silence and fairy-tale brilliance. At the Kennels in such years we recorded a temperature as low as my maxi-min thermometer would accept, a polar 38° of frost, when metal burnt your fingers on touch and calor gas refused to come out of its cylinder. These winters are exhilarating and vivid.

Somewhere in between is the third category of winter which is a product of these two airstreams locked in conflict. They are immediately recognizable as those of constant driving sleet and icy rain, searing winds and gales, sudden blinding blizzards followed a little later by overnight thaws, floods and driving rain again. These are the days when it is easier to creep back to bed than to face the howling wetness outside, and when the cattle stand dejectedly with their tails into the rain, and the river is brown and swollen and the rowdy mallard, congregating in packs of forty and fifty on the flooded field behind the house, struggle up the wind in tight formation, inching across the window as the gale resists their thrusting wings and then turn and sweep down on to the foam-flecked water like fighter jets.

Of the three possibilities it could only have been the last which hit us, full in the face, that roofless December at the Kennels. By Christmas we had experienced everything the Almighty could dream up and hurl at us. It remained only for the earth to split open and swallow us up or for the benign hump of Ben Sparra on the wooded horizon behind us to vomit molten lava over us. Neither would have been a surprise. One last twist of fate was the caravan. From the outside it was a perfectly normal, old, caravan. Even from the inside it appeared serviceable, if a little shabby, with good upholstery and all the usual fittings of cupboards and tables. We had used it all summer for storage and occasional accommodation, and it had presented no serious problem. I even rather liked it.

But now that we wanted to use it ourselves – had to use it as a last, desperate sanctuary from that weather – it revealed a side of its character hitherto unsuspected. That first night we lit the gas fire to air it, unrolled our familiar Lapland bedding on the double bunk, and tried to forget the horrors of our homecoming. As we lay there in the dark, with the warmth of our duck-down bags slowly restoring sanity to us, a large fat drip landed on Sorrel's face.

I snapped on the torch and looked up at the ceiling above us. There was a tiny droplet of water forming there, and I climbed out to inspect it more closely. The ceiling was sound enough and I assured myself that it was not a leak.

'I think it's only condensation,' I said. I wiped the ceiling above us with a towel and climbed back in. Half an hour later, just as we became unconscious, the same thing happened again.

Once again we struggled to dry the ceiling. Once again we set off for sleep. This time we made it and sank blissfully away from all our troubles – for about an hour.

When I awoke it was raining. Not outside, but inside the caravan. I got up and lit the gas lamp. The ceiling was studded with beads of moisture which fell regularly on to the table, floor, draining board, with a full range of unmusical plops and splashes. It was like standing in a cave from the roof of which water falls incessantly from no single source. The only answer was to open all the windows wide and prop the door open too, to get enough air going through to keep the humidity down. It was like sleeping in the open, and when it rained the rain came through the windows and ran down the walls. There were pools all over the floor in the morning, but at least we had stopped the dripping from the ceiling.

Months later, I attempted to sell the caravan back to the same dealer who had sold it to me.

'I'm sorry,' he said with exaggerated grief, 'I canna tak' that model, I'd never sell it again.'

'Why not?' I demanded. I had, after all, spent a long time cleaning it up.

'Oh, it's well known, that model,' he said, shaking his head.

'What's the matter with it?' I was indignant now.

'Och, it's a terrible caravan, that one, for the condescension. It was never a success. An awful model.'

So I went home, caravan, condescension and all, damp and disillusioned.

In all this very bad weather we turned our attention to the large kennel kitchen at the east end of the old cottage. The roof had not been opened at this end of the building since it had no upper storey and appeared to be much sounder than the rest. The kitchen was quite dry, but the reason we were not living in it was that when it had been a kennel kitchen it must have been estate policy to whitewash everything at least twice a year. The slaked lime used for this was caustic and unpleasant. Now, some thirty years after the last coat had been applied, it was flaking abominably. The flag-stone floor lay deep in fine white-grey powder which, if disturbed, choked the nose and throat. There must have been a hundred coats on those high walls. Preliminary excavation with a scraper revealed that the lime deposit was everywhere a quarter of an inch thick, and more where the sticky liquid had run down and accumulated.

We dressed like spacemen, tying cloths around our necks, plugging our ears with cotton-wool and encasing our heads in hats and masks of every description. We used garden hoes as scrapers, screaming them up and down the walls in a hideous cacophony. It was impossible to do it for more than twenty minutes at a time, and we would throw down our hoes and rush outside tearing at our face masks to suck in the clean fresh air. I can hear that noise now, six years later, cutting and scouring at my inner consciousness. It took us seven whole days to reduce the walls to flat plaster, seven days from early morning till evening, and no bath to wash in. Our eyes were red-ringed with soreness and our faces cracked and dehydrated by the pore-clogging lime. For a week or two we must have looked like leprous creatures, blotched and rashy, as we slunk in and out of the local shop to buy our provisions and disproportionate quantities of face cream.

I then washed the walls down with water and Sorrel hosed the flag-stones from corner to corner, swooshing the last of the wretched flakes away and out of the door forever. I got the builder to help me put in two new windows, huge squares, looking back across the flooded fields to the river, and a vast open fireplace. By Christmas we had a clean, dry, weatherproof room with a huge log fire and, for the moment, some semblance of comfort. With Sorrel's keenness for 'Christmas as it used to be' she had the room decorated with holly and a tree from the forest in no time at all. We ate capercaillie and venison, both products of a single dash to the west to shoot with a friend, and pigeons shot on the edge of the moor. The fact that the large double-glazed units for the windows had not come didn't really matter. We nailed sheets of polythene over them, inside and out, clamping the edges with batons, and with the fire like a furnace all seemed well.

It was with some surprise, then, that one morning not long after Christmas, when we awoke from our floor beds in front of the great fire, everything seemed strange and unusually cold. Having no torch to hand I slipped out of my sleeping bag and went to the table where I knew the hurricane lamp and matches were. To my astonishment my bare feet met with water on the flags, and, with another step, snow to the ankle. I could scarcely believe it. Then I heard the rustle of polythene. The window had split. As I crossed to the window I was suddenly up to my knees in snow and had to struggle to keep my balance. With an ember from the fire blown into a flame, I lit the lamp and turned the wick high. The light spread slowly across the grey room. Sorrel and Max lay stretched in front of the fire. Everywhere else was a fine covering of powdery snow; over our clothes, the sofa and chairs, our books and Christmas presents. From the two picture windows and the bleak outside stretched two huge snow drifts, spreading into the room as if a lorry had backed up and tipped a load of it through each. At the sill they were two feet deep, the same depth as covered the whole valley outside. When the blizzard had come it had done so with a wind so keen, so angry, that the polythene had been torn aside like the wrapping from a toy.

At first light, in pyjamas and gum-boots, I shovelled the snow back out of the window and replaced the polythene from the builder's roll. Sorrel stoked the fire high with pine logs till the whole room steamed, and we sat down to drink coffee and eat cold venison sandwiches as if it were all quite normal. After Lapland and our awful homecoming, such trifles as this no longer seemed cause for alarm or concern.

By the new year, it was clear that 1974 was going to be busy. Sorrel had worked miracles with marketing the courses and the spring weeks were filling well. In anticipation of this we had approached Peter Wortham, the silent botanist, at the end of the Lapland expedition, and asked him whether he would be interested in joining our venture. In fact we knew very little about him: he was shy and retiring by nature and contributed little to fireside conversation during our weeks of adventure in the snow and ice. But while he revealed little of himself in words he lost no time in showing the rest of us up. If there were a dirty job to be done or if we were all exhausted and cold, Peter, saying nothing, did it. When climbing into the Land Rover to drive all day along rough roads rutted with snow and ice, Peter went purposefully to the most uncomfortable seat at the back. When there was extra luggage to be carried and everyone dreaded the one piece of equipment which was awkward and heavy, Peter took it, first, when no one was looking.

There was never any question of offering him a job. 'Come and work for Highland Wildlife Enterprises, we live in a ruin at the end of a dirt road, have no money and made a roaring loss last year!' That was what it seemed like to me, and any approach we made had to embody all the hazard and risk inherent in such a situation. 'Come and try with us, we have some faith in it, and if there is a little money at the end we will share it with you; and if not, then you will have spent a year in the crisp Highland air.'

To my surprise he agreed, even eagerly, to join us in the early spring and we would do our best to have some accommodation prepared for him. By the new year it was clear that Peter's flat was not going to be ready. I began to foresee severe problems ahead.

We are forced by the timetables of the world at large to put a date to the beginning of our year and for convenience we use March 1st. But to Peter I said, come before the winter ends, before the lambs come and the winter migrants go, and you will be able to watch the year unfold from the very beginning. We were able to fit in one or two walks into the Affric mountains that busy February, into a wilderness as arctic as Sarek and with the same snow cornices and ice pinnacles and long sweeping glissades among the corries. We watched ptarmigan at the range of a few feet, pure white against the white snow but for one red wattle above the eye. We saw snow buntings amongst the high tops, pied sparrows busy amongst themselves in little troops of half a dozen and ten. And there were blue hares in their survival white, invisible until Max sniffed them out from their snow holes and sent them scurrying away over the snowfield far faster than he himself could struggle through the powdery drift. It was a natural sequel to the experience we had had together in Lapland, and I found Peter's experience and skill in the mountains comforting and satisfying. There are few people I would more trust to keep their cool in an ugly mountain situation, a fall or fracture, or a sudden blinding 'white-out' as mountaineers call a blizzard, or even a cloud descending unexpectedly so that one is completely surrounded by mist so dense that sound and vision are reduced to a few inches. After several years of working together and meeting new problems and crises as they have emerged, I would choose Peter to surmount a hazard before anyone else I know.

Inevitably his flat was not ready, nor for sometime afterwards. But he stowed his kit in an upper room and joined in cheerfully with the still daunting task of completing the building. My Highland builder did at last admit that he had bitten off more than he could chew. To complicate the poor man's life further, his mate, who was more of a labourer than a joiner, complained bitterly about having to work in the winter, or even having to work at all, and stamped about the site with total lack of good humour. After all those weeks of toil and hardship Sorrel was disinclined to pamper bad manners, and told him he could stop grumbling or go. He chose to go and I came to an amicable settlement with my builder friend to leave the job unfinished.

Out of nowhere, in response to the tiniest advertisement in the local paper, a magician arrived with a hammer and a saw and a bag of nails, and in one month the job was done. He came and went with neither fuss nor complaint, sometimes arriving so early in the morning that he caught us pyjama-clad and sleepy-eyed. He worked all day with his hammer and his mate, blows falling so fast and thick that the sound from the flats was a continuous thunder. He departed only when the light was too poor to place the next nail.

Peter, Sorrel and I spent two weeks solidly wallpapering, painting and dashing to and from the Inverness sale-rooms for furniture. By the time the grey geese had gone from Braelundie we had a home, an office and a base. Peter had his own flat and, give or take a little debris, we were home and dry – for the first time in eight months. Although Richard Frere and I had done the groundwork in those first speculative years, and it had been hard, unrewarding work, it was not until the

Lapwings

spring of 1974 that the enterprise crystallized into anything like a viable project, and it was sad that at this point, for domestic reasons of his own, Richard had to begin to take a smaller and smaller part. While from time to time he was able to work with us, taking his groups far into the distant hills with all his old vigour and enthusiasm, these occasions became rarer and rarer so that Peter took on the role of mountaineer in his place.

Easter and the lapwings came and went. We were busy with people anxious to fill their lungs with mountain air and watch the golden eagles spiral and tumble above them. Every day when Peter and I returned exhausted there was some new addition to our home. Sorrel worked ceaselessly to improve and equip it and we never knew what to expect next. One day we arrived back to find the kitchen, a practical white emulsion when we had left, wallpapered in a dozen different papers of every colour and pattern in the spectrum. Another day there were wall charts in the office, which had been completely rearranged, and covered with crosses and stars indicating the work which lay ahead. And yet another day, a bright sunlit day, when I returned wind-red in the face and fresh with the excitement of watching peregrine falcons stooping on curlew on the mud flats, as if to prove that her creativity was boundless after all the work and travail of the winter, Sorrel told me she was pregnant.

Chapter Five

That year marked a turning point. Following an enthusiastic piece of publicity in the *Sunday Times* written by Brian Jackman who had spent a few days with us in April, the public response was electric. For several weeks we laboured helplessly under the bulk of correspondence and our lives were run to the constant clatter of the typewriter and the telephone bell. Out of this maelstrom came almost more bookings than we could handle and a rush of full weeks so hard on each other's heels that in no time at all the summer was gone.

As well as the public interest from Britain came a new style of inquiry in the form of an American voice speaking down the telephone from the call-box in the village. He had come 'to check us out' we were told, in a tight drawl, from California. We drove to meet this gentleman at his hotel in Glenurquhart. He was tweedy with gold-rimmed spectacles and a frugal smile. He represented a Californian scientific foundation which arranged natural history travel programmes for its members. Our ears pricked up. After a great quantity of whisky and talk and of poring over maps, we departed with a booking. Not, as we had expected, for that year, but for the following summer, 1975. This, surely, was the stuff life was supposed to be made of. To have taken a booking fourteen months in advance was so unthought of, so unexpected, that we sang all the way home with the delight of the security it instantly supplied.

Knowing, therefore, that we were committed to a further year almost regardless of the success or failure of the one in hand, threw a new light on the whole exercise. It followed that it made sense to advertise in advance by sending out what we called 'long-shot' brochures to other American clubs and societies. Suddenly there were other fish tugging at other hooks on lines thrown out in several different directions. For the first time we glimpsed what the years ahead were to be like. From being a seasonal one-man show the thing had become a business – a living and future for the incipient family. That one American booking was probably the greatest single spur we received and it was not a little ironical that it should have come concurrently with Sorrel's first pregnancy. Without that impetus and with Sorrel effectively removed from the office by her child, the whole business might have easily slipped away so that our future would have been shaped quite differently. And it was tragic that the nice tweedy man in gold-rimmed spectacles never lived to bring his group to us. They came all right, and others since, but under new leadership, and it saddened us that we never had a chance to thank him.

Working with Peter was also a new experience that year. He was a scientist, I was not, and I found his scientific method reliable and reassuring. More than this, I had someone to compare notes with at the end of the day and with whom to exchange experiences, argue over identifications and to nurse me through the detail of his own science, botany, at which I was such a beginner. Together we shared the successes and the failures, commiserated with each other when it rained so hard that our groups saw nothing, and enjoyed the well-being which shone from those special days when we had happened upon some rare item like an eagle kill, or a goosander nest.

Complete failures were, happily, very rare, but one sticks obstinately in my memory. It was to do with capercaillie, the turkey-sized grouse, which frequented, and still does, all the woods at Guisachan and other areas nearby. These birds had fascinated me when I first came to live there and I had spent a lot of time stalking them up and watching them, around our home, mostly in the early morning. Occasionally they were to be seen from the windows of the house, and certainly whenever there was snow we became aware of their tracks on the edge of the forest which demonstrated that they were in greater numbers than our sightings suggested. One reason for this is because it is a bird which is on the move before dawn and I discovered by trial and error that, to watch them, one had to rise long before dawn and sit motionless in a chosen site where they were known to come to feed.

Quite apart from my own attempts at watching capercaillie, we often saw the bird silently winging away from us as we walked stealthily through the woods with our keen bird-watching followers. They became an assured highlight of our courses and I merrily committed myself to being able to find them at will. Then, early that year, came a group whose sole objective was to see these Leviathan grouse.

On the first day we set off confidently at an appropriate hour, and I had the group well seated by the time the first pale stripe of dawn appeared behind the countless erect stems of the pine plantation. The area where we sat was littered with the dry caterpillar-like excretions of capercaillie, and the forest floor was here and there pitted by their scratchings and dust baths. We sat very still. My party were experienced birdwatchers and knew well the disciplines required of them.

The first light of day spread along the sky and turned the pine-needle floor ginger-bread brown beside us. No caper-caillie came. The group looked to me for a signal to move, but I persisted, deadening any thought of movement by a finger pressed to my lips. We sat on. I felt sure that there were birds around us, but, after half an hour more, as the sun began to rise, I gave up and we left the wood.

'Never mind,' I said. 'A little disappointment whets the appetite even keener for tomorrow!' They all agreed and we went home for breakfast.

On our way back through the village we came across a little old man in a charcoal-grey suit advancing towards us on an elderly bicycle. He was a stranger, I knew, but he smiled brightly at us and stopped to talk.

'Good morning,' he offered, 'you look like birdwatchers.'

He stared at our strange clothing and unanimous agreement at his deduction. 'Where have you been this morning?'

'Up in the pinewoods,' I said, 'up there.' I pointed vaguely to the forested hills all round.

'Oh! How nice,' he smiled, as if pinewoods were rare, 'and what have you been looking for there?'

'Capercaillie,' I answered, not really wishing to go any further. It was clear from his expression that he had no idea what a capercaillie was, and to disguise his ignorance he changed the subject.

'I'm far too old to go birdwatching,' he said, 'but I love the countryside, and I come up here every year and cycle round the quiet roads enjoying it all.' Whereupon he began to re-mount his aged bicycle and with a cheery 'Good luck with your birdwatching!' he rode away.

The following morning we returned to the woods and tried again. To my annoyance the same thing happened. We saw a roe buck and some small forest birds, but not one feather of a capercaillie. That evening we were out again. Caper sometimes feed in the open in the dusk and we went to a place where I had seen them doing this. There was nothing to be seen. On the third morning I changed sites and moved ten miles to a whole new area, this time of old pine forest.

The pinewood was beautiful that morning and we watched crossbills right through the dawn, coming and going in the crowns above us, troops of them, males in bright scarlet and hens sometimes apple green in the sunlight and sometimes shining like the little parrots they resemble. There were crested tits, too, and tree creepers, and my group were ecstatic about that old wood with its twisted scaly branches and cushions of sphagnum moss. But there were no capercaillie.

Later that day I returned to these old woods and spent three hours on my own crawling around examining the needle litter, marking positions where fresh droppings were and where I could see the huge birds had been feeding and roosting. By the time I left for home I was sure I could position them in such a way as to bring success. But for the fourth time we saw nothing. Disgusted, we abandoned the woods and climbed a mountain instead.

As we returned in the Land Rover from our mountain on the evening of the fourth day, we passed through the village. The little old man with silver hair was standing outside the hotel. We waved to him and he signalled us to stop.

'Do tell me,' he said excitedly, 'what I have seen. I have been cycling round the forestry plantations on the tracks, and I keep seeing huge black birds flying up from among the trees. I've never seen birds so big, do you know what they could be?'

'Huge black birds?' I repeated painfully. 'As big as a turkey perhaps?'

'Oh yes! Huge birds. Like this!' He stretched his arms as wide as he could. I was conscious of a certain amount of shuffling going on in the Land Rover behind me and I cleared my throat.

'Er, yes,' I said. 'These are birds called capercaillie. They are grouse actually, very large forest grouse. Would you mind telling me exactly where you have seen them?'

'Oh, Everywhere!' came the enthusiastic reply. 'I've seen dozens of them almost everywhere I've been. Capercaillie are they? How interesting. Yes. Well! Well! Thank you, thank you so much. Very interesting to me, you know. I expect you see them all the time.'

'Not all the time,' I answered, and there was indelicate laughter from behind me.

Later that evening I returned secretly to the hotel with a map and sought out the little old man. I managed to extract the information I needed, and, on the fifth morning, since I had exhausted all my own ideas, we drove gently along the very tracks he had told me. To my conflicting chagrin and relief, just as the little old man had said, capercaillie arose from the track in front of and beside us all through the dawn. We saw the birds well, cocks and hens, and the group were very excited. Even as we left the forest in broad daylight to return to the Kennels for breakfast, we came round a corner to discover two great caper cocks fighting in the middle of the track. I stopped the Land Rover only fifteen feet from them and for fully five minutes we watched them circling and strutting, wings out and tails erect in a huge black fan. It was a most striking view and even though they impaled us fixedly with piercing glossy eyes, their blood was up and their quarrel was more important to them. Red wattles were gorged and the feathers on the back of their necks stood out until they looked like shimmering green scales belonging to some reptilian monster. They suddenly flew at each other striking heavily with fore-wings and powerful pine-plucking bills. They disengaged and circled again, now heads down like a fighting cock, now held high with dignity and arrogance. Without any warning one bird spun round and flew away. The victor, apparently not at all surprised by this turn of events, stood for a moment in full profile so that the world could admire his achievement and obvious mastery of that part of the forest, and then he strutted away, swaggering almost, off the road and into the needley darkness of the trees.

One of our earliest successes – if success can be quantified by the amount of pleasure gained from it – was the duck pond. I had long wanted to keep ducks and since there was a great congregation of wild mallard around us whenever the fields behind the house were flooded, I thought it would add to the appeal of the place to have a full-winged stock bred in captivity which could fly to and from the river with the wild birds. That part of the exercise was successful from the first. Mallard do very well in captivity, and in the rushy pen Peter and I constructed by fencing in half an acre of sloping ground in front of the house, they nested in baskets in the long grass and brought their fluffy broods to the water of a small round pond only a few yards from the kitchen door. These birds born in captivity were allowed the full use of their wings and were soon wheeling round the house from pond to riverfields and back again. They were a constant joy to us, planing in on vibrating pinions out of the dawning sky, often fifteen or twenty mallard at a time, haggling loudly over the grain we threw out for them daily. It gave me disproportionate pleasure to walk out to the duck pen in the semi-darkness of early morning, to call into the misty air and to hear my ducks answer from somewhere far out in the river-fields. Suddenly the air all round me would be roaring with the turbulence of banking wings and dark bodies would plummet into the pond beside me so thick and fast that they were impossible to count.

That part of the exercise was always a success, although we had had trouble enough lining the pond with polythene in the first instance. The area to be flooded measured some fifteen yards by eight with a large island in the middle. Peter and I bought a roll of industrial polythene and sat and wondered how we were to join the edges together to make a sheet of the right size and shape. After much disagreement amongst ourselves – and, incidentally, with the doubtful help of Roy Jonas, complete with Land Rover, who happened to be passing at the time – we decided to search Inverness for a polythene welding machine which would heat-seal the edges permanently together.

Before long we found one, possibly the only one, in a large commercial bakery where it was used for sealing sticky buns into bags. But unfortunately this machine, efficient though it was, was designed exclusively for the sealing of small polythene bags at most six inches wide. We had some forty yards of polythene to weld, which constituted some two hundred and forty separate welds on this tiny machine. Added to this complication, to make up the edges of our sheets satisfactorily, we had to unroll the polythene for several yards behind the machine in two parallel lines which could be fed evenly into the machine in a controlled fashion.

Luckily it was a Saturday and the bakery was not in operation. It was just as well. The three of us wound that wretched polythene into an inconceivable tangle of crumpled, snake-like coils which quickly became vilely sticky from the icing sugar with which the whole of the interior of the factory seemed to be coated. Everything we touched was sticky with it, particularly the welding machine, and the whole place gave off a sickly cake-shop smell which became so unpleasant after the first hour of working, mixed with the foul odour of burning polythene from the machine, that our tempers frayed and our language deteriorated.

Perhaps after two hours we neared the end of our huge, sticky serpent which lay in a crumpled heap in a corner of the bakery while the last lifeless feet of its tail were fed laboriously through the machine. We had reached the stage where we could only operate it for a few minutes at a time before rushing outside into the fresh air to rid our lungs of the acrid fumes. When at last it was finished we dragged the animal outside, past the incredulous janitor, in a fifty-yard procession of coming and going as it was bundled unceremoniously into the back of the Land Rover. The icing sugar was everywhere, all over our clothes and in our hair. It was days before we rid ourselves of its cloying stickiness and I retch instantly at the smell of a sticky bun to this day. In comparison to the welding, the laying of the polythene in the boggy bottom of a pit dug by a passing J.C.B. in return for a cup of tea for the driver, was easy. Peter and I slipped and floundered in the liquid mire and became so entangled in the folds of now greasy polythene that we had periodically to walk away in order to work out what we were actually doing; but the black peat-mud was fresh and clean-smelling, and we were out under the summer sky and felt none of the pressures which had so daunted us in the cake factory.

Finally, some days later, the pond was complete and full. We tapped a burn high on the hill above the Kennels and syphoned water in an alkathene pipe downhill to the pond. A gentle trickle kept the pond full and provided sufficient replacement to keep the water clear and pure. We erected a six-foot fence around the enclosure and imported some colourful species of duck to keep on the pond as an ornamental collection. We had garganey teal, pintail, wigeon, common teal, and gadwall as well as the mallard. They looked very fine perched on the island preening in the sun, glossy heads nodding to each other and their inverted reflections shimmering back from the surface of the water. They were ornamental and useful in that we could use them to teach wildfowl identification and illustrate various facets of bird behaviour and physiology, using the over-tame and ever-obliging mallard as a hand-held demonstration of feather structure and formation, or the mechanics of a webbed foot or dabbling bill. And that was that little project complete and working – so we thought.

Months slipped by until it was winter once again. That autumn brought us hard frost early on, in September, so that the trees turned into outrageous colour almost overnight and then the leaves fell, all together, so that autumn effectively lasted only a few days. The ducks were contented, well-fed and coping well with the ice which formed nightly on their pond and which Peter and I broke and removed every day. Suddenly one morning there was a pintail missing. We had expected some degree of predation sooner or later, but because the pond was so near the house and the road, and because Max patrolled the enclosure several times a day, urinating copiously on the fence-posts at the corners, we had thought it would take extremely dire circumstances to bring foxes in to steal from the pond itself.

On the following morning there was a gadwall drake missing. I began to worry. On the third morning another pintail had gone, and so, reluctantly, Peter and I decided to shut them up at night. We had built a night enclosure inside the main pen which was a veritable wire-netting fortress. It had double thickness netting all round the base and a ceiling netting and support wire right across the top. The doors were an excellent fit and there was no chance of a fox digging its way in because we had buried the netting deep in the peaty soil and placed a rim of stones around the outside. Nothing ever did get in. Nor, for that matter, did a duck ever get out.

The first night we herded the pinioned ducks into the night pen, and left one wigeon drake on the pond with the full-winged mallard. He had been obstinate and we reckoned that if we couldn't catch him a fox couldn't either. But we were wrong. In the morning he was gone. That day I smoothed large areas of mud around the pond and night pen to get a set of footprints, just to make sure it was not a local dog or perhaps a human. That night we got all the birds in except the mallard and all was well. In the morning there were no prints.

The sixth night was altogether more dramatic. I awoke at four in the morning to hear a great kevuffle going on amongst the mallard which were flying round and round the house quacking loudly. Since most of the other species in the pen were largely mute there was little sound from them, but I suspected that it was there the intruder was concentrating his efforts. I rushed out with a gun, a torch and Max, and stood barefoot on the track pointing my weapon and flashlight menacingly in all directions. I saw nothing. After several minutes I was so cold that I crept back to bed and nursed my frost-bitten toes back to life. In the morning one of my tamest full-winged mallard drakes was missing. This was getting serious.

In one week I had lost two pintail, a gadwall, a wigeon and a mallard, ducks worth some £40. Clearly I had to stop this or I would have no ducks at all. On the seventh night I sat all night in the Land Rover parked in the middle of the enclosure with the headlights pointing across to the pond and the night pen. I had a loaded shotgun across my lap and I nearly died of cold several times. My plan was to snap on the lights and shoot as soon as I heard a commotion, but nothing came near the place all night, and for all my woollies and jackets, socks and hat, I had to be resuscitated in the morning with massage and whisky.

This was injury added to insult and I was humiliated and angry. I sought to destroy the fox without further ado.

I procured a dead chicken and tied it to a stake in the ground in the middle of the pen. That night the fox came and took it. I procured another and the same thing happened.

Yet another boiling fowl was tied to the stake and once again the greedy raptor came and took it. Now, I thought, I have got you. The fox was so used to coming to this easy prey that all I had to do was to tie a string to the next chicken and retire to the house where I could sit in a window with the string tied to my finger.

Once again I lost a night's sleep, but no fox came. When I went out in the morning to my absolute disbelief a large fat mallard drake lay dead and headless inside the night pen. One mesh hole in the wire was larger than all the others. Some ultra-cunning predator had inserted a paw, grabbed the sleeping duck, dragged its head and neck out through the hole until it had jammed, bitten the head and neck off, and retreated abandoning the corpse on the inside.

I examined the wire and the ground around very carefully. I now knew this was not a fox. No fox, despite its largely mythological cunning, could hold a mallard head in one paw. It had to be an animal with a fully prehensile hand or with retractable claws of considerable strength. There were no footprints and there was not one hair left on the wire. It was still guesswork, although I strongly suspected my neighbour's cat.

The next night I pegged the mallard corpse to the ground and laid the string to the Land Rover parked fifteen yards away. I had the trap set by dusk and sat quietly in the vehicle until ten o'clock. I then slipped quietly out and back to the house for a quick reviving whisky and to say goodnight to Sorrel. I was in the house only ten minutes before slipping out again and tiptoeing back to the Land Rover. When I climbed in, taking special care not to let the door bang, I couldn't find the string. I snapped on my torch just in time to see the end of it disappearing through the front ventilator. I could scarcely believe my eyes. My hand jerked forward and jammed down the headlight switch. There, in a pool of dazzling light was a cat coolly eating the duck. I threw myself out of the Land Rover and fired both barrels simultaneously at the flashing green eyes in front of me. There was a hideous shriek and the cat bowled over like a skittle. Then to my horror, it bounded away like a tiger, sprung up on to the wire fence, leapt down again and disappeared into the dark forest beyond.

I stood there in total disbelief. My heart thumped so hard and so fast I thought it was going to break loose. It seemed incredible enough that the cat had come while I was in the house and not run away when I returned, but that I should have shot it at such close range and obviously only wounded it was cruelly unfair to me and the cat. I have always especially hated wounding anything. In the days when I did deer-control in the south-west of England I had prided myself on never wounding a deer. I had never been a good shot with a shotgun, but I had cleanly killed literally hundreds of rabbits at far greater distances than this cat, and running as well. I ran back to the house and fetched Max. He picked up the scent straight away, and, strapping a strong torch onto the barrels of my gun I reloaded and set off after him into the trees.

We thrashed about in that dark jungle for an hour. It was clear that the cat had headed up a steep bank and into a tangle of fallen trees and brushwood so thick that even Max couldn't penetrate it. I guessed that it would lie up there for some time, so I called Max off and returned to the house.

In the morning I was determined to find it, whether it had died of wounds in the night or whether it was still alive. I had a friend who was living at that time only a few miles away, who was expert at handling dogs. He had pointers and setters and could be relied upon to find almost any variety of game with them. I telephoned him at dawn and explained the situation to him. He kindly agreed to come straight over with two trained dogs.

When he arrived he was dressed as usual in a long tweed jacket and breeches and matching hat. He was a retired gentleman who had spent a lifetime in the country and was an expert on a great many country pursuits from wildfowling to fly-fishing. He was certain he could find the cat and we set off into the woods together. His dogs, a pointer and a setter, worked the ground back and forth, quartering the leaf-strewn forest floor until they found a scent. Then they were off, up into the woods so fast that my friend had to check them in order that we could catch up. Soon we came to the tangle where I had abandoned the chase the night before, and the dogs burst into it, pressing themselves flat to get beneath logs and between the spiky branches of fallen pine. Then they were out again, leading us up into a part of the dark forest I had never been to because it was so steep and dead. Dense conifer canopy high overhead had shut out the sun years before, and this dark place was the haunt of fungus and moss and smelt of rot and decay. Here the floor was leafless and bare, open soil with patches of emerald-green moss wherever the dim light filtered through. The dogs led us through this forest cave until we began to emerge again into a more mixed woodland. Here, on the fringe was a large dead pine tree, tipped over by the wind so that a huge platform of soil and roots torn from the earth stood ten feet high on its side. The great scaly trunk, supported by its broken branches, ran parallel to the ground obliquely away from us. At the foot of this fallen giant the dogs stood motionless, set in the classical gun-dog pose of noses outstretched, fore-paws raised and tails quivering stiffly behind. We came up breathlessly and as we did so a wounded cat sprang savagely from the dark cave beneath the roots, hissing and spitting at the dogs, mounted the root platform and ran awkwardly out along the horizontal trunk. I had taken the cartridges from my gun because the ground was so steep and slippery and now, as the cat paused to glare at us in full view and only twenty feet away, I was helpless.

My friend took in the situation at a glance. With a flick of his thumb he unbuttoned his jacket, his hand sped down his side and emerged with a sinister gleaming revolver. He levelled, and squeezed the trigger. A sharp report rang out and the cat fell dead from the tree. He quietly replaced the weapon in a deep leather holster and re-buttoned his jacket. Then he walked forward and picked up the cat by its tail. It had been shot neatly between the eyes.

'It's a wildcat,' he said, in his usual quiet voice, 'a young wild she-cat.'

And so it was. All along I had hoped that it was a domestic tabby cat gone wild. Wildcats, although common around Guisachan and Affric were special, and I would not have wished to destroy one unnecessarily. I stood there with my

Wildcat

mouth open at the action of my friend who had given me no inkling that he was armed at all, let alone with a revolver.

'I didn't know you had a gun!' I said, still bewildered.

'You weren't meant to,' came the quiet retort. And so ended the saga of the wildcat and the ducks. We never had any trouble after that, and soon we even gave up putting them away at night.

Chapter Six

'John! Wake up! On the skyline now!' I glanced at Peter to get the direction and lifted my own binoculars to my eyes. A black speck was drifting along the skyline a thousand feet above us. It seemed to hang on a string above the cliff and then it drifted on across the steep face so that we thought it was going past. Suddenly it folded its wings and rocketed down the face swerving left and right round protruding rocks, banking hard to turn in on itself, into a chimney and up again, vertically now, sweeping up the gulley to alight clumsily on a ledge fifty feet below the top of the cliff.

Peter and I had left home at dawn and driven to this lonely place to watch ravens. I had watched them in Wales in the Brecon Beacons some years before where I developed a high regard for these aerobats. We saw them constantly about us in our daily routine, and what we saw often puzzled us. The books told us they nested early in the year, sometimes February, yet we had definitely seen them carrying food to young in June. And in April, when they are all supposed to be busy with their progeny, we had seen huge flocks of them passing a thousand feet over the Kennels, thirty and forty birds at a time, tumbling and spinning and calling and arguing amongst themselves.

We had seen ravens on this cliff regularly all the year round for several years. Now, on a bright March morning we wanted to see exactly at what stage these ravens were in their unusual breeding cycle, and to watch them progress throughout the year.

When we arrived it was still too dark to see the cliff. We

positioned ourselves on a heathery knoll beneath the face, lay back and waited. I dozed off and must have slept for twenty minutes before the raven appeared.

'Bingo!' said Peter.

Our bird had done exactly what we had seen ravens do before – nonchalantly drift along past the site making sure they were unobserved, and then plummet down, twisting in and out round the scattered rocks and stacks on the face, then sneaking into the gully far below the nest and sweeping upwards against the rock to alight at the nest almost invisibly. On this occasion the ravens were nesting in an old eagle's eyrie, a huge mass of dead and sun-bleached twiggery composed largely of woody heather-stems, from which we had watched an eagle chick emerge two summers before. Huge though the adult raven is, beside this nest it looked a speck and was quickly lost from view as it settled inside the twiggy bowl. We watched in silence for half an hour.

'Well that seems fairly conclusive,' Peter said.

'Yes, she's incubating eggs, but we ought to find out for certain.'

It was a bit tricky right at the head of a gully and I was a little alarmed at the prospect of having to climb so high. We stared down our binoculars in silence for several seconds examining every possible approach from above, then left our heather beds and moved forward to the slope which curved steeply upward until it became scree and finally rock face. It was heavy going and we walked in silence to avoid alarming the raven on her nest so high above us. An hour later we stopped for breath. We were above the scree and among the rocks of the almost sheer face. It was veined horizontally with grassy ledges, many with connecting passages of steep and straggly heather, some accessible only by scrambling up the sharp rock for six or eight feet to the next grass ledge. The eagle's nest was out of sight still a long way above us and the glen stretched out like a photograph beneath us. A loch and the river feeding it sparkled silvery-grey in the rising light and the road wound, like a ribbon dropped by a child, this way and that along the shores of the loch and away out of sight to the east and west. The silence was so intense we could hear our own hearts thumping with the effort. A red-throated diver, calling from some invisible point far out on the loch, split the silence with its weird echoing cry like no other bird or animal.

Like Richard Frere before him, my new companion becomes quiet and introverted in the mountains. Peter is a compulsive hill-walker rather than the climber Richard was. Having walked the hills all week with our groups, on his day off Peter would be seen at dawn tiptoeing down the stairs with his boots in his hand, and without a word he would slip away in his car to some remote peak he needed to explore. On days like this he was in his element, and he allowed me little time to recover my wind before springing up and climbing on.

Soon we were rock-climbing the whole time. It was impossible to take a step without first finding a good hand-hold and the loch grew small and distant as the minutes sped by. Finally we reached the foot of the gully. Just as we stopped the raven appeared for a split-second as she darted away upwards and over the top of the cliff. It was obvious she was sneaking away as invisibly as possible which was a sure indication she had young or eggs.

'Here we go,' said Peter as he dug the toe of his heavy boot into the first crevice. There were no hand-holds for the first ten feet and then good luck after that. The eagle's nest was immediately above us now, a huge stack of sticks resembling a stork's nest more than an eagle's and the bottom layers were evidently many years old. A small birch sapling swerved ambitiously out of a crack in the rock wall and had grown to the remarkable height of fifteen feet. Its grip in the rock had withstood gale and storm on that exposed face so I was sure it would hold us. We swung up, Peter first and I quickly behind him, to the base of the small tree. Here and there were fragments of bone and feather, weather-bleached and bare with age. I spotted a withered grouse foot caught in some of the lower twigs of the nest, the remains of eagle prey perhaps decades old. I wondered how many eagle bones were built into the nest since many eaglets perish in the talons of their elder and stronger siblings.

We were now level with the base of the nest. It was six feet deep and occupied the whole of the shelf it was perched on. The walls either side were sheer and flat. The overhang loomed out above us blotting out the sky and the sunlight. There was suddenly a strong smell of decomposition.

'Where the hell do we go now?' asked Peter, searching the flat walls for a purchase of any kind.

'There's only one thing for it,' I said. 'I'll have to give you a leg up onto the nest shelf.' We shuffled around until I had got a good position and then Peter climbed up my back until he was standing on my shoulders. 'Can you see in?' I groaned as his boots dug into my neck.

'No, nowhere near,' came the strained reply, 'I need another two feet at least. Hang on.'

There was a heave which seemed to fracture both my collar bones and the weight was gone. I closed my eyes as a boot swept past my nose to an accompaniment of grunts and heavy breathing from above.

'Four eggs!' shouted Peter.

'Well done. Now come down and we'll let her get back to them.'

There was a good deal of shuffling going on up there and a constant fall-out of dust and small twigs rained down on me, but I dared not look up for fear of getting dust in my eyes – one of the most hazardous things that can happen to you on a rock face.

'What are you doing?' I shouted.

'Trying to turn round.'

Seconds ticked by. All sign of Peter had vanished.

'Peter?'

'Yes?'

'Are you hatching the bloody eggs?'

'No. I'm turning round, I tell you.'

'It's taking a hell of a long time.'

'It's all right for you down there, there happens to be two hundred years of eagle junk in my way.'

Another minute went by painfully slowly.

'John?' came a timid voice.

'Hullo!'

'I'm stuck.'

'You're what?'

'Stuck!'

'What do you mean, stuck? You got up there, didn't you? Do the same thing in reverse.'

'I can't.'

'Why not?'

'Because I can't. There's nothing to hang on to.'

'Well you can't stay there forever.'

'I'm glad you realize that.'

'What do you want me to do?' I asked. Silence, while Peter thought. 'Shall I go for help?' No reply.

It began to rain.

'Bugger!'

'What's the matter?' I asked.

'It's raining up here.'

'Oddly enough it is down here, too. You'd better hurry up and find a way down or the rock will be as treacherous as hell.' No comment from above. Suddenly a thought occurred to me. 'Peter, if I climb the birch and bend it over towards you do you think you could jump into it?'

'Yes, but do you think it will hold the weight of both of us?'

'I don't know,' I replied, 'but at least if it broke it would bend us a long way down towards the ledge first.' I looked down the thousand or so feet below to the scree slope and the brooding loch. 'I don't much fancy missing the ledge,' I said to myself but evidently loud enough for Peter to hear.

'Bloody hell!' I heard him expostulate.

'What's the matter?'

'I hadn't looked down before.'

'Well don't look again,' I said. I began to climb the tree.

We were almost level now and about eight feet apart. I was swaying alarmingly in a ridiculously small tree, and Peter was standing beside the nest as white as a sheet and looking very unhappy. He was on a shelf of rock about the size of a small tea-tray, with the rickety pile of debris jamming him back against the overhanging rock above. He could see nothing below except the scree at the bottom of the mountain, the rest being hidden by the ledge he stood on and his boots.

I leant over towards him. The tree swayed across and we joined hands.

'Now then, make a grab for the tree below me.'

There was a moment of all-blinding fear as the little tree lurched, swaying out from the face of the rock as if to pitch us both into the loch below. Then it swayed back again, in to the rock and the gulley. As it did so we both slithered frantically down the shiny stem to the ledge. We were a tangle of gripping hands and stabbing boots as we struggled to hold on. A few seconds later we were seated on the shelf, both perfectly safe, both suddenly exhausted and cold. The rain spat icily on us and a chill wind whined up the face so that we shivered and buttoned our collars to the top. The same gust spread across the loch below, ruffling the surface in a wide arc like the wrinkles in a counterpane.

That year was memorable for some of the characters who joined us. There was Mr Howard, a parks' superintendent from Berkshire, whom we booked into a family hotel in Drumnadrochit. When I went down to meet him he was standing in the foyer choosing postcards. Birdwatchers tend to stand out in a crowd, and although there was no crowd, this one stood out well. He was a short man with thick-lensed spectacles and just-got-out-of-bed hair. He wore a dark green cotton anorak with the badges of many bird and nature conservation societies bachelor-stitched on at random wherever there happened to be a space. Out of his top pocket bulged a field-guide to British birds, and round his neck hung a well-used pair of binoculars. There was no doubt that this was my man so I strode forward to greet him.

'How do you do?' I said, sticking out my hand, 'you must be Mr Howard.'

'Yeah. That's right,' he said. 'Arry 'Oward's the name. I don't know why I bother with the H's I never use 'em.' Harry actually turned out to be a very keen and experienced bird-watcher, and he kept the group in hysterical laughter throughout his week.

A second and very different character to emerge that year was Roddy Miller. Roddy had come to us first in 1973 as a schoolboy of fourteen. He and a friend had stayed in the condensating caravan at the Kennels while they attended a course. After they had left Roddy wrote thanking us for having him and offering his services as a general helper during his future school holidays. We received many such requests and it was inevitable that we had to turn most of them down. Whether it was that Roddy had impressed himself on us with his remarkable schoolboy knowledge of ornithology, or whether he was just lucky, I don't know, but the answer was yes and he lost no time in taking us up on it. It was one of the best acts of Fate to fall our way during those formative years and he has added greatly to the quality of our activities ever since.

That year he came back in the summer for several weeks. He busied himself with whatever needed doing at the time, from painting the outside of the house and himself a powerful shade of champagne cream, to tending the ducks and their numerous broods of chicks which were always in trouble of some kind. Whatever he was supposed to be doing he was also birdwatching, perpetually and tirelessly. He performed no task without his Zeiss binoculars round his neck or at least within reach, and by his constant vigilance and skilled scrutiny of every stirring feather within his vision, we came to accumulate information about our surroundings on a far more intense scale than I had ever managed to achieve alone. In those early days I was very much the tutor to Roddy, helping him as much as I could, giving him reading lists to take back to school, and encouraging him to take every opportunity of getting experience in the field. He worked so hard at this that within two years his knowledge had increased to a level beyond my own. I had never specialized so particularly in ornithology as he chose to, and after a while I found myself

Heather and bog asphodel

using his encyclopaedic knowledge of bird records to supplement my own observations. Later on, when Roddy became a full-blooded member of the staff, it often amused me to introduce him to the groups which were to be in his charge. More than once I saw indignation rise in their faces at being palmed off with a schoolboy. Far more than once they came to me in the evenings, taking me quietly to one side to tell me how remarkable they considered his knowledge to be.

One day after some particularly arduous chore I had thrown myself down on the grass outside the Kennels and was staring blankly up at the blue sky when I fancied I saw a bird. I reached out for my binoculars and focused in on the speck. Even through my x8 glasses it was barely discernible. I called for Peter and Roddy and we lay on our backs, all three, and stared at it. The light was so bright and the speck so minute that it was almost impossible to get any real definition on the image. It could possibly have been an eagle, but we knew eagles well and we weren't happy with that answer. It appeared to be osprey-shaped, but we weren't satisfied with that either. Finally we dismissed it as a mystery and thought no more about it.

Several days later, quite by chance, the same thing happened again. Examining some gulls passing over I picked up a speck far higher, thousands of feet higher, drifting across the sky. It was so high that when Peter came to examine it he never managed to find it before I, too, had lost sight of it. When it happened a third time, and it was Roddy who found it this time I think, our interest was galvanized. We now examined the sky at every opportunity when there was no cloud and we had a moment to spare. It was remarkable how many times we did manage to locate this extraordinary bird. During that summer we must have seen it seven or eight times, but never well enough to be sure of its identity. Always it appeared to be drifting – it was too high to tell whether it was beating its wings or not – from east to west on the same flight-line, and always at this extreme height.

I was talking to Roy Dennis, Highlands Officer for the Royal Society for the Protection of Birds, one day and I remembered to ask him his opinion of our mystery. He told me that a similar phenomenon had occurred in south Scotland between the Clyde and the Forth, and birdwatchers there had finally identified these mysterious high-flyers as gannets and kittiwakes crossing from one coast to the other. It just so happens that one of the shortest routes across the Highlands would be from the Beauly Firth to Loch Duich, a distance in a straight line of about fifty miles, and Guisachan lies mid-way between the two. Although we never verified this theory it seems the most likely explanation, and the fact that we picked the speck up so often suggests that it is a route regularly used by many birds. Ever since then I have watched gannets closely at sea and I have never seen one rise higher than about one and a half thousand feet nor have I yet seen one over land except at their breeding colonies. Perhaps we know far less about gannets than we think.

Because the Arab states began to throw their weight around at about that time and world petrol prices went crazy, we began to run up dramatically high fuel bills for our vehicles. From the Kennels to the two hotels we habitually used in Drumnadrochit was eighteen miles and so we were often having to do four times that distance even before we had travelled to our destination for the day. The total was often well over a hundred miles a day and the Land Rover was one of the worst possible vehicles for consumption. When the prices started to escalate I did a quick projection and worked out that our motoring costs would certainly double, and possibly treble.

Sorrel, Peter and I held an emergency meeting and decided to use the two flats as accommodation at the Kennels, thereby saving on two scores. The petrol bill was slashed by not having to run a collection service, and the fees we were paying out to hotels now contributed substantially towards the ever-increasing costs of the Kennels. We did a quick conversion of one or two rooms, poor old Peter was evicted from his nice new flat, and got pushed into a cramped upper room in the house, and his flat supplied us with another series of bedrooms for guests.

For the first time Sorrel was actively involved with the course members. It was ironical that this should have come at a time when she was, as the Bible puts it, 'great with child'.

But it bothered her not a whit, as she dashed about the house red-cheeked and vulgarly healthy. It meant that for the first time we got to know our visitors as people rather than as names in a hotel register, and we liked it. The evenings around the fire were rewarding and the day's activities were often relived over and over again in the friendly glow of the pine-log in the hearth.

It meant, too, that Sorrel suddenly became a cook. The necessity to produce seven traditionally Scottish dinners and seven farmhouse breakfasts every week for maybe a dozen or more hungry people made our little kitchen sing with activity and Sorrel revelled in it. Quite without planning it the future of our business was reshaping itself around us, and after we had run it as a residential Field Centre for a few weeks I was sure that I wanted nothing else. It was the obvious, logical way to operate and I found myself idly planning newer and larger centres in any old building I came across. The country-house dream I had harboured back in the early days loomed large once again. But I had much to think about in the immediate future and I had to make a conscious effort to abandon dreams and cope with the present day by day.

Suddenly the season was over. The people had gone and our rambling house was our own again. Peter and I spent a few days tying up odds and ends, painting the eaves and the window frames which had never got done before the season started, and then he too was gone. He was away south to Kent to his family for a holiday and a break. One of the great satisfactions of a seasonal business is the wonderful feeling of release when it ends. While it doesn't last long because we are essentially active, those first few days after everyone has gone are magical. That year they were extra special because of the imminence of an infant. Those were the last evenings we could spend around the fire together as a couple, rather than as a family. The winter came early that year and there was snow on the fields all round us before November was out. I stoked the log pile high with dead pine from the woods, and when I brought them in to bank up the fire they often sizzled and spat with the melting snow and ice on them.

By December the frost was with us and the valley silent in its grip. Sorrel grew so great with child that it seemed she could expand no further. The date came and went and still she grew until it was thought unwise for her to stay at the Kennels any longer. We drove to Inverness and I left her in the hospital where she was to remain for several days. One evening I went in to see her as usual and the nurses let me stay until late. At ten o'clock I got up to go. On my way out the Sister said that the baby would be induced if it did not come soon. Sorrel was still writing advertisements for the coming season when I passed by her window on my way to the car.

By eleven I was home and undressing to go to bed. Suddenly the phone was ringing. 'If you want to be present at the birth of your child you must come very quickly,' said the nurse. Snatching only a coat I rushed out to the car. Because of the cold the roads were empty and the villagers asleep in front of their televisions as I roared through. As I arrived at the delivery room I heard the consultant ask 'Where is the husband?'

'He won't be here for half an hour,' came the reply. 'I have just phoned him.'

Ten minutes later our son was born. Warwick, we called him, and Sorrel was triumphant as she held the newborn infant to her, seconds after its birth. It took me the rest of the night to get home. Much whisky and celebration later, I arrived in the dawn to greet the startled dogs and the wide-flung doors as I had left them.

I only just had time to dismantle and remake an old worm-eaten cradle before they came home. I had found it in a sale-room in Inverness, an old Scottish rocking cradle with a hood and high sides. I took it apart and re-fashioned it painstakingly from white pine. I spent those last fireside evenings sanding it to perfection and lining it with pink silk and braid. I was finished not a day too soon.

Chapter Seven

Early in 1975 I received a letter from a man who wanted to come and talk to me about our business. He mentioned starting a project of his own on the west coast and wanted to see if we could be mutually helpful to each other in any way. Sorrel and I viewed this approach with suspicion, since a year never went by without several approaches by pie-in-the-sky-eating nutters who made us wild proposals of every bizarre nature. One man offered himself as a fully fledged profit-sharing partner without any capital introduction or expertise of any sort. When, at the end of this proposal, we asked him in what way we were going to benefit from his presence he admitted that this was something he had not given much thought to.

But this new approach was clearly not a partnership deal. When he arrived in a smart city suit and white shirt I found myself apologizing for my own ragged and patched tweeds and darned stockings. I might have guessed he was an ex-Naval officer. His name was Charles Barrington and his venture was mildly comparable but far from being in conflict with our own. He had bought the first of a series of modern ocean-going yachts, a Rival 34, in fact, with which to start a yacht charter business on the Isle of Skye. He showed me his plans and proposals neatly laid out in a portfolio and I was struck with the efficiency of them. Later on, with a new project, I copied this approach myself and I am grateful to Charlie for that lesson. Perhaps we were able to help him a little that day, perhaps not. All these ventures work or fail only by the narrowest of margins and often, I have come to realize, succeed not so much as a result of hard work, but of sheer gambling courage. We have seen many come and go now, ventures of many different kinds, some set up by Highlanders, and many more by immigrants from the south like ourselves. It is hard when after perhaps two years of real toil and glowing enthusiasm one sees a project fail and the owners creep away in disillusionment.

Predictably, Seol Alba, as Charlie named his enterprise, hicupped once, twice, and settled down to an active and busy existence.

In the spring, when Charlie Barrington had arrived, so to speak, on Skye, he came to visit us again with the suggestion that we collaborate on a small expedition to some of the more remote Hebridean Isles to study grey seals which came ashore there every autumn to calve and to mate. I had long wanted to do just that and we quickly agreed. The date was fixed, not by us but by the seals, since there would be little point in going when they were not there, and we chose the first week in October. Since it was an exploratory expedition we decided to restrict our numbers to seven, the number of berths in his Rival, two of whom would be Peter and I. We worked our way through that summer with the new and rising excitement of our Hebridean voyage ahead. Like Lapland it required a good deal of research and our evenings were busy with it.

Of the several possible grey seal breeding stations we could have chosen, many were impossible because of their extreme exposure to the elements. North Rona, the most northerly of the Hebridean Isles, is constantly storm-battered and requires a major expedition to visit, although it is there that the greatest congregation of grey seals in the world assembles every year to breed. The government have recently launched a control programme (1978) for seals around the north, including North Rona and Orkney which together form the bulk of the population, so figures available now may not be relevant any more, but it was certainly correct that some eight thousand seals visited North Rona each year. Compared with this, all the other Hebridean colonies are small, mostly representing an annual haul out of under one thousand seals.

One by one we considered the possibilities, the Monach Isles, Oidhsgeir, Gunna, Haskeir, and the Treshnish Isles. The main problem was that the grey seal breeds on the autumnal equinox, between mid-September and the end of October. The actual date of birth of most calves in a colony seems to fluctuate from year to year, but always falls in that season. Since this is the only time of year that the seals do come properly ashore for any length of time, it is, apart from being the most interesting, the only time available for study.

In the Hebrides the equinox means spring tides and high incidence of Atlantic gales. That rules out all those unprotected westerly islets without an anchorage. Only the Treshnish Isles offered any sort of protection for a yacht and that was scant. But the formation of the islands, of volcanic origin, has permitted the erosion of the basalt lava to form cliffs falling sheer to the sea with a platform at approximately sea level, so that it was possible to lie in the lee of these cliffs, and to camp on the wave-cut platform amongst the breeding seals, with a certain amount of protection from the prevailing westerly and south-westerly winds.

We set sail on 29 September from Armadale on the Isle of Skye. There was a steady drizzle and the grey waters of the harbour sizzled with the impact of rain on the oily-calm surface. Beyond the pier the Sound of Sleat looked cold and chill. There was little wind and the mainland loomed dully from over the water. We had first to cross the Sound to the port of Mallaig on the mainland to collect one of the crew and we did so on engine power alone, donking along through the rain with the yacht on an even keel.

Below decks there was a for'ard cabin with two bunks and chain locker, a tiny lavatory, mysteriously called 'the heads', the only reason for which seemed to be that in order to use the machine one almost certainly cracked one's head on the ceiling. This arrangement was scantily separated from the for'ard cabin and the main galley by two thin plywood doors which provided such scant privacy that Peter and I took one look at it and at the two girls who had the misfortune of being allocated the for'ard cabin, and decided that we would actually arrange to be constipated for the entire week.

The main cabin slept four by an ingenious conversion of seats and a table into bunks. There was also a cooker and a sink and ample space for storage. On my first visit below decks a cursory inspection revealed these six bunks straight away, but the seventh eluded me completely. Charlie Barrington allocated the accommodation with a Naval air and left himself out.

'Where are you going to sleep?' I asked him, thinking that either he could not count or that he didn't know there were only six bunks in his boat.

'In the skipper's bunk,' came the cheery reply.

'The skipper's bunk?' I asked.

'Yes. Down here,' he said, pointing to nothing in particular. I peered in the direction of his finger.

There was a small hole disappearing back towards the stern of the boat in which one might have thought of stowing a fishing-rod or a pair of oars, or, with difficulty, a small child. The prospect of Charlie, a close-on six foot, burly sailor, getting a night's sleep stowed, like luggage, in that damp slot between the engine and the chart table, seemed to me to be incredible. But he did it, regularly, without either a shoe-horn to get him in or a cork-screw to get him out, and with no fuss. The whole Naval institution rose considerably in my estimation.

When we arrived at Mallaig our crew member was standing on the quay with his kit-bag on his shoulder like the time-honoured mariner and Peter and I were instructed to prepare to throw a line ashore. A Norwegian trawler lay between us and the quay and my first attempt with a coil of wet rope so entangled an unsuspecting Norwegian sailor that a stream of Norse was smartly returned with the now badly knotted cord. I mumbled apologies and set to re-coiling my rope.

'Anti-clockwise!' roared Charlie and I looked about me to see who was doing what wrong.

'Coil it the other way!' he screamed again from the cockpit

and I suddenly realized it might be me he was addressing.

Peter, meanwhile, had done better and his coil of rope had landed ashore. Suddenly our crew was aboard, Charlie and the Norwegian were sharing another private exchange and we were pulling away again out of the harbour and into the Sound. I was still untying knots and re-coiling my confused coil. It was clear that I was not going to be a great success at sailing.

As we struck out into open sea the swell increased and our yacht began to pitch and roll. A little wind sprang up and there was a great call from the cockpit for sail. People hauled on ropes (called sheets, I discovered) and ratchets clicked and churned. Shiny white sails appeared and were whisked into the sky with a flurry where they filled and bowed in high bulging curves. I was just beginning to think that it was all rather beautiful and that there might be something in this sailing game after all when to my total surprise the yacht keeled over and the deck disappeared from beneath my feet. More by good luck than design I was hanging on to a shroud and as my bottom hit the hard glass-fibre deck I found myself face to face with a large wave. I ducked and it went away, to my relief without wetting me. I looked up to see five faces laughing at me from the cockpit.

After an hour or so at sea I had got the hang, literally, of the antics such vessels play, and had learnt to keep well clear of ropes and pulleys and acres of flapping canvas. I found a position in the bows where I was largely untroubled by all the activity and where I could concentrate on the water ahead.

It is the silence of sail which, even to the hardened land-lubber like myself, makes the whole experience so captivating. After the thudding engine and the diesel exhaust in our faces as the wind whipped it along the length of the boat, this gentle swish of water and the occasional flap of cloth above were greatly soothing and relaxing. Manx shearwaters skimmed across the surface of the waves beside us and black guillemots scuttled like tiny penguins to get out of our path. The horizon all round was studded with the looming bulk of mountains and islands, Rhum, Canna, Skye, and the mainland behind. It no longer mattered that it was drizzling, or that my feet were wet from occasional waves which broke over the bows with quick stinging spray. I could feel the incipient adventure rising within me as all the toils and pressures of our busy season dropped away.

We spent that night in the anchorage at Kinloch on Rhum. It was sheltered and still and the wind echoed down to us from the high cloud-lost corries of the mountains above. The shrouds rattled gently and gulls cried softly overhead as darkness crept up to our tiny vessel and overtook it. We had rowed ashore in the dinghy and collected a young Nature Conservancy zoologist who was to accompany us to the Treshnish Isles. She was sent to the for'ard cabin to bunk with the cook. I hope she enjoyed her one calm night at anchor in that quiet bay, because she enjoyed little else. We unkindly nicknamed her 'The Green Maiden' the following day when, like most of us, she became badly sea-sick. She remained variously green and yellow for a week until we set her ashore again.

In the morning I was awoken by Charlie who brought us mugs of steaming tea. On deck it was barely raining, and there was a slight breeze. The sun was not yet up and the island surrounded us like a huge enveloping backcloth, featureless and foreboding. It is here on these black cliffs that the Nature Conservancy Council are attempting to re-introduce the white-tailed eagle, several of which we had watched at close quarters in Lapland. I could think of no more suitable site for such an attempt, and I look forward to the day when they might be seen again around those soaring heights and stark brooding faces.

After breakfast we, that is to say I, hauled up the anchor since I had flatly refused to partake in any of the other rope-pulling exercises Charlie had proffered my way. What he did not tell me about the anchor was that it had to be raised by hand, leaning out over the water in an inadequate steel cradle, and that as if the iron itself was not heavy enough, it would bring up with it several hundredweight of weed and silt which I had to disentangle and clean before stowing it on his spotless white deck.

He also failed to explain that there is a way of handling an anchor. If you pick it up in the wrong place it turns smartly round, like a snake, and bites your hand. If you attempt to pick it up by its ring-end it is too heavy to lift, and so one automatically goes to raise it by its neck. But modern anchors, unlike the good old solid models seen only nowadays on pub signs, are articulated at the head. If you are unaware of this and pick the thing up logically and sensibly, to disperse .the weight of your load evenly, the heavy steel head swivels viciously round and crushes your fingers against the shaft. I let out a yell of anger and pain as blood spurted from three fingernails at once. So I was relieved of that task, and retired below to nurse my wound and talk to the cook.

When I next emerged some little while later to deliver coffee to the crew, we were under way, motoring out of the anchorage down the long loch to the open sea again. To my delight I arrived in time to witness a piercing shaft of sunlight strike the russet headland and turn it bright gold. At the same moment a huge double rainbow appeared above us, arching from the gilt headland to an orange sea far over to the north.

Soon we were out of the shelter of the Rhum hills, and a brisk wind was whipping the sea into a swell: deep grey troughs and bubbling green crests just creaming at the very peak. Those who knew how to, were again busy with sheets and booms and there were shouts of 'Belay that!' and 'Stow that boathook properly!' from Charlie.

In minutes we were sizzling through the water, all roll gone, the white vessel tossing its head high and pounding down again, flinging the luminous green water into the air where it sparkled and fell in a glitter of sunlit spray. We were passing between Rhum and Eigg, close under the sheer cliffs where in May many thousands of shearwaters breed. As we swept silently along the edge of this fertile island we passed its broad bay with the houses dotted about on their own square fields of multiple hue, and the yellow sand curving round in a great arc with small boats pulled high above the tide and figures moving about them so small and distant as to seem part of another world and another age.

The wind was favourable and we sailed hard all day. Muck slipped by us as a single volcanic hump on our starboard side. Its dark cliffs looked savage and hostile against the grey sky and no birds seemed to wheel above it as we had seen on Eigg and Rhum. As the small isles faded behind us and the open expanse of sea spread out, unsheltered now by any outer isles, the full Atlantic swell swept in from the ocean to meet us. Spray flew from the surging prow, lashing the sails and the cockpit with stinging water, so that as the wind dried our faces the salt collected in our eyebrows and beards.

Somewhere out to the south-west was the Isle of Coll and its partner Tiree beyond it, but their profile is so low that no land was visible to seaward at all. Only the mass of Ardna-murchan and Mull remained on the mainland side to link us with civilization at all. Charlie fiddled with dividers at his charts and came back to the cockpit with a new bearing and we altered course, sailing as close to the wind as would allow us to make good time, for Lunga, the main Treshnish Isle.

Lunch was soup bravely manufactured by the cook in a galley which pitched and tossed beneath her, and a giro-stove which swung alarmingly beneath the brewing pot. Peter and I ate biscuits and pretended that we felt fine. The Green Maiden ate nothing and spent her time either stuck out over the stern like a corpse ready to be buried at sea, or with her head in a bright yellow polythene bucket which made her already green face look as though she had also contracted some especially virulent breed of jaundice.

By mid-afternoon we had sighted land ahead. The islands were as yet indistinct and merged together to form one mass, but they were undisputably land and our spirits rose accordingly. There was still no sign of Coll, and Mull itself was a blurr on the port helm. The wind was still brisk and we estimated reaching our anchorage before nightfall.

One by one the islands took shape. We could soon identify Lunga, the main island with its single hill, and the Dutchman's Cap, far beyond, unmistakable with its hat-like outline. Sgeir nan Chaisteil, too, appropriately named the castellated rock, soon became clear to the west of Lunga, providing a hard battlement silhouette against the falling light on the western horizon.

Suddenly Charlie was barking orders to get the sails down and bagged as we came in amongst the first outlying islets and reefs. It was too risky to sail into these waters in the half-light, and as we stuffed the wet canvas into the stowage bags the engine churned and throbbed into life beneath us. With the decks clear, and Peter and I peering ahead for rocks, we motored slowly between the skerries into calm and sheltered water. Even as we did so the wind seemed to drop away, and a great silence fell over the archipelago. Shags and gulls panicked at our approach and flapped away; the hard slap of cormorant feet on the water and the cries of indignant gulls echoed round about us, intensifying the calm and the absence of the wind we had heard in the sails all day. An hour later, at anchor off Lunga, only a stone's throw from the shore, that same silence was broken by the soft crying of seals on the rocks round about us. It was unmistakably a seal colony. As we drifted quietly into our anchorage, gauging the depth as we neared the silhouette of the land, the first inquisitive seals had come out to watch us. Their glossy faces were all round us, round wet eyes reflecting the lights from the cabin and rising and disappearing with only a deep melancholy sigh to betray their presence. Every now and again a seal would come too close and suddenly panic, crashing away in a wild dive leaving a gaping whirlpool and spray falling all around.

As I leant out over the bows, peering down into the clear water with a torch to see the bottom, these same faces seemed drawn to the beam and by focusing it on the surface I could attract them in until I had a ring of staring eyes around me, eight or ten of them transfixed at the distance they dared to come, and not a whisker nearer. But if I moved the beam on to one of them, they spun away with a great commotion and turbulence so that I could no longer see down through the water. I had to abandon my game for fear of rebuke from Charlie at the helm.

Seals around boat in sea

Late that night, after supper and laughter as we all began to relax from the pitch and toss of the open ocean, as the crew turned into their bunks and the boat lay quiet at her anchor, I slipped over the side and rowed away in the rubber dinghy. The oars scarcely needed to touch the water to slide me gently over the oily calm, until I was mid-way between the yacht and the black, kelp-fringed island of Sgeir nan Chaisteil where the bulk of the seals were.

There is something quintessentially wild and unobtainable about the Hebrides, and I had felt it before during my sojourn on Kyleakin Island. It is an undefinable quality which is as deeply manifest in the moaning of grey seal cows to their newborn pups as in the sight of the land itself, a fractured and storm-battered rock hard against the afterglow on a western horizon.

On the one side lay the yacht surrounded by the shimmering reflection of her cabin lights, and the occasional laughing voices echoing out of the darkness at me. To the other side, and a little nearer, lay fifty or perhaps a hundred grey seal cows invisible on the wet lava shelf among rock-pools and shingle banks thrown up by a thousand years of storm. Their voices, the seal song of timeless Hebridean folklore, rose and fell in a perpetual concert of woodwind and cello. I was transfixed. I felt the absurd desire to abandon my dinghy and slip into the dark water as if by so doing I could shed my ancestry and rejoin the seals as a fellow subordinate to the common enemy of all wild animals. I rowed myself slowly and quietly back to the yacht and the warmth of the yellow cabin lights.

Our skipper brought us tea again at first light. But this time I was out of my bunk before he could pass it to me. We had made a plan to go ashore before breakfast, very quietly, just Charlie and I. We planned to row round Sgeir nan Chaisteil and examine the lava platform to get some idea of how the colony lay. In minutes we had swallowed our scalding tea, swilled our faces in cold water and dressed. The day was mild and dry, but with sufficient cloud to make some rain a strong possibility. Luckily the water was still completely calm in between the islands and there was no need for oilskins. They are noisy and cumbersome to wear in a dinghy, and we wanted to be as unobtrusive as possible.

Already we could see the seals hauled out like cigars on the lava shelf two hundred yards from the Rival, and with binoculars one could easily distinguish the huge volume of bull seals lying apart from the cows and apparently indifferent to them.

The grey seal is Britain's largest mammal. The bulls grow to over nine feet in length and attain a gargantuan weight of up to 630 lbs. The cows are smaller and much sleeker, reaching little over seven feet in length and weighing up to 550 lbs. It is a common and numerous seal in British waters but probably has a world population of under 120,000 animals, over 60 per cent of which are to be found around Britain. In world terms this represents a small population and the grey seal is listed among the rarer species.

It is the seal which, from time to time, is the centre of passionate argument and debate. On the one hand it is damned for diminishing fish stocks, particularly coastal salmon, and for wrecking fishermen's nets. On the other, it is defended by the perennial upsurge of public feeling against the government policy of culling, which is seen as degrading to the humans who kill in cold blood a trusting infant of emotionally appealing appearance.

While the argument rages back and forward the grey seal population happily continues to rise; but conservationists have not been slow to point out that the most dangerous feature of the situation is the habit of the grey seal – and for that matter, puffins and gannets – to congregate in a few huge colonies to breed. There is little doubt that, if commercial considerations became too great and legal protection was relaxed, whole populations could be wiped out with ease at this time of year when they are so vulnerable.

At our approach in the dinghy many of the cows heaved off the rock and submerged. The reef was ringed with turbulence for a few moments as they crashed into the water. Then again we found ourselves ringed in by the dappled blue and grey heads with wide intelligent eyes and long Roman noses gazing intently at us from only a few yards away. Their nostrils flared and clamped shut again, and I could see them pulling back beneath the surface and ghosting through the clear green water beneath the dinghy to rise again on the other side without a ripple and only that melancholy exhalation to give them away.

We stopped rowing and drifted quietly among them. They were sublimely graceful, more so by far than most fish, rolling and spinning in their voiceless underworld, hanging vertically in the water with heads out to watch us, or torpedoing along beneath us in one sinuous power-drive of effortless grace.

Charlie and I completed our reconnaissance and returned to the Rival for Peter. We had found a good place to land where we would not disturb any obvious accumulation of calving seals, and from where we could plan a survey of the colony. We collected our various cameras and lenses and set out again for the lava platform. This time the cows largely ignored us as we rowed up the length of the island still some way out from the shore. A thick band of olive-green kelp waved in the gentle swell and we had to find a channel through it to reach the rock. In a little while we had found an opening and Charlie sculled us in with ease and skill. We pulled ourselves up onto the smooth red rock and quietly hauled the dinghy up behind us.

The platform we were now standing on was wave-cut from a solid volcanic intrusion which had welled up from the earth's crust some fifty million years ago. In West Highland terms it is a new formation, a mere third of the age of the ancient rocks which form the bulk of Highland scenery. On Sgeir nan Chaisteil the rock has been eroded into terraces which correspond to the actual flows of the molten lava. The wave action has polished the surface of the rock to a fine finish so that we were standing on a wide flat platform almost exactly at sea level. At the equinox the high spring tides cover the platform, but for the bulk of the year they are only marginally covered in periods of storm and high swell. Because of this there was no weed on the bare rock, only a fine peppering of barnacles which gave us a good grip on the slippery surface.

To the rear of the platform the lava cliffs rose sheer for fifty feet to a flat top. Here the rock was slowly being broken up by wind and sea action, and huge chunks of basalt had fallen away from the face leaving gaps against the sky and providing excellent cover at the base of the cliffs. In places these boulders, often as large as a house, were jumbled together to form caves and deep chasms, and we were able to move along the cliff face creeping from boulder to boulder in order to get amongst the calving cows without their knowledge of our presence.

Even as we crossed the open terrace on our way to the cliff

face we came across pups asleep on the rock. They lay about like large white maggots until one came close and the soft fleece became distinct. Many were asleep on their bellies, full of rich seal-milk, snoring quietly with tight-shut eyes and nostrils opening and closing like the adults in the water. We found that if we tickled their tummies very gently they stretched their flippers up to their whiskery faces, and yawned widely revealing an array of needle milk teeth like a puppy, and then they settled back to sleep again without ever opening an eye or a tremor of fear or awareness.

We found one newborn fellow with a pale yellow tinge to his white fur and we named him Daffodil. He crooned softly in his sleep as we tickled him and when he awoke he raised his head to examine us with large round eyes, deep sea-weed brown and white-less and gently weeping down his puppy face with the necessary constant tears that prevent his pupils from drying up. Daffodil was newborn, perhaps only a day old, and his umbilical cord was as yet pink and undried. He examined us passively, shifting his gaze from face to face quite without any sign of fear or aggression. He was quite incapable of movement across the rock and seemed resigned to it. I wondered how many thousands of times these liquid seal eyes had looked up into the faces of parties like ours, not with cameras, but with clubs to crush the soft skulls and harvest the fine soft wool pelts.

We climbed carefully over the rocks beneath the cliff and split up, working individually now so as not to miss any cow calving in the crevices below. There were many cows on shore, far more than we could survey at first. There were those which were perhaps not imminent calvers and which were content to lie out on the shelf immediately beside the water, ever ready for a quick retreat into the sanctuary of the sea. These we could count readily and there were fifty or more just on our visible stretch of Sgeir nan Chaisteil. As well as these, there were the cows which had already given birth and which lay alongside their newborn pups sleeping and suckling. The third category were those in which we were really interested – the imminent calvers. These were cows which had come well inshore, perhaps fifty or sixty yards from the sea, right up to the boulder-strewn ground beneath the cliff. We came across several such animals, fast asleep and so heavy in pup that their whole abdomen down to their tail flippers was one huge bulge.

One by one we passed them by. We reckoned that if they were asleep they were probably not immediately ready to give birth. Grey seal birth is dramatically fast, some witnesses report as little as fifteen seconds, and we were anxious to see it for ourselves. Certainly none of these sleeping ladies was showing any signs of contraction or discomfort.

Occasionally we rounded a boulder and came face to face with a cow and suckling pup. When this happened there were two reactions. Either the cow lay inert and rumbled quietly at us, never taking her eyes off us for a second, but making no move away from her offspring; or, alternatively, she would snarl and lunge at us with wide gaping jaws revealing the rows of savagely pointed fish-grabbing teeth in perfect carnivore style. These ladies we allowed to pass. We scrambled back up the rocks to get out of their way as they shuffled angrily away down the shelf to the sea. The departing cow invariably spread alarm amongst the others and there would be a general commotion as they all floundered off into the water. When this happened we had to hide amongst the rocks and lie low for up to half an hour to allow the colony to settle again, before moving on.

Once, as I was rounding a rock backwards, sneaking away from a cow I had disturbed but which had not seen me, I walked right into the jaws of another cow with a tiny pup beside her. I leapt sideways just in time to miss the initial lunge, but tripped and fell as I tried to sprint away over the jumble of boulders and shingle underfoot. In a second, and before I had time to get to my feet, the cow was on me, a rushing snarling carnivore twice my weight and infinitely more powerful. The smell of her hot fishy breath was wet on my face as I kicked wildly at her, showering shingle and stones in her eyes. Grabbing up a large stone I thrust it purposefully into her face less than a yard from me so that she snatched at it and I heard her teeth grate on the hard rock as it was wrenched from my hand. At the same time I scrambled to my feet and leapt away, wildly jumping from rock to rock, my cameras and film disappearing beneath her as she came on again.

In a few more seconds I was out of reach and she returned to her pup only occasionally turning back to snarl at me as I sat on the top of a huge square boulder, heart thumping madly and my chest heaving with exertion. I lay there for many minutes before creeping back to collect my camera, miraculously undamaged, from where it lay pressed into the shingle by the huge weight of her body.

From another prominent position Peter signalled to me that he had seen something interesting, and Charlie and I hurried over to join him. There was a cow a hundred yards or more down the island which Peter had been watching for some minutes. She was alone and high up from the sea. He had noticed her twisting back and forth and writhing on the shingle. This was almost certainly what we were looking for and we climbed down to close in on her.

It took us some minutes to cover the ground which was deeply pitted with chasms and gorges, and when we arrived within some twenty yards or so it was clear that we were just too late. A tiny white pup lay at her tail, wet and bloody and inert. The cow herself was covered in blood from the belly down and had just evicted the afterbirth, in which she lay. She was quite unaware of our presence and, to our surprise, instead of turning to her pup she shuffled slowly off down the shelf and plummeted into the sea. A red stain arose from where she dived and there was a gory trail down the rock where she had travelled.

In a moment or two, quite clean now, she re-emerged, clambered back up the rock and came on towards us and her pup. Now, however, she saw us and turned back. Success had eluded us twice. Not only had we missed the birth by seconds but also we had allowed our enthusiasm to lose us the chance of witnessing the first behaviour of a mother to her newborn pup. She disappeared into the sea and, realizing that she would now not reappear for some minutes, we moved forward to photograph the pup and the afterbirth and then quickly went away.

Although we have sent a study group to the Treshnish Isles every year since then, I have never yet witnessed the birth. Weather conditions and the problems of living on the islands without disturbing the seals make the chances of being in the right spot at such a precise moment, usually just after dawn, very slim.

By lunch-time that first day we had surveyed Sgeir nan Chaisteil in its entirety; watched huge bulls, as yet uninterested in the calving cows, roaring and challenging each other for territory; we had counted pups and adults and, in the last sunlight we were to get, we rowed quietly back to the yacht.

In the afternoon Charlie sent the crew ashore to Lunga to survey that island, and Peter and I set up a base camp on the beach nearest the yacht. We planned to work from there so that we could be in a watching position before dawn. We erected our camouflaged tents and laid out our bedrolls with a few dry stores to keep body and soul together. At nightfall we returned to the vessel for supper and to listen to the shipping forecast.

'. . . Malin, Rockall, Faeroes, . . . Hebrides, Tiree . . . west-south-west force five or six rising.' Charlie looked grave.

'How does that place us?' Peter asked.

'All right at the moment,' came the confident reply, 'but if it rises beyond force six we're going to know all about it here.'

'Is the anchorage safe?' I queried.

'So far,' Charlie said. 'It seems good holding ground, and we can put out another one, but there's no land between us and the West Indies to break the force of this gale if it is going to be a gale. And if it veers round to the north at all this anchorage will be worse than useless.'

'What do we do then?' asked Peter who was in charge of the shore-base.

'We must be ready to move out at a moment's notice,' said Charlie. 'Leave everything packed and ready to snatch up if we have to run for it. I'll keep you posted with the walkie-talkie.'

'Yessir!' said Peter, carefully avoiding the Naval expression. After supper Charlie rowed us ashore to our camp and then returned to the boat to brood over his charts and the radio.

We slept soundly as the wind built up around us and our remarkable skipper was with us again half an hour before dawn, shaking us from our sleep and offering us steaming tea from a flask.

Three minutes later we were standing outside in a bitter wind with icy rain spattering diagonally at us out of a dark brooding sky. To the east the first streaks of dawn were spreading somewhere behind the hills of Mull, now invisible in the mist and rain. Charlie had secured his dinghy and was walking up the beach to meet us.

'I don't much like the look of the weather,' he said. 'This wind is rising fast, so we must make the best of the time we've got.'

Charlie and I decided to take the windward side of Lunga and we set off up the hill while Peter went east along the shore. We would be in contact periodically over the walkie-talkie and if we found anything interesting we could report to each other.

The tide was at low water and had just turned and we spent the morning counting pups all along the now wind-battered south and western shores. We searched constantly for a cow due to give birth but all the pups in this area appeared to be a week old or more and there were none newborn or, as far as we could see, about to be born. The only adult seals were one or two bulls in charge of an empty territory later to become a mating harem, and the mothers of those pups already born.

At lunch-time we found a large flat-topped rock overlooking

the water and sat down to enjoy our dry rations as best we could.

'Look at this,' said Charlie tapping my arm and pointing out to sea. A seal cow was treading water fifty yards out watching us intently. Every few seconds she rose high out of the water, vertically, so that her head and shoulders were well clear of the surface. She was clearly straining to get a better look at us.

'What do you think she's up to?' I asked. 'I haven't seen one doing that before.'

'No, it's funny that she should be so keen on us.'

Slowly she came nearer until she was only a few yards from our rock.

'She must have a pup here we can't see,' I said; 'it must be right underneath us.' Charlie nodded in agreement and at that moment the cow levelled out and swam purposefully up to the rock. We had to crane over the edge to see her and to our delight she flounced up alongside a small ledge, crooned softly to the pup which was sheltering there, and contrived to get it on to her back. We held our breath in excitement as they were only seven or eight feet from us.

At that point I expected the two of them to disappear out to sea, but to our amazement the cow moved gently round the rock until she was alongside us in a more sheltered position. Here she helped the pup climb on to a small rock protruding from the sea by only a few inches.

The swell was now considerable and the force-seven wind was sending in large curling waves which broke angrily over the rocks and swirled into hollows and pockets with a great slap and swoosh. We suddenly realized that we had witnessed a normal behavioural procedure. The cow had sensed the oncoming storm and knew that her pup was in a vulnerable position, for, while grey seal pups can swim in calm water from birth, they have no hope of managing to steer or control themselves in any sort of current or swell. Storms undoubtedly do account for a great many natural deaths every year and the behaviour we were witnessing has certainly evolved to counter this toll.

For half an hour we watched the two together. The pup was carefully positioned in the lee of the rock and the cow lay across in front of it in precisely the best position for taking the full force of each incoming wave as it curled and crashed down smothering them both in boiling spume. During this time the tide was rising and after a while the rock no longer gave the shelter it had done when the cow chose it; waiting for a lull in the waves she drew her floating pup to her, submerged and rose beneath it so that it could grip her back with its acutely prehensile fore-flippers, and then bore it away to another rock better positioned for the new water level.

We shifted our own positions to keep them in view. We had both been photographing despite the bad light and the lashing rain, and we were soaked through, although we barely noticed it. Again we managed to lie on a flat-topped rock directly above the cow and her pup. By now the sea was angrily rough and although she was aware of our presence she barely glanced at us any more. It appeared that she had made up her mind that we were less of a threat to her child than the storm and it was the storm she was going to concentrate on.

Again she placed her pup on the landward side of the rock and drew herself up on to it across his nose so that he was doubly protected by the bulk of her body. It was most noticeable that he drew himself in to her as soon as she was in position, not to her head, but to her arm-pit, as it were, just behind her powerful fore-flipper which we could see was gripping the rock with the long claws curled over and round the edge. There they remained, as the waves came and went and the storm battered down on them; the obvious survival value in this position was abundantly clear. Twice more we watched this attentive parent move her infant from rock to rock until the tide had forced them right back against the cliff where they could retreat no further. Now she was constantly on guard. Her dappled head rose up to meet the oncoming breakers and every few seconds they were engulfed in an avalanche of water, ton upon ton of it hurtling down, shattering into boiling white foam which seethed and hissed over the head of the invisible pup and then sucked out again revealing them high and dry and the cow glaring out to sea to gauge the force and timing of the next one.

Charlie and I lay there in all that storm and wind, our cameras now back in polythene bags, enthralled by the little drama below us. We had lost all idea of time and had quite forgotten the rest of the party. Suddenly Charlie looked out to sea and saw the angry swell and the row upon row of marching white horses stretching away as far as the eye could see.

'Christ!' He expostulated. 'This sea is rising fast! I must get back to the boat and check our position.' With that he was up and away, heading back across the island at full tilt.

I lay on, watching our seals for an hour or more. Slowly the tide receded and fewer and fewer breakers smashed over the steadfast pair. I was fascinated to see when she was going to relax, and I waited on. Spring tides fall quickly once they are under way, and within a further half-hour the water had dropped so that my seals were beyond its snatching grasp. Finally, when no wave had done more than splash them with spray for several minutes, the cow rolled over and crooned softly to the pup. It nuzzled up to her and with its tiny black nose it searched her fur down the flank to a nipple near her tail-flippers. As it shuffled forward to draw heavily on the life-giving milk, the cow rolled back to allow easier access and yawned and closed her eyes. I struggled to look at my watch beneath my oilskins. It was eight hours to our certain knowledge since this pup suckled last. Eight hours of grimly hanging on while the pounding waves smashed down on him and then tried to pluck him off his rock and suck him away and out to sea. Little wonder he was hungry, and even as I watched I could see his shoulders working with the vigour he was putting into his feed.

Suddenly I saw a red-oilskinned figure signalling to me from the hill. It was Charlie and I guessed that he was anxious to leave. I ran back down the island as fast as I could. I badly needed the run to get the blood circulating again after lying still so long, and when I arrived at our camp it was gone.

Peter and Charlie were standing at the water's edge signalling urgently to me. I glanced out at the bay and could scarcely believe my eyes. The calm anchorage was a field of angry water. The yacht was plunging and bucking at her anchor, and on the beach itself where there had been no waves to speak of at all in the morning there were now rows of curling breakers ramming in to the shore one after another.

Peter and Charlie were holding the dinghy, already laden with our equipment.

'Wrap your cameras up tightly,' Charlie said, 'this is going to be wet.'

I held the painter and followed them out into the water. The waves were pitching and falling so severely that just as we thought we could climb in, a trough arrived and plonked the little boat firmly on a rock. We struggled even further out into the slippery weed-strewn sea so that as each wave broke we were up to our waists in icy swirling water.

'Wait for it . . .' shouted Charlie above the whine of the wind, '. . . now!' And we all jumped in as a large wave picked the dinghy up high above the rocks. For a second we hung suspended as if the wave was going to dash us forward on to the beach again, but the force of the three of us jumping from landward had given us sufficient motion to counter the wave. Charlie slammed the oars into position and pulled savagely away. As we moved out the bottom of the boat just scraped over the last slippery rock.

Charlie rowed like an Oxford blue possessed. The oars bit and swirled in the heaving water and the waves broke over us, slapping up against the sides and filling the little dinghy to overflowing. There was no point in baling. Our camera gear was, we prayed, in waterproof containers and everything else was soaked anyway. We just ploughed on.

Once on board the Rival we set all hands to preparing to leave. The radio had issued a gale warning for the Hebrides which, to our horror, was veering to the north-west. In a dizzy spin of action the dinghy was shipped and lashed to the bulkhead, the engines churned and idled, the cabin was cleared and the storm sails prepared. Hauling in the two anchors was a mammoth task as the yacht reared high in the air and then plunged down again, and at times I thought my arms would be plucked from their sockets. Peter was stowing the chain behind me as it came in, and, as soon as I was sure we were clear of the bottom, I yelled the word back to Charlie at the helm. The engine thudded into action and we gradually backed away from the threatening rocks of Lunga.

Once we were under way the rest of the chain came aboard quickly, and we lashed the anchors down firmly to the deck. Up went a storm jibsail and we turned out towards the open sea.

'We'll run for Coll,' shouted Charlie, 'there's a good harbour there which will give us shelter even if the wind does veer.' It was clear that we were going to find out what sort of stuff Charlie and his Rival were made of.

'What wind-speed is this?' I asked him shouting through the singing shrouds and roaring wind.

'It must be force eight now,' he yelled back. 'God knows what we're in for out there.' He pointed to out beyond the last land shelter of Sgeir nan Chaisteil. 'Now everyone must harness up with safety lines. Quickly now! We've only a few minutes left before we're out in the open sea.'

We snapped our spring clips on to the safety lines and buckled our harnesses tightly round waist and shoulders.

'Everyone secure?' he shouted again.

'Yes,' came the unanimous reply.

'Right, mainsail up. And Peter, get winding that reefing handle!'

In a few seconds the mainsail was tightly reefed in and humming like a top. The storm jib, a mere slip of a sail was bowing out in a delicate arc as steady and secure as the mast itself.

I had no idea what was to hit us once we cleared the shelter of Sgeir nan Chaisteil. I did not know such seas existed in inshore waters, and I certainly had no idea that a yacht could sail in them. When the first squall hit us I thought we were going straight over. The deck rose to within a few degrees of vertical and the sails clipped the waves on the lee side. I held my breath and hung on. To my astonishment the implacable Charlie Barrington was wedged firmly in the cockpit, leaning heavily on the tiller and apparently loving it. The Rival came back surely and slowly as her keel, some eight tons of lead, corrected her trim. From then on it was a straight screaming race across the eleven miles of ocean to the Isle of Coll. We were sailing obliquely across the wind at a frightening speed. Charlie told us we were making ten knots and the angle of the deck was never less than 45°, often a good deal steeper.

Wave after huge wave smashed into us. Swirling green water deluged down the decks filling the cockpit and lashing us until our faces were raw with stinging and cutting salt spray. We were so completely wet that no one thought about it. The waves bearing down on us were fifteen and twenty feet from trough to crest and the yacht seemed to disappear in among them like entering a valley. And then we soared up the other side, high into the turbulent sky and the rain, only to crash down again as the water was suddenly sucked from under us. There was not time to be ill or to think about it. Hanging on, grimly and determinedly, was the foremost issue.

For a moment, out in the middle there, with no visible escape from each monstrous engulfing wave, and with my white fingers crying out with the ache of hanging on, I thought, just fleetingly, that I knew what it was like to be a seal pup, one of the hundreds still battling for their lives out there in the foaming surf of Treshnish.

In 1975 we spread further afield even than the Treshnish Isles. We led two groups to the Shetlands to watch and observe the spectacular congregation of sea-birds which come ashore each spring to breed on the gaunt wind-carved headlands of those remote isles. I took a group out to St Kilda, the farthest flung of all our inhabitable islands, where a million puffins whirr and glide with their orange feet outstretched and their comic bills crowded with shiny fish; and to Skye where, with ravens croaking and tumbling high above us, we swam in the mineral-green water of Loch Coruisk ringed in by the stark Cuillin peaks.

Epilogue

Almost without noticing them five years had gone by. They had been years of trial and error, of success and failure and a gradual process of evolution of what we thought to be the right way to run our business.

Courses came and went. Some full, some slack, but there was always something new to see, something extra to record and enter in our precious log. The duck pond now was so crowded with boisterous mallard that we had to encourage them to go wild and shoo them away. Feeding in the morning brought a rush of wings from out in the river-fields as thirty ducks, all haggling loudly in the morning sky, wheeled in around us with a roar of vibrant pinions and planing feet on the water.

The Kennels was changing, too. We had outgrown the office and our typist sat among cardboard boxes of files and correspondence piled high up the walls. We had no work-room or laboratory facilities, and the showing of slide lectures, now a part of every course, was hampered and made amateur by lack of space. Warwick and a second employee to help Sorrel with the running of the house had removed two bedrooms from those available for guests. It was difficult to envisage where we could build on. It had become a very different dwelling from the deserted semi-ruin I had first walked into four years before.

One afternoon that summer our friend and annual visitor, Paul Johnson, came to see us at the Kennels. He was working on a book in a cottage nearby and periodically emerged to re-vitalize his wits and engage in a little oral sparring with us.

We recounted our year to him and outlined the pressures we suffered at the Kennels.

'There's a big house standing empty down near my cottage,' he announced quite casually.

'Whereabouts?' We asked in unison.

'Only a few miles down the valley. It's in a beautiful position.'

For a moment I relived the old dream of a large country-house in its own grounds: a vision of space and rooms especially designed for library, lecture room, laboratory and workshop, dining-room and sitting-room, in which we could house our groups in comfort and build up an atmosphere unhindered by our own living space and the restrictions of a young family.

That evening, against the setting sun, Sorrel and I drove down the valley to look at it. Empty it certainly was; we had seen it from the road many times. Its turrets and towers stood out against the flaming sky in a fairy-tale silhouette of Gothic architecture. A young roe deer watched us attentively from a laurel shrubbery and swifts hawked and screamed round the towers above us. I made a mental note that they must be nesting in the roof.

As I write, more than a year later, after a long and desperate campaign to persuade the owners to sell it before neglect took too great a toll, we have won through. The place is ours. Aigas it is called, and its pink sandstone silhouette gives little indication of the urgent work to be done. In the meantime it is winter, and another year crowded with events and person-alities has passed us by. The Kennels is quiet now and Peter has gone off for a long deserved holiday and a rest. Warwick and the dogs are playing in front of a huge crackling fire in the big drawing-room and I can hear the ducks arguing and bickering on the pond outside. The wigeon nested this year in the rushes at the top of the enclosure and her six young are now fully fledged and flying. They will leave us, I am sure, for the firth any day now, where tens of thousands of wigeon are congregating for the winter. It will be a test for our birds